The employees of THORNDIKE PRESS hope you have enjoyed this Large Print book. All our Large Print titles are designed for easy reading, and all our books are made to last. Other Thorndike Large Print books are available at your library, through selected bookstores, or directly from us. For more information about current and upcoming titles, please call or mail your name and address to:

THORNDIKE PRESS
PO Box 159
Thorndike, Maine 04986
800/223-6121
207/948-2962

THE FOUNDING AND DEVELOPMENT OF THE PROGRAM OF AFFILIATION OF THE CATHOLIC UNIVERSITY OF AMERICA: 1912 TO 1939

by

Rita Watrin, M.A.

The Catholic University of America Press
Washington, D. C. 20017

INTRODUCTION

There is today on the campus of The Catholic University of America a Program of Affiliation which services over seven hundred Catholic secondary schools and colleges of the United States. In establishing and maintaining such an educational center, the Catholic University, as a national pontifical university, recognizes its own unique position within the American Catholic educational system and its resulting obligation to assist the general cause of Catholic education throughout the country. Thus the present Program of Affiliation defines itself as "a voluntary and organized cooperative effort to place the resources of the University at the disposal of Catholic secondary schools and colleges seeking professional assistance within the framework of a Catholic philosophy of education."[1] In keeping with this primary purpose of service to Catholic education, University Affiliation seeks to assist its affiliates, individually and collectively, to meet first the minimal standards of state and regional accrediting agencies and then to work systematically and continuously toward higher levels of academic excellence. Emphasis accordingly is placed on capable leadership from within the affiliate and on a genuine willingness on the part of these school authorities to work cooperatively toward the strengthening of both the academic outcomes and the Catholic character of the institution. Rigid uniformity, standardization, or any form of control by the University is carefully avoided by making the essence of Affiliation a series of flexible and individualized services of a consultative and cooperative nature. Thus the specific purposes of each affiliate, as well as the common objectives of Catholic education, are fully respected at all times.

While the Program of Affiliation in its present form is centered on educational evaluation and embodies a variety of

modern evaluative and self-study techniques, affiliation as a
function of the Catholic University is not new. The Univer-
sity's original Constitutions, approved by the Sacred Congre-
gation of Seminaries and Universities in 1889, empowered the
University to affiliate other Catholic educational institutions.
To this authority was added the personal exhortation of Pope
Leo XIII, who wrote in his apostolic letter, Magni Nobis
Gaudii, on March 7, 1889:

> We exhort you all that you should take care to
> affiliate with your University your seminaries,
> colleges, and other Catholic institutions, accord-
> ing to the plan suggested in the Constitutions, in
> such a manner, however, as not to destroy their
> autonomy. [2]

In the early developmental years of the University, efforts to
implement this directive were confined almost entirely to
seminary affiliation, so it was not until 1912, twenty-three
years after the University's founding, that a plan for the affiliation of Catholic high schools and colleges was initiated.

The Reverend Doctor Thomas E. Shields, Professor of
Education at the University and Dean of the then new Catholic
Sisters College, is largely credited with working out a practical plan. Dr. Shields was keenly aware in the early 1900's
of the serious and pressing needs of the emerging and rapidly
growing Catholic school system. He recognized in the University a potential guiding force through which the problems of
unification, articulation, standardization, and general academic improvement could be met. With determination and un-
wavering energy he sought solutions in a variety of approaches,
among them primarily the providing of programs and facilities
for the professional and academic training of the teaching sisters, the production of Catholic pedagogical literature, and a
scheme of affiliation that would reach down to the classroom
teacher and his students. Through a set of relatively well-
defined standards, course outlines, and sanctions of required
reports and testing, the several levels of Catholic education
were to be clarified, and their overall quality as Catholic

educational endeavors was to be raised throughout the country.
It was this plan of affiliation that the University Trustees approved on April 17, 1912, creating the first standardization
program under Catholic auspices in the United States.

When the first pioneering work of unification and standardization of Catholic education had been accomplished, with
the Shields' plan serving well during this period, Catholic educators found themselves facing new but equally complex problems. It then became evident that if Affiliation were to meet
these changing needs, the original program would have to be
generally over-hauled. Thus in 1939, Doctor Roy J.
Deferrari, then Secretary General of the University, and a
new Committee on Affiliation and Extension took on the task
of reorganization. As Dr. Shields and his collaborators had
so ably met the problems of their day, so also Dr. Deferrari
and his Committee saw clearly the needs of Catholic education
at the end of the 1930's and sought to devise a plan that could
grow and develop at whatever pace or direction the "new"
education would properly take. The old idea of standardization or accreditation was abandoned entirely, and in its place
was established the basic principle of cooperative servicing
and the flexible procedures and policies which characterize
the present Program of Affiliation. The Committee made its
core service a series of individualized evaluations through
inspections and written progress reports, so that a systematic plan of improvement could be put into operation by each
affiliate. The other services initiated at that time were supplementary in nature, providing educational principles and
know-how for the successful carrying out of these developmental plans by the affiliates.

During the 1940's and 1950's, the Program's earlier
promise of making the University a source of educational information and assistance on a variety of educational matters
was fulfilled. New services were developed and those already
existing were strengthened. Its steady, healthy growth in the
number and kinds of affiliates and its general reputation within
many Catholic and non-Catholic educational circles attest both
to the value of its achievements in working with affiliates and
to its overall influence on Catholic education in the United

States.

As a function of the Catholic University then of some
duration and considerable scope, the historical development
of Affiliation would seem to be of importance not only as an
integral part of the history of the University but also of
American Catholic education in the twentieth century. Existing studies of the foundation and early years of the University
by Ellis, Ahern, Hogan, and Barry traced the concept of affiliation as it existed in the idea of a national Catholic university
and, during the first three rectorships, its first implementation in the form of the affiliation of theological seminaries to
the University.[3] O'Connor, in her Master's dissertation of
1941 on Dr. Shields' influence on Catholic education, sketched
briefly the founder's work and thinking regarding his 1912 affiliation plan,[4] and Deferrari, in his more recent memoirs,
gave his recollections, also briefly, of the development of
Affiliation from 1938 to 1960.[5] No comprehensive historical
investigation of the Program, however, has been made.

This present study,[6] therefore, after following the concept of affiliation as a function of the Catholic University from
its founding to the 1910's, traces the establishment of the
Program of Affiliation and its development through the first
twenty-seven years of its existence. In so doing, an effort
has been made to identify the general educational problems
and events leading to the 1912 plan, its original and primary
aims, its nature and working procedures, its growth and development, and those individuals who made substantial contributions to its structure and implementation. The years following the death of Dr. Shields, from 1921 to the reorganization
of Affiliation in 1938, are shown as a static period and, in
some ways, as a period during which Affiliation failed to keep
pace with the changing needs of Catholic education. The last
chapter, devoted to the 1938 and 1939 work of reorganization,
treats the same general factors of the new plan as were identi-
fied for the old, demonstrating by contrast its considerable
potential for meeting the varying, future needs of Catholic
schools and colleges.

No attempt has been made to evaluate or measure the influence of Affiliation during these years. The study is confined

rather to a modified chronological recording of the thinking
and events which shaped the Shields plan and brought about its
present form of operation. Nor does this investigation include
the historical development of the other program of affiliation
which the University maintains, entirely distinct, for the theological curricula of the major seminary. The term "affiliation, " therefore, is used generically throughout this study to
describe the relationship of "a school closely associated with
another, usually larger, school but separately operated, " 7
and, as a proper name, to refer to the Catholic University's
Program of Affiliation for secondary schools and colleges.
While the six-year minor seminary, classified as a secondary
school and a junior college, and the philosophy division of a
major seminary, classified as a general college, were eventually included within this Program of Affiliation, any reference to the affiliation of theological curricula as it may touch
on the topic of the present study is always clearly qualified as
"theological" or "seminary" affiliation.

In a search for primary source material, two limiting
factors became apparent: no Affiliation files per se from 1912
to 1938 could be located and the available Shields' papers dealt
comparatively meagerly with matters pertaining directly to
Affiliation. Four major sources, however, proved most valuable. (1) The Archives of The Catholic University of America
provided Affiliation data in the form of correspondence and
documents by Drs. Shields and Pace and by the several Rectors
and Vice Rectors who served during the 1912-1939 period,
minutes of the meetings of the Board of Trustees from 1885 to
1933, and such official printed records as the annual Affiliation
booklet or "syllabus, " the Rector's annual report, and the University Year Books. (2) A survey of the periodical literature
of the same period was also fruitful, not only in relating Affiliation to the contemporary educational scene but in locating
many articles and notes, by both Shields and Pace, concerning
the early concepts and procedures of Affiliation. Issues of the
Catholic Educational Review, the Catholic University Bulletin,
and the Bulletin of the Catholic Educational Association were
particularly valuable. (3) For the 1938 and 1939 years, the
files and records of the Office of Affiliation provided extensive

and specific information in the form of minutes, reports, correspondence, and miscellaneous records. (4) To fill some of the many gaps which exist in the written materials, a series of interviews with Dr. Roy J. Deferrari, the present Director of the Program who has been associated with the work of Affiliation since the early 1920's, was most helpful.

The writer wishes to express sincere appreciation to the Right Reverend Joseph A. Gorham for his encouragement, guidance, and helpful criticism in the directing of this study and to the Reverend Aubert J. Clark for his critical reading of it. Thanks are due also to Mr. Charles Ritter for his generous assistance in the University Archives. A special debt of gratitude to Dr. Roy J. Deferrari is fully acknowledged. His kindly interest in the study and the time which he gave to evaluating sources and providing additional data and insights regarding the development of Affiliation contributed much to a fuller history of the Program than would otherwise have been possible.

FOOTNOTES

[1]Program of Affiliation (Washington, D. C.: The Catholic University of America Press, 1964), p. 7.

[2]ACUA, Constitutions of the Catholic University of America, translated from the Latin (Washington, D.C., n.d.), p. 3.

[3]John Tracy Ellis, The Formative Years of the Catholic University of America (Washington, D. C.: American Catholic Historical Association, 1946); Patrick H. Ahern, The Catholic University of America, 1887-1896. The Rectorship of John J. Keane (Washington, D. C.: Catholic University of America Press, 1948); Peter E. Hogan, S.S.J., The Catholic University of America, 1896-1903. The Rectorship of Thomas J. Conaty (Washington, D.C. Catholic University of America Press, 1949); Colman J. Barry, O.S.B., The Catholic University of America, 1903-1909. The Rectorship of Denis J. O'Connell (Washington, D.C.: Catholic University of America Press, 1950).

[4]Sister M. Augustine O'Connor, "The Influence of Very Reverend Doctor Thomas E. Shields on Catholic Education in the United States" (unpublished Master's dissertation, Depart-

ment of Education, The Catholic University of America, 1941).

[5] Roy J. Deferrari, <u>Memoirs of The Catholic University of America, 1918-1960</u> (Boston: Daughters of St. Paul, 1962).

[6] In its original form this study was a dissertation submitted to the Faculty of the Graduate School of Arts and Sciences, Department of Education, of The Catholic University of America in partial fulfillment of the requirements for the degree of Master of Arts, June, 1964.

[7] Carter V. Good (ed.), <u>Dictionary of Education</u> (New York: McGraw Hill Book Co., 1959), p. 19.

KEY TO ABBREVIATIONS

ACUA . . . . Archives of The Catholic University of
                America

AF . . . . Affiliation Files
ASF . . . . . . Academic Senate Files
BTEM . . . . . Board of Trustees Exhibits of Meetings
CSCF . . . . . Catholic Sisters College Files
MMBT . . . . . Minutes of the Meetings of the Board of
                Trustees
MMCAE . . . . Minutes of the Meetings of the Committee
                on Affiliation and Extension
RF . . . . Rector's Files
VRF . . . . . . Vice Rector's Files

ARR . . . . Annual Report of the Rector

AHSC . . . . Affiliation of High Schools and Colleges

CEAB . . . . Catholic Educational Association Bulletin

CER . . . . Catholic Educational Review

CUB . . . . Catholic University Bulletin

OAF . . . . Office of Affiliation Files

TABLE OF CONTENTS

Page

INTRODUCTION   iii

KEY TO ABBREVIATIONS   x

Chapter
  I. THE GROWTH OF A CONCEPT   1
       Affiliation as a Function of the Catholic
           University
       Growth of the Concept: 1889-1896
       Growth of the Concept: 1896-1903
       Growth of the Concept: 1903-1909

  II. DR. SHIELDS AND THE 1912 AFFILIATION
           PLAN: 1909-1912.   34
       A Master Plan for Catholic Education
       First Steps in Carrying Out the Plan
       The Catholic Educational Association's
           Failure to Act
       Action of the Catholic University

  III. THE 1912 PROGRAM OF AFFILIATION.   60
       The Affiliation of Colleges
       The Affiliation of High Schools
       Execution of the Plan of Affiliation
       The High School Examination Program

  IV. THE PIONEERING YEARS: 1912-1921   89
       Early Organization and Growth
       High School Testing and Curriculum
           Development
       Early Recognition, Benefits, and Evaluations
       Internal Problems and Dr. Shields' Death

xi

V. THE STATIC YEARS: 1921-1937. 121
  The Program of Affiliation from 1921-1927
  The Program of Affiliation from 1928-1937

VI. THE REORGANIZATION YEARS: 1938 and 1939. 154
  A New Committee on Affiliation and
      Extension
  Reorganizational Work: The College Plan
  Reorganizational Work: The High School Plan
  Procedural and Promotional Work
  The High School Testing Program and
      Course Outlines
  The Initiation of New Services

CONCLUSION 193

APPENDICES
  A. The 1912 Plan of Affiliation. 197

  B. The 1939 Plan of Affiliation. 202

  C. Table Showing Number of Affiliates by
        Academic Classifications, 1913-1939. 211

  D. Table Showing Number of High School
        Tests and Certificates Distributed
        from 1913-1939 212

BIBLIOGRAPHY. 213

INDEX. 231

CHAPTER I

THE GROWTH OF A CONCEPT

With the beginning of the high school movement in the mid nineteenth century, the public schools of the United States were gradually being united into a system, one which permitted the student to move with comparative ease from the elementary level into the high school and then on to the college and university. The number of public high schools grew in the years from 1860 to 1880 alone from a mere forty-some to nearly eight hundred schools. The process of unification, however, was not without conflict. The rigid demands of the colleges for purposes of admission restricted the new and more practical curriculum offerings of the high schools. While some attempt was made to secure greater flexibility within college admission practices in order to give the high school some freedom in developing its own objectives, college entrance examinations remained a formidable weapon in controlling the curriculum of the secondary school. Problems of cramming and of teaching merely for these examinations were often greatly multiplied by the lack of uniformity among the colleges and led to seeking solutions through a process of standardization or accreditation.[1]

The University of Michigan was the first to attempt by this method to breach the widening gap between the two levels of education. In 1871 it initiated a plan of accreditation whereby the graduates of high schools approved by the University would be admitted to the University on the basis of a certificate issued by the approved schools. The weight of the certificate lay in the fact that a University committee had visited the high school to ascertain that its preparatory curriculum and the quality of its instruction were acceptable in terms of the University's admission requirements. On this pattern similar accreditation plans were adopted by other universities and state departments of education, so that by

1

1890 the standardization process was well underway throughout the country.[2] About this time, the voluntary regional accrediting associations took up the problem of articulation between college and high school, promoting also the general clarification and strengthening of both kinds of institutions.[3]

In general, the state accrediting systems at first made no provision for the approval of private schools but were concerned only with public high schools. Three Catholic high schools, however, were accredited as early as 1888 by the University of California and another so approved by the University of Wisconsin in 1893.[4] At the regional level, the private schools participated from the beginning, although the extent of Catholic school participation varied from region to region.[5]

Within the Catholic school "system" of the same period there was little by way of mass coordination. Catholic educational endeavors were primarily in the hands of religious communities, and efforts to attain uniformity among institutions were scattered, confined mostly to each community's connecting its own schools to its own colleges. Thus Catholic institutions existed to a large extent in isolation so that in fact it could not be said there was an all-embracing Catholic system.[6] The secularization of the public schools and the general materialistic philosophy that permeated the country had served to emphasize the need of Catholics for an education not divorced from religion. With the flood of Catholic immigrants at the middle of the nineteenth century, the growth of the number of Catholic parochial schools had been steady, but more were needed and the Catholic high school as a connecting link between elementary and higher education was generally missing. Moreover, the number of well-trained religious teachers had not been able to keep pace with the growth, and the already existing schools were meeting with difficulty the competition of the public school system in academic efficiency. Thus the providing of additional Catholic educational institutions at all levels, a greater unity of purpose and action, and the more thorough preparation of teachers were the problems facing the emerging Catholic system by the 1880's.[7]

Affiliation as a Function of the Catholic University

It was concern for this overall status of Catholic education as well as the general good of the Church of this country
that prompted the bishops of the Third Plenary Council of
Baltimore, in 1884, to set up the machinery for enlarging and
improving Catholic educational opportunities. Both the Schema
decretorum and the official Acta et decreta of the 1884 Council
reflected, by the nature of the deliberations and by the volume
of the minutes devoted to education, the keen awareness of the
hierarchy to the educational problems of the times and to the
need for a more complete Catholic system. The decrees dealing with improved supervision, training, and certification of
teachers showed equal concern for the quality of the education
to be offered under Catholic auspices.[8] In this connection
also the founding of a national Catholic university was viewed
as a necessary step, a university that would serve not only as
a crown for the total system but also as the very keystone to
hold all its parts together.[9]

> Nothing was overlooked by them in their efforts
> to raise the standards of Catholic schools. . . .
> The fathers of the Council recognized the necessity,
> not only of multiplying parish schools, but of in-
> creasing Catholic high schools, academies, and
> colleges as well, so that a complete system of
> Catholic education would be afforded the Catholic
> youth of the land. A significant advance in higher
> education began with the appointment in the Council
> of a committee for the purpose of instituting the
> means necessary for the establishment of a central
> Catholic university.[10]

Archbishop Martin John Spalding, who is generally credited with the idea of an American Catholic national university,
had expressed this hope earlier at the Second Plenary Council
of Baltimore in 1866, but it was his nephew, John Lancaster
Spalding, Bishop of Peoria, who at the third Council was able
to head the movement that brought the university into existence.

The university committee constituted by the Council included among its members several, besides Bishop Spalding, who were destined to play major roles in the development of the new university: Archbishop James Gibbons of Baltimore, the first Chancellor of Catholic University; Bishop John Ireland of St. Paul, a loyal and active supporter of the University for many years; and Bishop John J. Keane of Richmond, the University's first Rector.[11] Over their names and those of the other members of the committee, an appeal to the Catholics of the United States was made in the year immediately following the Council. This twenty-four page, printed document included a definition of the envisioned scope of the proposed university:

> It is obvious that the dignity of the Church in America demands that it should have at least one institution which, transcending local needs and interests, shall assume a national and representative character; and what other institution can so well take this position as a great intellectual centre of Catholic intelligence and influence, which will unify and complete our educational system, and be a crown of honor and a focus of light for our schools, colleges and seminaries?[12]

While no documentary evidence was found to substantiate that the founding fathers actually had already in mind at that time some practical plan through which the University was to effect educational unification and harmony, the concept of affiliation as a then popular trend and as a promising working approach to the problem must have been a part of their considerations sometime before the summer of 1888. When Bishop Keane was formally appointed the Rector of the Catholic University on September 7, 1887, among his first official tasks was the preparation of the University constitutions. To this end he devoted much of the following summer.[13] His preliminary draft, which was submitted first to Bishops Ireland and Spalding and then to Archbishop Gibbons, included a specific reference to University affiliation:

The statutes stated that the officials of the university
were to "assiduously cultivate" friendly relations
with the Catholic colleges and seminaries of the
United States and these institutions might be affiliated
with the university by the board of trustees. In case
of affiliation the certificates of the students of such
institutions would be regarded as equivalent to entrance examinations to the university. [14]

Bishop Keane's first draft of the constitutions, with
minor changes only, was approved by the Board of Trustees
on November 13, 1888. It was then to be translated into
"first-rate Latin" and submitted to the Holy See for approval. [15]
The Rector, who was encharged with carrying out these plans,
left almost immediately for Rome, but while he waited in New
York to sail on November seventeenth, the matter of affiliation
was given some prominence. The event was recorded by Keane
himself:

> Shortly after the meeting of Nov. 11th, [sic]
> I again started for Rome. In New York I met Bp.
> O'Connor of Omaha, who told me he had taken
> that long journey in order to confer with me about
> the practicability of supervision and direction over
> the Seminaries & Colleges of the country, in order
> to, as it were, coerce them into elevating the
> standards of their studies. The need for such im-
> provement he considered deplorable, and unless it
> came from outside coercion, it seemed to him
> hopeless. I showed him the many difficulties and
> the inevitable resistance in the way of such super-
> vision. But I promised to use my influence to in-
> duce the Holy See to at least plant the germ of it,
> by recommending affiliation of those institutions
> with the University. This explains a sentence to
> that effect in the Holy Father's Brief of March 7th,
> '89. [16]

Bishop Keane was apparently astonished by being thus

approached by Bishop James O'Connor, the Vicar Apostolate
of Nebraska. As a member of the Third Plenary Council of
Baltimore, O'Connor had been in favor of postponing the establishment of a national university until the already existing
seminaries were sufficiently improved to feed and maintain a
university of high quality.[17] To Keane, therefore, his suggestion concerning affiliation represented "a change of front on his
part towards the University."[18] Moreover, O'Connor's conviction that the University should act in a supervisory capacity
for Catholic higher education of the country must have been
strong; not only had he made the trip to New York to confer
with Keane but also he followed up the matter a little later by
a long letter to the Rector in Rome. Bishop Keane was frankly
doubtful of the reception any plan of coerced supervision would
receive by the Holy See.[19] Evidently it was not acceptable,
for the Constitutions as approved by Pope Leo XIII on March 7,
1889, contained two sections on affiliation in which institutional independence and cooperation were the key principles:

> 3. The authorities of the University should take
> care to confer with the Directors of Catholic col-
> leges and seminaries in our country so that all may
> labor unitedly to advance the education of our
> Catholic youth.
> 4. Colleges and seminaries, without prejudice to
> their autonomy, may by authority of the Board of
> Trustees be affiliated to the University. When this
> has been done the diplomas conferred by such
> colleges as evidence of the acquirements of their
> students shall be accepted in lieu of an examination
> for admission to the University.[20]

Bishop O'Connor's insistence on a University plan for
the improvement of Catholic seminaries and colleges did,
however, have a direct result. As Keane pointed out in his
"Chronicles," it was responsible for the special recognition
of and emphasis on affiliation as a University function in the
Pope's apostolic letter to James Cardinal Gibbons, on March
7, 1889, approving the Constitutions:

> We exhort you all that you should take care to
> affiliate with your University, your seminaries,
> colleges, and other Catholic institutions, accord-
> ing to the plan suggested in the Constitutions, in
> such a way, however, as not to destroy their
> autonomy.[21]

The press of the late 1880's showed a keen interest in
the new Catholic University in Washington, and its relationship
to the other Catholic educational institutions of the country received substantial attention. The idea of a strong bond between
the University and other Catholic colleges and seminaries in
order to unify and strengthen the system seems to have been
sympathetically and even enthusiastically received by many.
Within a few months after the Pope's approval of the Constitutions and before the opening of the University in the fall of
1889, the Catholic World carried an unsigned article which
raised the question of the nature of this relationship if
through the influence of the University a greater harmony
within the system were to result.

> It may be safely said that seminaries will be
> helped every way. . . . This much, however, is
> certain: no change is desired which will not benefit
> the seminaries and the colleges of the Church in
> America. When the Holy Father speaks of their
> affiliating with the University, he does not mean
> that they shall become succursal to it. There is
> no disposition whatever to lower their standards,
> or in any way to abridge the present scope of their
> activity as seats of learning. There shall be no
> curtailment of their present power of conferring
> degrees. The words of the Holy Father and of the
> Statutes plainly indicate that there should be some
> harmonious relationship established between all
> Catholic institutions of learning in the United
> States, for the advancement of education in all its
> grades. Seminaries in particular will feel an
> immediate benefit from the influence of the

University.[22]

The writer of the article offered no working plan. On the contrary, he felt that it was too early to go beyond the general principles of the Constitutions by any commitment to a particular method, that experimentation and experience, "time and opportunity to learn how to accommodate various educational interests" were needed.[23]

The American Ecclesiastical Review that same summer expressed a similar acceptance of this aspect of the University's work. Also unsigned, the article stressed the growing danger of infidelity in the country and particularly in the Protestant universities. In poetic terms, the author viewed the University as a life-giving stream that

. . .will act upon the river system of our colleges and schools, which become its tributaries. . . . It has been said that our educational system is still in many ways defective, and that nearly all the lower grades of schools need much reforming. . . . Now we believe it true that our Catholic schools and colleges are by no means what they could be made to be. But they certainly exist, and no one will deny that, of late years much advance has been made, though not in every place alike. The University Commission emphasize this fact when, in their letter to the Holy Father, they say that their attention is being constantly devoted to the allsided improvement of our common Catholic schools, no less than to those of higher grade. We don't paint and finish our houses until the roof is on. The entire educational system is a complete edifice and each part helps to suggest the proportionate improvement of the rest. . . . The University, once that its existence has become a fact, will necessarily act as a regulator and promoter of all other education in the land. . . . Thus, the idea of a central source of Catholic thought is shown in its usefulness as regulating at once, and keeping in healthy activity, the teaching organism of the American Church.[24]

Very soon after the opening of the University, John T. Murphy, C.S.Sp., of Holy Ghost College in Pittsburgh, also discussed the same problem at some length. He saw the relationship primarily one of mutual benefits: while it would bring about higher standards in existing colleges and the "stamp of excellence" for those deserving, it would at the same time secure for the University a supply of well-trained students for advanced studies. Murphy offered a practical plan based on a system of examinations similar to those of Oxford and Cambridge, using local colleges as testing centers with subjects, fees, and procedures to be set. The two objections which he foresaw, he proceeded to answer. To the first, that the University would be going out of its true sphere, he replied that since the state and the Church had made no attempt to set college standards, the University should do so because of its unique and influential position in the American Catholic educational system. The second objection foreseen by Murphy was that the interests of the colleges were so varied that colleges could not be expected to submit to any kind of "iron-clad" system of studies or examinations. To this his answer was that the plan would not be "iron-clad" in regard to ways and means of education and that the examinations would represent only the net result of the teaching given. If the proposed scheme, or a similar one, were carried out judiciously and liberally by the University, Murphy felt that colleges would be glad to cooperate, in fact that they could not afford to disregard what he considered to be one of the most practically important functions of the new University.[25]

Growth of the Concept: 1889-1896

When the Catholic University was officially opened and dedicated on November 13, 1889, its faculty was limited to theology and its student body to thirty-two divinity students.[26] Growth and expansion were naturally its first concern, permitting little consideration of any systematic development of the affiliation concept. Nor was the first rectorship an easy one.

The work of building up a distinguished faculty as well as the
student enrollment, financial problems, and internal and external controversies exacted much personal attention on the
part of the Rector. Under these conditions, it seems apparent that any attempt to initiate an overall plan of affiliation for
the Catholic school system would have been entirely impracti-
cal. Certainly Bishop Keane, in his aversion to affiliation
based on coercion, must have realized, as the Catholic World
article pointed out, [27] that a sound and acceptable scheme of
affiliation would take time and experience; that for affiliation
to be well-received voluntarily by other Catholic institutions,
the University would have to be academically strong and comprehensive in its own right. For this period, then, the general
development of the University may be considered also an advancement of the cause of affiliation. In this regard, probably
the most significant achievement was the addition of two new
graduate schools in 1895, the School of Philosophy, which included science and letters, and the School of Social Sciences.[28]
The resultant opening of the University to laymen was of fundamental importance in building a closer relationship between
the University and the other Catholic colleges for men in this
country.

    There were, however, several other events of particular
importance for affiliation. In 1891-1892, the third academic
year of the University's existence, Fathers Edward A. Pace
and Thomas Shahan joined the faculty, the former in the field
of psychology and the latter in ecclesiastical history.[29] Both
of these professors not only contributed substantially to the
University's development and scholarship in the years which
followed, but they also became directly involved in the formation and promotion of the 1912 plan of affiliation: Dr. Pace as
a close collaborator of Dr. Shields and Dr. Shahan as the University Rector at that time.

    It was, moreover, during the first rectorship that semi-
nary affiliation in two distinct forms was introduced. Just
before the opening of the University in 1889, the Reverend P.
J. Garrigan, Vice Rector of the University, wrote that the
Paulist Fathers were to open a house of studies near the University as of September, 1890, and that other religious com-

munities had also been invited to do so, at the express wish of
the Holy Father, in an effort to attain uniformity of teaching
in all the ecclesiastical schools of the country.[30] Ellis, in
noting this same development, cited a letter from Augustine F.
Hewit, the Superior General of the Paulist Fathers, to Cardinal Gibbons, on February 13, 1889, in which permission was
sought to establish a Paulist House,

> . . .distinct but affiliated, in the expectation that
> the ordinary seminary course will be carried on
> under the direction of the rector [of the Paulist
> House], but hoping to engage the services of
> University professors for instruction, and to give
> young priests and alumni who are prepared, the
> benefits of the higher courses in the University.[31]

Such a house was established in temporary quarters by the
opening of the University, and similar negotiations with the
Dominicans, Marists, and Holy Cross Fathers were entered
upon before 1895.[32]

In the fall of 1894, St. Paul Seminary of St. Paul, Minnesota, under Archbishop Ireland became the first major seminary located any distance from the University to affiliate.
Keane noted the event and described the relationship in his
annual report for that year:

> An admirable example has been given to the
> Seminaries and Colleges of the country by the affi-
> liation to the University of the Seminary of St.
> Paul, at St. Paul, Minnesota. In virtue of this
> affiliation, the University has the right to preside
> over and pass upon the examinations for degrees
> held in the Seminary; and the Seminary has the
> privilege of having the Baccalaureate of the Uni-
> versity conferred on students who pass said
> examinations satisfactorily. The advantages of
> such an arrangement, both for the University and
> for the seminaries, are manifest.[33]

In this affiliation of St. Paul Seminary was seen "another link in the chain which should bind to the University all the leading Catholic institutions of learning."[34] This early promise, however, was not fulfilled. While the number of neighboring houses of studies increased steadily in the next two decades, St. Paul Seminary still remained in 1912 the only affiliated seminary not located in Washington, [35] and the examination-degree plan which it represented continued to be a matter of some concern to the Rector, Trustees, and Academic Senate for many years to come.[36]

Growth of the Concept: 1896-1903

By the time the Reverend Doctor Thomas J. Conaty became Rector of the University in 1896, the University was in a somewhat better position to consider acting more positively in its efforts to unite and coordinate the Catholic educational system on a national basis.

The Catholic University of America may thus be said to have fairly commenced its work and to have taken the position of "a great central college or university. . .in which all arts and sciences" should eventually be taught. In the natural development of its different Schools and Departments as now established, in the inevitable increase of its buildings, teachers, and students, in the ultimate affiliation to and coordination with it of the Catholic academies and colleges now engaged in undergraduate instruction, the hope and prophecy of the Fathers of the Second Plenary Council of Baltimore in 1866 is approaching fulfillment, and there is every reason to believe that after a few more years of united effort the Catholics of America will possess a University worthy of any nation and of any age.[37]

One of the problems which Conaty hoped to solve by affiliation was the gap between the seminary program and University studies. Seminary students, especially those from

seminaries that did not confer the Baccalaureate, were found
frequently to be in need of review and special study before
they were able to follow regular University courses.[38] The
same was true of lay students, who often required several
months to repair the defects of undergraduate work. Both
Conaty and Pace expressed concern for the lack of standards
and the need for greater cooperation between the two levels of
education if the upgrading of collegiate work were to be accomplished.[39]   While the St. Paul Seminary arrangement of
1894 had not caught on, Conaty felt that this kind of affiliation,
tied in with the supervision of examinations for the Baccalaureate, was a possible solution to the articulation problem.[40]
He decided to give the total matter further consideration.

At the March 9, 1897, meeting of the Academic Senate
of the University, the deans of the Schools of Theology and of
Philosophy were instructed to call a meeting of their faculties
to study and report on the question of affiliation.[41]   At the
next meeting of the Senate, Dr. Pace, Dean of the Faculty of
Philosophy, reported on the affiliation of colleges. He first
reviewed the general principles and plan laid down by the
University Constitutions: that the authorities were to confer
with college and seminary directors to promote the education
of youth, that the University may affiliate colleges and seminaries with the authorization of the Board of Trustees, and
that in such cases where affiliation was granted, the diplomas
issued by the affiliate were to take the place of examinations
for admission to the University. The recommendations of his
report included: (1) that the University confer with college
authorities regarding affiliation; (2) that prior to consultation,
it be ascertained what are the qualifications of the colleges as
to completeness of the curriculum, the methods of teaching,
the corps of teachers, equipment, and the attainment of
graduates; (3) if the college was empowered to grant degrees,
that it be required to grant the Baccalaureate degree and that
the work leading to the degree be of such a quality and extent
as the University may require of candidates for matriculation;
and (4) if the college is not empowered to give degrees, that
the second part of the third recommendation be enforced. The
report closed with a statement that the University's granting

of a degree to a graduate of an affiliate depended on the legality of the procedure or likelihood of friction with civil authorities of states in which the colleges were located and on the college graduate's intention of pursuing his studies at Catholic University or another institution.[42]   The report was discussed in regard to the legal aspects involved but no action was forthcoming that spring.[43]   In the fall of 1897 at the first meeting of the Senate, the Rector noted that Pace's report had been referred to a special committee of the Rector and deans and that the matter was of first importance.[44]   No second and final report, however, was located.

The records on the debate of seminary affiliation, which was carried on that same spring by the Faculty of Theology, are also incomplete but a report did reach completion and was presented to the Board of Trustees at its April 10, 1897, meeting. The faculty recommended the continuing of the original examination requirements set in connection with the affiliation of St. Paul Seminary and the conferring of the degree of S.T.B.   While the Trustees adopted the report, the matter was not closed. In the hope of solving the examination diffi-culties in a manner more favorable to the seminaries, the Rector was directed to confer with seminary presidents on the conditions of affiliation.[45]   The result was an invitational conference in May of 1898, held at St. Joseph's Seminary in New York. This meeting proved to be of historical impor-tance, not only for its re-clarification of the University's position in regard to the other segments of the Catholic edu-cational system but also as the beginning of other similar conferences under University auspices leading to the formation of the national Catholic Educational Association.

In presiding over this first conference, Conaty called for the organization of Catholic educational leaders in a con-scious effort to unite. He re-emphasized that the University was an integral part of the system, closely bound up with and dependent on the other parts, and that the Holy Father had clearly expressed in the University's Constitutions his desire that unity be attained through a scheme of affiliation under University leadership.[46]   The general favorable reaction to and spirit of the seminary meeting encouraged the Rector to

initiate a similar conference for the presidents of Catholic
colleges. Thus on April 12 and 13, 1899, in Chicago, the
first meeting of the Association of Catholic Colleges of the
United States was held. Again Conaty spoke, stressing that
efficiency was dependent on system and that system in education must include all its parts, from the lowest to the highest
with no breach in continuity. He pointed out also that, while
uniformity in certain essentials was to be desired, this did not
imply a stereotyped curriculum, inviolable regulations, nor
any singly approved textbook. The existing variations in college entrance requirements, however, were a serious obstacle
to unification, the remedy for which lay in the improved
training of teachers and the adjusting of the Catholic schools
into a cooperative system.[47]

The reaction of this group was also favorable and a second meeting was called for the following April. Unification
without destroying individual effort remained Conaty's theme.[48]
At a third meeting in 1901, Conaty carried his argument further, noting the rapid development of the state school system
and its resulting attraction for Catholics because of the comparative ease of transition from one educational level to the
next, the trend in educational legislation for control over
private schools through the state university, and the dangers
of submitting Catholic students to some of the secular literature of the time. The greatest danger, he felt, lay in the
ignoring of the high school movement by the Catholic system.
This would force parochial school graduates into the public
high schools and would lose them henceforth to non-Catholic
colleges and universities. As a solution, he proposed the
better coordination of the entire Catholic system and the development of the University's graduate programs so as to
make it possible to compete with the non-Catholic institutions.[49]

This idea of perfecting Catholic education in scope and
quality with the Catholic University playing a major role was
well supported. Cardinal Martinelli, the Apostolic Delegate,
in writing his regrets at not being able to attend the conference, had said:

Unification and co-ordination of educational work,

so that a complete and perfect system shall exist,
based on the strong and broad foundation of good
parochial schools, the superstructure consisting
of well and highly perfected academies, colleges,
seminaries and under-graduate universities, all
culminating in the Institution, the foundation of
which our Holy Father counts as one of the glories
of his Pontificate, are, it would seem to me, the
thing most to be desired at present to enable the
Catholic efforts to cope successfully with those
being made by secular or sectarian forces.[50]

This letter as well as one from Cardinal Gibbons, urging
concerted action toward unification on the part of Catholic educational leaders,[51] had been read at the opening of the conference. The overall results were encouraging. Before the end
of the meetings ten resolutions were passed, reflecting the
several points made by Conaty in his address. The sixth
resolution was especially pertinent to the University's status
among the other institutions:

Sixth--That we call upon all Catholics to recognize
the imperative need of a more perfect organization
of our educational system, and we assure them that
with a fuller development of the Catholic high school
we shall have a complete system, with its headship
in the University, and shall thus continue to maintain a high collegiate standard.[52]

The 1902 conference of the Association carried the discussion along similar lines, but with the presence of representatives from the diocesan school systems even greater
emphasis was placed on the importance of the Catholic high
school movement.[53] At the 1903 meeting, Conaty, who had
in the meantime been made the Bishop of Monterey-Los
Angeles, presided as president of the Association for the last
time, turning the organization over to the new and third Rector
of the University. However, it was under Conaty that the
ground work for the unification of the three separate educa-

tional conferences -- seminary, college, and parish school --
had been accomplished, making possible in 1904 the first
meeting of a united, national Catholic Educational Association.[54]

Perhaps Conaty had hoped that by establishing a national
association of Catholic educators he would place the University
in such a position as to create by its influence and his own
diplomacy a demand for a comprehensive program of University affiliation. There is no evidence, however, that he made
any positive, overt effort in this direction, but the close relationship between the two projects, especially as to purpose
and source of impetus, was obvious. Thus Cardinal Gibbons
in reporting to Pope Leo XIII in 1901 wrote:

> An effort was made with encouraging results,
> on the part of the Rector of the University, towards
> the unification of our educational system and the
> co-ordination of work in the different departments
> of the system. By the Conference of the Presidents
> of Seminaries, . . .the great bond of union and
> sympathy has been established between the differ-
> ent seminaries while the University has been
> regarded as not only a stimulus to excellent work
> but also a kind assistant and guide. . . . The
> Conference of the Catholic Colleges. . .has been
> the means of bringing together representatives of
> Catholic collegiate work, for the purpose of unify-
> ing the different systems as far as possible, and
> bringing everything in line with the suggestions of
> the Pontifical letter by which His Holiness expresses
> the desire that the colleges and seminaries should
> look to the University for direction and guidance as
> head of the system.[55]

In spite of this close relationship, there seemed to have
been no inclination on the part of the Rector to feel that a well-
organized national association led by the University might be
properly considered as a possible substitute for the less
prospering concept of affiliation. For while his external
activities regarding educational unification were enjoying a

healthy degree of success, he was continuing efforts within the
University to solve the seminary affiliation problem. In the
autumn of 1900, the Faculty of Theology prepared an exhaus-
tive statement on this subject, submitting it to the Board of
Trustees at its fall meeting.[56] Conaty, however, noted
rather tartly at a later meeting of the Academic Senate that
nothing had been settled by the report and that the faculty was
to take up the matter again in cooperation with a special committee appointed by the Trustees.[57] The second report was
also negative since the faculty would concede nothing, under
the University Constitutions, that would permit the more
practical plan sought by the Trustees.[58]

In the meantime the question of the affiliation of colleges
was revived in the form of a petition by the School Sisters of
Notre Dame to affiliate their college in Baltimore. At the
October 11, 1899, meeting of the Trustees the request was de-
bated, with Archbishop Ireland and Bishop Spalding favoring
affirmative action. It was generally felt, however, that
Trinity College, about to be established near the University
campus by the Sisters of Notre Dame de Namur, should be the
first "female" college to be granted affiliation, not only because
of its proximity to the University, but also because of the sac-
rifices entailed in its founding. A committee of Archbishop
Keane, Bishop Spalding, and the Rector was appointed by
Cardinal Gibbons to give further consideration to the broader
question of conditions for the possible affiliation of "female"
colleges.[59] But the following fall the Board came to the conclusion that it was not prepared to affiliate such colleges,
"considering what it means and what it may imply."[60]

In making this decision, the difficulties in settling the
seminary affiliation problem had played an important part.
The letter to Sister Theophia of the College of Notre Dame of
Maryland, in reply to the original request for affiliation,
brought this out.

> . . . The decision arrived at was that as the larger
> question of the affiliation of seminaries was as yet
> in an unsettled condition, it was difficult to reach
> any conclusion concerning the meaning and benefits

of affiliation with female colleges. The whole
matter was consequently referred back again to
the Committee for further consideration.

It is not an easy matter to determine just in
what affiliation consists, or what advantages may
accrue to colleges whose students cannot attend
the regular courses of the University. The matter will certainly receive the most careful consideration. It is only when one begins to study it
in all its bearings that the difficulties of the question are made manifest.[61]

The affiliation of high schools does not seem to have been
discussed during the Conaty rectorship, probably for two very
practical reasons in addition to the one already stated in connection with the proposed affiliation of colleges for women.
First, the Catholic high school movement was just beginning
to gather momentum and, secondly, the University was still
without a department of pedagogy through which to exert influence at the secondary-school level. For some time and as
early as 1897-1898, Dr. Pace had recommended such a department to meet a felt need of all Catholic schools and colleges. He considered the training of teachers an important
function of the University and one of the best means of improving the educational system in all its grades.[62] In 1899 he
pressed the matter further in view of the then current developments in Catholic secondary education.[63] Conaty's own views
of the importance of good teachers to the overall quality
of Catholic education were well known. Moreover, the Second
Annual Conference of Catholic Colleges had formally requested
a chair of pedagogy at the University to counteract the false
philosophies then prevalent outside the Church and to insure
thus the correct formation of Catholic teachers. Conaty had
recommended such a chair to the University Trustees for their
immediate attention.[64] He had also taken a direct and active
part in the high school movement. In 1901, for example, he
requested the appointment of an Academic Senate committee
of advice to assist him in the matter of promoting Catholic
high schools. While he did not wish to imply that the move-

ment belonged to the University, he felt strongly that the University, as head of the system, must exert its leadership and hoped also to solicit the support of the Trustees at their next meeting.[65]

Although urgent and repeated were the recommendations for a department of pedagogy, no action by the Trustees was forthcoming at that time. In the spring of 1902, however, an Institute of Pedagogy, to be located in New York as a University extension, was approved, primarily through the determination of Bishop Spalding. Its success, under Pace and the Dean of the Institute, supplied later the impetus needed for securing the long-desired department of education[66] and thus also served as a stepping stone to the 1912 plan of affiliation.

In this same regard, another important event of the last year of Conaty's rectorship was the arrival of the Reverend Thomas E. Shields on the University campus. In the fall of 1902, he was appointed instructor of psychology in the Department of Philosophy.[67] With this appointment, the three key figures of the 1912 affiliation plan (Shields, Pace, and Shahan) were now on hand.

Growth of the Concept: 1903-1909

When Denis J. O'Connell took over as the third Rector of the University on April 22, 1903, he faced an almost immediate crisis. The University was in a state of "arrested" development: the student body was decreasing, faculties were incomplete, and general financial support was lacking.[68] With the advent of the new Rector, however, Peoria's Bishop Spalding, among others, saw hope again for the fuller development of the University in its role as unifier of the whole American Catholic educational system.[69] While the internal conflicts of this period were serious and bitter, centered on financial problems and faculty dissension, yet by the end of the O'Connell regime in 1909 certain foundations had been laid which were to make possible the future security and expansion of the University so necessary for its leadership role. Among these more general advancements may be included the providing of undergraduate courses in all branches of learning except theology, with Pace, Shahan, and Shields taking prominent parts in the planning work;[70] the strengthening of the academic organization of the University by the division of its program into the five faculties of theology, philosophy, letters, science, and law;[71] and the continued growth in the number of "affiliated" neighboring houses of studies.[72] More specifically important to the present study were two additional accomplishments of this period: the bringing of the seminary affiliation problem to at least a temporary solution and the establishing of a department of education.

The lack of success in getting the seminary affiliation plan moving had long remained an obstacle to the extension of affiliation to other Catholic educational institutions. The Board of Trustees had appointed in the last fall of Conaty's rectorship a special committee to take up once again the problems of seminary affiliation, and, on a motion made by Archbishop Ireland, the matter of the affiliation of colleges for women had been re-opened and referred to the same committee.[73] While continued study had been given to the seminary plan in the months that followed and a slightly modified scheme had been approved by the Trustees at their April meeting in 1903, the committee had requested additional time to consider the affiliation of "female" colleges.[74] No record of a second report, however, was found. Conaty's resignation that spring and the almost immediate financial crisis faced by the new Rector and the Trustees probably accounted for the lack of further action at that time.

Nor did seminary affiliation apparently receive any extensive consideration again until the academic year 1906-1907. At the fall meeting of the Board of Trustees in 1906, a request for affiliation by Dunwoodie, the New York Seminary, re-opened the debate on the impracticality of the modified seminary plan, which still had not found enthusiastic support among seminary authorities.[75] The committee appointed at this meeting made its report the following spring. A new plan was proposed in which the previous rigid supervision of programs and examinations by the University was somewhat relaxed, and the affiliated seminary was given greater latitude in maintaining the degree standards as approved by the University. The Trustees adopted the report unanimously, directing the Rector to issue an invitation to seminary presidents to affiliate under this revised plan.[76]   Thus, for the time being at least, seminary affiliation as one of the pressing problems of the University was laid to rest.

About this same time O'Connell re-petitioned the University Trustees for a department of education. Drs. Pace and Shields prepared a statement for presentation to the Board, a statement which reflected not only a keen awareness of the then common problems of Catholic education but also of the total contemporary educational picture. Their brief included the need for improved training of Catholic teachers, the perforced seeking of such training in non-Catholic institutions of higher education, the dangers inherent in the use of secular and naturalistic textbooks and in following too closely the public schools, and the desirability of coordination, through systematic cooperation, among all the levels of the Catholic system. The two professors argued that the University's position was now such that it could be used to shape and raise standards throughout the country if it maintained a strong department of education, one which could take on the work of coordinating curriculums, methods, and textbooks through a program of professional training and a scheme of inspection. The Trustees were evidently convinced of the general need for such a program, and favorable action was taken on November 16, 1907.[77]

A degree of pedagogy was likewise approved the following year, but the first work of the new department was limited to the training of priests as teachers and as future diocesan superintendents and supervisors.[78] The professional needs of the teaching sisters, however, were not being completely ignored by the University. In 1902 an extension center, called the New York School of Pedagogy, had been established in New York City for the purpose of offering educational courses to the sisters and others who were seeking the New York teacher's certificate. When the University withdrew from this work in 1904, Archbishop Farley continued it under the name of the Institute of Scientific Study. In the fall of 1907 he requested and received University affiliation.[79] Pace and Shields

worked out the details which were primarily a matter of curriculum standardization, since the basic purpose of the affiliation was University recognition of course credits toward a
University Baccalaureate degree.[80]

Throughout the University documents of this time relating to the development of professional education programs, the
University's commitment to the concept of affiliation as a highly desirable function of the University remained firm, and its
dependency on a strong program for the professional and academic training of Catholic teachers became increasingly clear-
er. Thus once the Department of Education had been brought
into existence, O'Connell, Shields, and Pace began giving
serious study to the establishing of a Catholic teachers college
for the sisters. Such an institution was not only vital to any
overall qualitative improvement of Catholic education but also
essential for the counteracting of the secular affiliation trend
growing among Catholic schools. With a sisters' college,
they felt, it would be possible, through the joint efforts of the
University and the Catholic Educational Association, to set up
a cooperative accrediting plan. To be effective, however, any
proposed plan of standardization called for sufficient strength
and comprehensiveness within the University's own pedagogical programs to permit the setting of standards at a level that
would earn the respect of non-Catholic educators.[81]

These hopes for a Catholic sisters' college were not realized under O'Connell, but his efforts as well as his more
successful external educational activities underscored his genuine dedication to the promotion of the general cause of
Catholic education under University leadership. In the new
Catholic Educational Association especially, he saw a vehicle
of great promise for achieving this end. In spite of the fact
that the opening of the Catholic University to undergraduate
laymen in the fall of 1904 had repercussions among Catholic
educators in general, alienating the support of some individual
Catholic colleges that felt the University was placing itself in
competition with the other Catholic colleges of the country, [82]
O'Connell was able to carry on with great success the "new
unity movement" started by his predecessor. Accepting the
presidency of the Catholic College Association after Conaty

resigned at the 1903 meeting, he continued forward the project
of uniting the seminary, college, and parochial school conferences into one central organization. The 1904 meeting was a
good one. The newly formed organization entitled itself the
Catholic Educational Association of the United States, installed
O'Connell as its president, and proceeded with its business in
a spirit of general, harmonious cooperation.[83] Thus it was
within the framework of this Association that O'Connell was
able to carry on a multi-sided program

> . . .aimed at preparing teachers for the Catholic
> schools, affiliating seminaries to the University,
> arousing support among the Catholic colleges for the
> University cause, developing feeders for the Univer-
> sity and stemming Catholic student attendance at
> secular institutions of learning. Behind all these
> undertakings was the basic aim of establishing the
> University as the head and heart of the whole Ameri-
> can Catholic educational system.[84]

Unification of the Catholic Educational Association having
been successfully accomplished, O'Connell and its other members turned their full attention to the most pressing problems
of Catholic education. Thus at this point the activities of the
Association and the developments at the University as already
mentioned became closely interrelated. Both were primarily
devoted to the completion and unification of the Catholic system and to a clarification of the several levels of that system
through a better definition of curriculums and standards for
each level. The high school especially figured prominently
in the discussions. It was generally recognized as the missing
link of the system, and, as the middle link, that its standardization and general upgrading could be used to help bring about
curricular and other qualitative reforms within both the parochial schools and the colleges.[85]
    The quantitative and qualitative defects of the Catholic
secondary schools were felt by many to be the reason for the
increasing attendance of Catholic students at non-Catholic
colleges and universities. This undesirable trend was viewed

as the result of the failure of Catholic education to keep up with the successful public high school movement and its standardization process. The latter was gradually providing for the comparatively smooth transition of the student to each higher level of education, a characteristic still lacking in the Catholic system. The problem was further complicated by the fact that prospective religious teachers were also being trained in non-Catholic institutions and that Catholic academies and high schools were seeking to affiliate with these same institutions in order to compete more favorably in the public eye with the public school system. To emphasize merely the duty of the laity to support Catholic education was neither sufficient nor logical under these circumstances. More basic remedies would have to be applied.[86]

Dr. Shields noted that the papers and discussions of the fourth annual convention of the Association in 1907 manifested not only a growing desire for the completing and unification of the Catholic system but also a general recognition that "the permanency and efficiency of the Catholic school system imperatively demand that it produce its own textbooks and train its own teachers and establish its own standard of excellence for each grade of educational work."[87] Dr. Pace too pressed the issue. At the 1908 meeting of the Association he spoke on many of these general conditions, placing some emphasis on the dangers involved in the affiliation of Catholic schools with secular colleges and universities. Such a practice, he felt, was bound to influence the Catholic schools adversely, since the dissemination of literature and advice on textbooks, curriculums, and methods was an integral part of the affiliation procedure. Why then would not a Catholic parent question the need for Catholic schools per se if those very schools drew their strength from institutions outside the Catholic system? While Pace did not propose University affiliation in his 1908 paper, he did suggest general steps in remedy: better coordination and articulation from parochial school to the University, the preparation of good teachers, more Catholic grade and high schools, and improved college standards.[88]

In the discussion that followed Dr. Pace's speech, Father James A. Burns, C.S.C., one of the leaders of the

Catholic high school movement, endorsed heartily what had
been said and stated optimistically that eventually a practical
form of coordination and cooperation would be worked out.
However, he offered no specific plan.[89]

At the next Association meeting, the last at which
O'Connell presided, the Reverend Matthew Schumacher,
C.S.C., of the University of Notre Dame, continued the discussion of affiliation from the college point of view.   He defined affiliation as a closer relationship than accreditation,
with the main institution having direction of and control over
the work of the affiliate and providing active help.   Accreditation, on the other hand, implied sufficiently high standards
on the part of a school to meet the entrance requirements of
the college and a certain continuity of the curriculum.   For
the latter, therefore, uniform standards for admission to the
college freshman year were needed.   Father Schumacher
favored an accredited list of colleges and high schools, and he
proposed a committee of the Association to examine the
school's curriculum, teaching, and equipment and to apply
defined criteria.   Where state accrediting groups were functioning well, their lists could also be used.   The by-products
of such a plan, as he saw it, would include coordination, cooperation, and organic unity for the Catholic school system,
keeping students in Catholic schools as they advanced to each
new level.[90]

The Very Reverend Bernard P. O'Reilly, S.M., of Dayton, raised several obstacles to an accreditation plan.   He
felt that the high school diploma was not sufficient evidence of
actual, satisfactory college preparation and that a college certificate was also needed.   Nor would this work in admitting
students to college unless the college requirements were clarified and made uniform.[91]

No major agreements were reached and no action was
taken at that time.   This was, however, the beginning of a
dialogue which was to continue during the next decade in
Catholic educational circles and especially at the annual meetings of the CEA under its new president, Thomas J. Shahan,
also fourth Rector of the University.   It was this very prominence and a continuing lack of agreement among Catholic

educators as to an acceptable solution to the problem that were eventually to prove an impetus to separate action on the part of the University, action under Shahan through Drs. Shields and Pace in the form of the 1912 University plan for the affiliation of Catholic high schools and colleges.

FOOTNOTES

[1]Rev. James T. O'Dowd, Standardization and Its Influence on Catholic Secondary Education in the United States (Washington, D. C.: Catholic Education Press, 1935), pp. 11-13. O'Dowd defined "standardization" of schools as involving two steps: the drawing up of a list of minimum standards or norms to be met and the devising of sanctions to make these standards effective. The latter usually included machinery for inspection, evaluation, and certification by means of which the rank and excellence of an educational institution was determined and a list of schools so approved was published. In addition to personal inspections, other evaluative techniques used have been school reports, scholarship ratings, and examinations (ibid., pp. 30-39). Cf. Patrick J. McCormick, "Standards in Education," CEAB, XIV (November, 1917), 70-83.

[2]O'Dowd, op. cit., pp. 13-17.

[3]Ibid., pp. 19-25. The New England Association of Colleges and Preparatory Schools was established in 1885, followed by the Association of Colleges and Preparatory Schools in the Middle States and Maryland in 1892 and the North Central Association of Colleges and Secondary Schools and the Southern Association of Colleges and Secondary Schools in 1895.

[4]Ibid., pp. 15, 17.

[5]Ibid., pp. 19-25.

[6]ACUA, Pace Papers, Edward A. Pace, "The Development of the Catholic University of America, 1889-1917," p. 1.

[7]Rev. James A. Burns, C.S.C., The Growth and Development of the Catholic School System in the United States (New York: Benziger Bros., 1912), pp. 17-19, 201-202.

[8]Francis P. Cassidy, "Catholic Education in the Third Plenary Council of Baltimore," Catholic Historical Review,

XXXIV (January, 1949), 260-261.

[9] Theodore Maynard, The Story of American Catholicism (New York: Macmillan Co., 1951), p. 486.

[10] Cassidy, op. cit., p. 326.

[11] Ellis, op. cit., pp. 110, 149.

[12] ACUA, "An Appeal to the Catholics of the United States in Behalf of the University which the Late Council of Baltimore Resolved to Create" (New York: Catholic Publications Society Co., 1885), p. 5.

[13] Ellis, op. cit., pp. 244, 309.

[14] Ibid., p. 315.

[15] Ibid., pp. 309-321.

[16] ACUA, "Chronicles of the Catholic University of America from 1885," pp. 28-29. This document, written in Keane's hand, is dated January 9, 1894; the lapse of time since the event cited here probably accounts for the error in the date of the Trustees' meeting.

[17] Ellis, op. cit., p. 130. Much emphasis was placed during the Council on a university program of advanced studies in theology for the clergy; thus the direct tie-in of seminary programs with the success of a university as seen by O'Connor. Cf. Cassidy, op. cit., pp. 289-290.

[18] Ellis, op. cit., p. 339.

[19] Ibid.

[20] ACUA, Constitutions of the Catholic University of America, translated from the Latin (Washington, D. C.: n.d.), p. 10.

[21] Ibid., p. 3.

[22] "The Catholic University and Its Constitutions," Catholic World, XLIX (July, 1889), 429.

[23] Ibid.

[24] "Present Aspect of the Catholic University," American Ecclesiastical Review, I (August, 1889), 289-290. Ellis, op. cit., p. 364, attributes this article presumably to Herman Heuser, the editor of the Review at that time.

[25] John T. Murphy, C.S.Sp., "The New University and the Existing Colleges," Catholic World, L (December, 1889), 302-306.

[26] Ahern, op. cit., pp. 30-31.

[27]See pp. 7-8 of this study.

[28]Ahern, op. cit., pp. 95-106.

[29]Ibid., p. 50.

[30]Rev. P. J. Garrigan, "The First Lustrum of the Catholic University," American Ecclesiastical Review, I (September, 1889), 345.

[31]Ellis, op. cit., p. 341.

[32]ARR, April 1891 (1891), p. 24; ARR, April, 1892, (1892), pp. 7-8; ARR, September, 1895 (1895), pp. 5-6.

[33]Ibid., p. 6.

[34]"University Chronicle," CUB, I (January, 1895), 93.

[35]Year Book of the Catholic University of America, 1912-13 (Washington: 1912), p. 196.

[36]While the term "affiliated" was used both in relation to the local houses of studies and to St. Paul Seminary with no clear distinction made between the two, the relationship of each to the University was not identical. The arrangement described above in Fr. Hewit's letter applied to some of the houses, but in other cases the "affiliation" to the University was no more definite than mere proximity of location (ACUA, MMCAE, January 20, 1939, p. 24). By 1939, the term "affiliated" for these institutions was dropped in favor of "neighboring" and the arrangement was described as a "crystallization of the house-college idea of Harvard and Yale," to provide living and study quarters for advanced students under the discipline of their own religious community while following studies at the University (The Catholic University of America: A Half Century of Progress, 1939, p. 7). Cf. Ahern, op. cit., pp. 84-88.

[37]Year Book of the Catholic University of America, 1896-'97 (Washington: 1896), p. 11.

[38]ARR, October, 1897 (1897), p. 8.

[39]Ibid., pp. 10, 35-36.

[40]One other seminary, St. John's of Boston, had sought affiliation but an impasse had been reached over the nature of the required examinations (Hogan, op. cit., p. 66).

[41]ACUA, Academic Senate Records, March 9, 1897.

[42]ACUA, ASF, "Report of the Dean of the Faculty of Philosophy," April 7, 1897.

[43]ACUA, Academic Senate Records, May 6, 1897; May 11, 1897; June 3, 1897.

[44]Ibid., October 18, 1897.

[45]ACUA, MMBT, April 10, 1897, pp. 70-71.

[46]"Educational Conference of Seminary Presidents," CUB, IV (July, 1898), 399-402.

[47]"The Association of Catholic Colleges: Report of the First Annual Conference of the Association of Catholic Colleges of the United States," CUB, V (July, 1899), 358.

[48]Thomas J. Conaty, "The College Teacher," CUB, VI (July, 1900), 292-293.

[49]Thomas J. Conaty, "The Catholic College of the Twentieth Century," CUB, VII (July, 1901), 309-315.

[50]CUB, VII (July, 1901), 386, Sebastian Martinelli to Thomas J. Conaty, April 23, 1901.

[51]Ibid., 387, J. Cardinal Gibbons to Thomas J. Conaty, Easter Sunday, 1901.

[52]"Third Annual Conference of Catholic Colleges," CUB, VII (July, 1901), 385.

[53]ACUA, ASF, "Proceedings of the Fourth Annual Conference of the Association of Catholic Colleges of the United States, July 9-10, 1902."

[54]Hogan, op. cit., pp. 79-80.

[55]ACUA, ASF, Report, J. Cardinal Gibbons to "Your Holiness," May, 1901, pp. 5-6.

[56]ACUA, ASF, Rector's Report, October 9, 1900.

[57]Ibid., November 13, 1900.

[58]Ibid., January 8, 1901; "Report of the Senate Committee," February, 1901.

[59]ACUA, MMBT, October 11, 1899, p. 84.

[60]Ibid., October 10, 1900, p. 90. Women were not at that time being admitted to the University.

[61]ACUA, ASF, Thomas J. Conaty to Sister Theophia, Govanstown, Maryland, November 5, 1900.

[62]ARR, October, 1898 (1898), p. 25.

[63]ARR, October 1899 (1899), p. 31.

[64]ARR, October, 1900 (1900), p. 5.

[65]ACUA, ASF, April 25, 1901. A Senate committee was appointed with Pace as a member, but no further reference to

the committee's report was found.

[66]Hogan, op. cit., pp. 83-86. Cf. "Supplementary Report on the Institute of Pedagogy," ARR, November, 1902 (1902).

[67]Ibid., p. 4.

[68]Barry, op. cit., pp. 24-25.

[69]Ibid., pp. 40-42.

[70]Ibid., pp. 68-69.

[71]Ibid., p. 162.

[72]Ibid., pp. 109-122.

[73]ACUA, MMBT, November 12, 1902, p. 103.

[74]Ibid., April 22, 1903, p. 105. Cf. ACUA, ASF, "Report of the Board of Studies on Affiliation," January 13, 1903.

[75]ACUA, MMBT, November 27, 1906, pp. 149-150.

[76]Ibid., April 10, 1907, p. 153. Cf. ACUA, ASF, "Conditions of Affiliation," June 20, 1907. Barry (op. cit., p. 222) reported on similar action taken by the Trustees at their April 10, 1907, meeting on a plan for the affiliation of Catholic colleges and high schools. His reference is to a single document in the Board of Trustees files entitled "For the Affiliation of Colleges and High Schools to the University." The document is a four-page printed leaflet, marked by hand "Document C, April 10, 1907," and located now in the Catholic University Archives, Exhibits of the Meetings of the Board of Trustees, Meeting of April 10, 1907. It describes in some detail the need for affiliation of Catholic educational institutions under Catholic auspices, the standards to be met for the affiliation of colleges and high schools, and a proposed procedure for effecting the affiliation of applying institutions to the University.

This investigator, however, rejects this document as an authentic 1907 record for the following reasons. (1) There is no mention in the minutes of the Board of Trustees for its meeting of April 10, 1907, of any discussion or action regarding such a plan, although the seminary plan of the same date is fully recorded. (2) There is no mention of a University plan for the affiliation of colleges and high schools in any of the University records of that time, either just prior to April, 1907, or in the several years immediately following. A careful search was made not only of the minutes of the meetings of the Board of Trustees but also of Academic Senate records and reports of the Rector. (3) In the Board of Trustees files, ACUA, there is a document by Pace and Shields, written two years later and dated April 10, 1909, in which the establishment of a teachers college for the teaching sisters by the University was proposed. The authors showed concern therein for the then current trend among Catholic schools and academies to seek affiliation with secular institutions in order to gain any kind of educational recognition. Not only was no mention made of the availability of a similar affiliation program at the University but a major argument made for the establishing of a Catholic teachers college was that it would permit such a plan under University auspices (cf. Barry, op. cit., p. 221). (4) There is also no mention of an existing Catholic University plan of affiliation in the printed proceedings of the Catholic Educational Association meetings of this period, even though the overall problem of affiliation was discussed by this group at length during this time. In fact, as will be shown later in the present study, in several instances mention was made at Association meetings of the need for a practical Catholic program of affiliation, with at least one direct proposal that it be placed under University auspices (see p. 43 of the present study). Moreover, both Shahan, then Rector of the University, and Shields were present at that particular meeting. (5) The content of the questioned document is substantially the same and almost identically worded as the first four pages of the 1912-1913 Course of Study for Affiliated High Schools, which was issued by Shields after the approval of the 1912 plan. While it is possible that the same plan was submitted in 1907 and again in 1912, with action taken only at the later date, it seems highly unlikely that over the five-year interim period neither Shields or Pace would have made no modifications. (6) The original 1912 plan, as submitted to the Trustees by the Rector at their April 17, 1912, meeting was designated in the minutes of the Board also as "Document C" (ACUA, MMBT, p. 199). This document, however, could not be located in the University Archives and was noted as missing as early as 1938 (ACUA, AF, George Johnson to Roy J. Deferrari, n.d.). Since the "Document C" in question was clipped to the back of the seminary affiliation document of April 10, 1907, and so filed, a possible and highly probable explanation for the incorrect date on it is that the misfiling occurred considerably after 1907 and that the April 10, 1907, date was placed on the 1912 document at that time.

[77]Barry, op. cit., p. 219.

[78]O'Connor, op. cit., p. 72.

[79]ACUA, MMBT, November 13, 1907, p. 159.

[80]ACUA, BTEM, November 13, 1907, Document K. Cf. Barry, op. cit., footnote 78, pp. 219-220.

[81]Ibid., p. 221.

[82]Ibid., pp. 126-132.

[83]Ibid., pp. 214-218.

[84]Ibid., p. 213.

[85]James A. Burns, C.S.C., "Coordination and Cooperation in Catholic Educational Work," CEAB, III (November, 1906), 41-45.

[86]Barry, op. cit., pp. 225-228.

[87]Thomas E. Shields, "Notes on Education," CUB, XIV (January, 1908), 79.

[88]Edward A. Pace, "The Present Status of Education," CEAB, V (November, 1908), 43-44.

[89]"Discussion," ibid., 48.

[90]Matthew Schumacher, C.S.C., "The Affiliating and Accrediting of Catholic High Schools and Academies to Colleges," CEAB, VI (November, 1909), 132-140.

[91]"Discussion," ibid., 141-142.

CHAPTER II

DR. SHIELDS AND THE 1912 AFFILIATION PLAN: 1909-1912

A Master Plan for Catholic Education

It was within the fourth rectorship of The Catholic University of America that a practical, working plan for the affiliation of Catholic high schools and colleges came into existence. The Right Reverend Thomas J. Shahan was appointed Rector on May 7, 1909, having served as Pro-Rector since February 25th of that year.[1] As a member of the Faculty of Theology since 1891, he had earned a reputation both as a scholar and teacher and was the first rector to be chosen from the professorial ranks. With Dr. Pace, Shahan had worked closely on many University affairs, and his name was linked sympathetically with University development as a pedagogical center of national scope. It was not surprising then that he continued the efforts of the former rectors toward the unification and coordination of the country's Catholic school system and that in him Drs. Pace and Shields found support in their various educational activities.[2] Moreover his position in this regard was a forceful one:

> It has always been felt in the University that it owed the most earnest service to Catholic education, not alone within its own borders, but throughout the country. . . . Indeed, there is no service which the University prizes more highly or is more anxious to render than the service due Catholic education. This is its highest merit, its broadest field of action, its very raison d'etre.[3]

Another important figure for this study was Monsignor Edward A. Pace. He too had joined the University faculty in 1891 and over the years held such important positions as Dean

of the School of Philosophy, Director of Studies, General Secretary, and Vice Rector. Nationally he was recognized as a
Catholic philosopher, psychologist, and educator and, as the
latter, contributed substantially to most of the important educational movements of his life time: the Catholic Educational
Association, the Department of Education of the National
Catholic Welfare Conference, the American Council on Education, the Catholic Encyclopedia, the Catholic Educational
Review, and the professional training of religious teachers.[4]

It was through Pace and Shahan that the attention of the
University was drawn in the 1890's to the promising work of
a graduate student at Johns Hopkins University, that of the
Reverend Thomas E. Shields. On their recommendation, the
Rector persuaded Archbishop Ireland of St. Paul to give the
University his seminary biology teacher, and in 1902 Dr.
Shields joined the faculty as an instructor of physiological
psychology in the Department of Philosophy.[5] The close col-
laboration of Drs. Pace and Shields on many and various edu-
cational endeavors thus ensued.

Among these endeavors were several of major importance to the success of a plan of affiliation. In an undated
typescript among Pace's papers was found a brief résumé of
the events which took place after 1907 as an outgrowth of the
University's new Department of Education. Pace noted first
that from 1907 to December, 1910, a series of articles on the
science and history of education was published in the Catholic
University Bulletin. The authors, Dr. Shields and the
Reverend Patrick J. McCormick, then of the Department of
Education and later a rector of the University, hoped to build
a body of educational literature for the Catholic teacher and
student and to bring at the same time the cause of Catholic
education before a broader general public. To serve these
same purposes, the Catholic Educational Review was started
in January of 1911 by Shields, who had also recently organized
the Catholic Education Press for the publication of textbooks.
In that same year, at their April meeting, the Trustees authorized a summer school for sisters and, at their November
meeting, the Catholic Sisters College, both with Dr. Shields
as Dean. Formal approval of the Shields' plan for the affilia-

tion of Catholic high schools and colleges followed in the
spring of 1912. Of this rapid succession of achievements,
Pace stated: "The significant facts in the whole development
are, first, that Dr. Shields was the prime mover and contro
ling influence of these undertakings; second, that all were
sanctioned by the Trustees of the University."[6]

Nor was the close timing of these events mere coinci-
dence. While each was promoted separately, they were all
part of a master plan in the mind of Dr. Shields: "Through
the Catholic Sisters College, the Summer School, affiliation,
the Review, the textbooks, we are endeavoring to unify and
strengthen Catholic education and to help all of our schools."
This many-sided attack, moreover, represented an equally
broad vision of Catholic education on the part of Dr. Shields
and an untiring energy poured into the projects of his master
plan. By his writings, which were voluminous and diversi-
fied, Shields revealed himself as an educator of both depth
and breadth, realizing that "any effective measure taken by
Catholic educators must be purposive, well-directed, concerted, and of such a comprehensive nature as to stimulate,
strengthen, and properly orientate every phase and plane of
educational life and endeavor."[8]

Dr. George Johnson, a student and colleague of Shields,
called the mission of Dr. Shields a "providential one." Since
the structuring of the Catholic school system by the Fathers
of the Third Plenary Council of Baltimore in 1884, steady
quantitative and organizational progress had been made at the
diocesan level; the Catholic high school movement had been
gotten underway, and the first efforts at national unification
had been accomplished through the founding of a central
Catholic university and a national Catholic educational association. But the emerging Catholic system, in its concern
for external developmental activities during this period, had
given less time to translating fundamental Catholic principles
into pedagogical practice, and non-sectarianism, as adopted
by the public schools, was seen to be dangerously infiltrating
the Catholic schools through the textbooks and curricula.
Shields realized fully that any superficial or negative approach
to the problem would be useless.

He saw the need of a Catholic philosophy of
education, of an expression of the Catholic philosophy of life in terms of the classroom. Furthermore, he realized the necessity of embodying
this Catholic philosophy of education and curricula
and textbooks, in details of administration and
supervision, in teacher-training and school policy,
were it to become really effective in the lives of
the learners.[9]

While Shields admitted that the state had rights in the
education of its youth, he saw a tendency toward monopoliza-
tion in its sytem of affiliation and state university entrance
requirements and was prompted to warn, because of the ex-
clusion of religion from the state system, that "every approach toward state control should be jealously looked into."[10]
He agreed fully with Dr. Pace that Catholic teachers must be
given aid from within their own system if that system were to
be Catholic in more than name only.[11] Dr. Shields, however,
was not adverse to change. It was becoming increasingly
evident, he said,

> that any school, whether private or public, that
> fails to adjust itself to the new conditions must
> cease to exist. The college that adheres rigidly
> to the traditions of the past soon finds its halls
> deserted, and the elementary or secondary school
> that fails to give adequate training to the pupils
> which it receives will very soon meet a similar
> fate.[12]

The changes he emphasized for Catholic education were in
the form of improved teacher training, methods, and curriculum, but these changes to be effective for a truly Catholic
education would have to come from internal forces, not
through coercive legal enactments.[13] Thus teacher training
institutions, standards, and standardization procedures had
to be made integral parts of the Catholic system itself.[14]

First Steps in Carrying Out the Plan

Drs. Shields and Pace were doing more than merely theorizing and hoping during this 1908-1909 period. They were also presenting forcible arguments, first to O'Connell and then to Shahan, why the University should provide professional programs for the teaching sisterhoods. A six-page document, dated March 1, 1908, addressed to Monsignor O'Connell and signed by both Shields and Pace, outlined the Catholic educational situation as they saw it. The document was divided into four distinct parts: (1) the general realization of Catholic school teachers of a need for better academic and professional training if their schools were to compete successfully with the public schools and keep Catholic youth within the Catholic system; (2) the desire on the part of these teachers to receive this training under Catholic auspices as evidenced by their strong support of and interest in Catholic educational activities; (3) the preference of Catholic University as a center of teacher-training as shown by the success of the University's various summer institutes and its correspondence courses and by the number of petitions made to the University and Trinity College by bishops, superintendents, and communities for pedagogical instruction for their teachers; and (4) the success of non-Catholic educational work due to systematic organization and cooperation to an extent not present in the Catholic system, a fact which was resulting in the affiliation of Catholic institutions with non-Catholic institutions. The latter situation was observed as placing the non-Catholic institution in a position to dictate to Catholic schools on matters of curriculum, methods, and textbooks, making it impossible for Catholic educators to shape the policy and character of their own schools. Thus not only were the Catholic schools becoming mere annexes of the public system but the situation was blocking efforts toward coordination within the Catholic system, since some schools were under diocesan supervision while others were under the supervision of the affiliating non-Catholic institution.[15]

A similar document by the same two professors, dated April 18, 1909, and entitled "Some Relations of Catholic to

Non-Catholic Schools," covered much of the same ground as
the earlier document but enlarged considerably on the affiliation condition and ended with a concrete plan for a Catholic
sisters' college at the University. While the statements on
non-Catholic affiliation were directed as arguments for the establishing of a sisters' college, they reveal at the same time
the authors' recognition of the great potential within the affiliation movement for Catholic education, if such a plan were
completely under Catholic auspices.

> A systematic effort is being made by the non-
> Catholic universities to dominate the whole public
> school system and to control all the primary and
> secondary schools within the radius of their influ-
> ences, whether such schools be Catholic schools
> or State schools. The chief means employed have
> been the system of affiliation and accrediting and
> the training of teachers. The universities in this
> way have fixed the standards for high schools and
> colleges and for all other schools of similar rank
> which comply with their requirements. In this
> affiliation the textbooks, methods, curriculum and
> the qualifications of the teachers in the schools
> seeking affiliation all pass under the jurisdiction
> of the institution granting the affiliation. Where
> such affiliation is granted the pupils may pass
> without examination from grammar school to high
> school and from high school to the university.
> Moreover, such affiliation is frequently made the
> condition upon which the graduates of such a school
> may obtain positions as teachers in the public
> school system. To gain these advantages a large
> number of our academies and Sisters' colleges
> have sought and obtained affiliation with the non-
> Catholic universities.
> . . . .

> The conditions upon which the university grants
> affiliation or upon which it accredits a school vary

somewhat in different parts of the country, but in
general the procedure is as follows: a deputy,
usually a member of the academic staff of the university, visits the affiliated school once a year.
He examines text-books used, the curriculum in
force, the methods employed, the equipment of the
school, and the efficiency of the teachers. If in
all these aspects the school meets with his appro-
bation it is put on the accredited list or retained
there, as the case may be. If in anything the
schools fail to meet the requirements, suggestions
are made for suitable changes; if these are not duly
complied with, the school is dropped from the accredited list.

. . . .

The practice of affiliation still further empha-
sizes the fact that Catholic schools are turning to
non-Catholic sources for their ideals and for their
standards. The logical conclusion from this, as
many see it, is that since the public school system
is the end towards which our schools shape their
courses, the sooner the child enters the public
school system the better. It amounts to a public
confession of the inferiority of our schools.

A further consequence of the attendance of
Sisters at non-Catholic schools and of the affiliation of Catholic schools to non-Catholic universities is that it is gradually leading to the adoption
of the text-books in use in the public school system and which have been written with the avowed
purpose of excluding all religious teaching and
all reference to Christ. In these books the world
with its phenomena is presented as sufficient in
itself, having no need of a creator and no room
for Divine Providence. The mere addition of formal religious instruction during one period of the
day and the religious garb of the teacher are

scarcely sufficient to offset the effect of such textbooks.[16]

Shahan warmly supported the plan for a Catholic sisters'
college and submitted the two documents by Shields and Pace
at his first Trustees meeting on April 21, 1909. The Trustees, who also felt the matter to be of great importance, set
up a special committee to study the proposal and to report at
the next meeting.[17] The recommendations of the committee
were most favorable and were adopted unanimously by the
Board on November 17, 1909. The Rector was directed
through the University's Department of Education to offer a
complete course of pedagogical training and to open a summer
normal school for religious and lay women the following summer. He was further authorized to communicate with the
principal teaching sisterhoods to learn their reactions to such
programs and the prospects of support.[18]

Dr. Shields was evidently commissioned by the Rector
to carry out this last directive. He made an extensive trip
in the late spring of 1909, visiting bishops, priests, and sisters, and was well received by all. While his first aim was
to ascertain the amount of support a sisters' college at the
University could expect, one can be sure that Shields did not
miss the opportunity to discuss his other related projects,
affiliation among them. Thus he wrote to the Rector in regard to his audience in Detroit:

> I had quite a long talk with the Bishop and with the
> priests, all of whom seemed eager to welcome our
> projects. They will, I think, adopt our textbooks
> and methods. Many of them stated that the only
> hope, in their opinion, of bringing about unification
> in our Catholic schools lay in the University.[19]

and of his meeting in Buffalo:

> At a dinner following the commencement exercises,
> there were a number of priests present, among
> them a Jesuit Father whom I did not know, a

German I think. This man was very much interested both in my talk to the Sisters and in the
conversation at the dinner table, which consisted
largely of a fire of questions from the priests and
my answers concerning our present school policies.

. . .Everywhere the priests and Bishops look
to the immediate future of the University with great
hope. There is beginning to be a realization of the
great need of the University's influence in uniting
and uplifting all our Catholic schools. In this I
believe we have an earnest of success.[20]

Because of preparation difficulties, the opening date of
the summer school was postponed until the summer of 1911,
but the formal, though humble, beginnings of the Catholic
Sisters College followed immediately in October of the same
year.[21] Dr. Shields, as Dean of both, saw thus the achievement of the most important first step of his master plan, with
the other parts falling rapidly into place.

Shields had always felt strongly the need for Catholic
educational literature and textbooks to combat the general
movements of materialism and agnosticism, thinking that a
body of Catholic educational literature would do much to eli-
minate the very need for affiliation with outside institutions.[22]
Nor did he feel that Catholic University could be a genuine
center of Catholic education unless it had the necessary organs
to extend its influence throughout the country and to offer
guidance and safeguards against encroachments by other educational and philosophical systems.[23] In 1905, therefore, he
had started a Catholic Educational News Service to supply
articles on educational topics to the Catholic weeklies and
other periodicals, and in 1909, the Catholic Education Press
to publish textbooks and other educational materials for the
schools.[24] By the 1910's, however, Shields, Pace, and
Shahan were laying foundations for a more extensive and considerably more challenging activity, a regularly published
periodical devoted entirely to Catholic educational interests.
Such a publication was to have direct benefits for the unifica-

tion movement, not only by reaching the individual classroom teacher on whom the competence of the Catholic system depended, but also through arousing the active cooperation of the secular clergy and religious orders in the form of written contributions by their best educators. With the Rector's whole-hearted endorsement and under joint editorship, Shields and Pace published the first number of The Catholic Educational Review in January, 1911.[25] The Review was to serve in the years that followed as an important line of communication between the University and its affiliates on a variety of educational matters and also as a means of disseminating information pertaining to specific policies and procedures of Affiliation.

The Catholic Educational Association's Failure to Act

In addition to these achievements on the University campus, the continuing activities of the Catholic Educational Association during 1910 and 1911 also gave impetus to the University's 1912 affiliation plan: positively, by their increasing emphasis on Catholic educational problems of unification and standardization and, negatively, by the inability of the Association to take any practical steps toward the solution of these problems.

After Father Schumacher's urgent request for a form of Catholic accreditation in 1909,[26] Shahan again took up the theme of unification at the 1910 conference. In warning of the dangers of isolation, he emphasized that the needed coordination must result from influences that were thoroughly Catholic and so comprehensive as to include every level and aspect of Catholic education.[27] In the discussion which immediately followed the paper, the Very Reverend F. A. O'Brien of Kalamazoo, Michigan, suggested that the entire Catholic school system would benefit by a bureau or department set up at the Catholic University, the University being the center of learning and head of all Catholic education in the United States. Through this bureau, the University should then send authorized agents to visit every parochial school to determine how it was being conducted and to encourage its development.[28] Dr. Shields then spoke, re-emphasizing that the schools must be standardized but that the standards must not be set by a system essentially different from the Catholic one.[29] To this, Monsignor Joseph Schrembs of Grand Rapids concurred but stated that he would go a step further than Father O'Brien. Catholic University should also establish uniform course standards, fixing principles and limits for the various courses in parochial schools and providing examinations to enforce these standards.[30] Out of Shahan's paper and its discussion came a general resolution adopted by the Association: that the betterment of the Catholic educational system depended on the correlation of parish schools with Catholic secondary and higher educational institutions and that pastors must, therefore, interest themselves also in the higher schools.[31]

Another paper at the same meeting dealt with college entrance requirements as a standard. Father O'Mahoney, president of St. Viator College in Bourbonnais, Illinois, felt that no picture of the present status of Catholic college requirements nor agreement on a standard could be reached unless the high school unit was clearly and precisely defined.[32] A motion resulted and was carried that a committee be appointed to look into the matter of standardizing entrance requirements for the colleges.[33]

The 1911 meeting of the Catholic Educational Association brought affiliation and standardization forward as the major topic. Reporting for a committee on high schools appointed in 1908, Father James A. Burns, C.S.C., summarized the Catholic high school situation. The report in general reflected a phenomenal growth at this level, but a spontaneous one to meet immediate needs rather than a systematized trend. The danger of modeling the Catholic high school after public schools was shown by several statistics: of 295 high schools responding to a questionnaire, a total of 56 were affiliated with some type of non-Catholic institution of higher education, while only 19 were so affiliated with a Catholic college.[34] Commenting on these figures, Father Burns said:

> Here, surely is a situation full of significance.
> For it means that our secondary schools, which
> ought to form a natural and easy passageway from

the parish school to the Catholic college, are, in
steadily increasing numbers, being drawn into such
academic relationships as will make it a most easy
if not inevitable thing for the Catholic boy, on fin-
ishing his course in our schools, to pass up into a
non-Catholic college. . . . I need not point out that
it is full of danger for the future of our colleges.[35]

Among his recommendations to stem this undesirable affiliation trend, Burns included that Catholic colleges affiliate the
stronger Catholic high schools and admit their graduates
without examination.[36]

The report brought forth considerable discussion. Dr.
Pace opened it by stating that the most significant aspects of
the report were the facts regarding the affiliation of Catholic
high schools to non-Catholic colleges. The question which he
raised was whether these affiliations were concerned only
with external work and policy or with the inner life of the
school, ejecting into the work of the Catholic school the principles, methods, examinations, and textbooks of the state
systems.[37] There were several who, on the basis of personal experiences, defended the situation and disclaimed the
internal influences which Pace feared,[38] but Father Green,
the president of St. Rita College in Chicago, denounced the
practice roundly as an unqualified abuse, a "heterodoxical
spectacle" and "a stultification of our claim of the necessity
of Catholic education."[39] Two other papers at the 1911
meeting also discussed the nature of the high school and its
general improvement. Their recommendations included the
establishing of Catholic central or diocesan high schools, improved curricula, and the elimination of the preparatory departments conducted by the colleges.[40] The only general
agreement reached, however, as a result of all these papers
seems to have been that further study of the high school was
called for.

From the college point of view, the 1911 meeting of the
Association was more specifically productive. Father
Schumacher reported on the work of his committee on Catholic
college entrance requirements as had been requested the

previous year. From this report came the adoption of the
first college standard by the Association: that the standard
college should require sixteen high school units for entrance.
The implications for the high school were not without importance, since in setting this standard the group also defined a
high school unit as "a subject in secondary work pursued for a
year of at least thirty-six weeks, taught five periods a week,
each period at least forty-five minutes." Moreover, the
standard college was urged to require that the amount of work
represented by a unit be formulated in detail and fully outlined.[41]

Drs. Shields and Pace must have been disappointed that
out of all this discussion and sometimes heated debate on the
affiliation problem there evolved no general "demand" on the
part of the Association that the Catholic University take steps
to establish a comprehensive program of affiliation for the
Catholic system. By the same token, however, three facts
must have been apparent to them at this time. First, this
very lack of agreement among Catholic educators on the secular affiliation problem which prevented the drafting of the
University for the job would also hamper for some time any
definitive solution by the Association. Secondly, and because
of the first, the growing desire in Catholic educational circles
for standardization and recognition was making it increasingly
urgent, and opportune, that the University put into effect
Rome's original mandate that the University affiliate other
Catholic educational institutions. And thirdly, this same lack
of agreement underscored once again the necessity that any
affiliation plan attempted by the University would have to be
on a strictly voluntary basis and in no way prejudicial to the
autonomy of the affiliate.

Action of the Catholic University

The records of just what took place at the University by
way of preparing a plan of affiliation for submission to the
Trustees in the spring of 1912 or the actual developmental
steps which followed the approval of the plan are meager.
From a variety of sources only a general outline could be

pieced together. The decision to reopen high school and college affiliation as a matter for consideration by the Trustees
was made in the fall of 1910, the minutes of the Board's meeting at that time noting that "incidentally the Right Reverend
Rector promises to take up the matter of affiliation of other
institutions in earnest and report at the next meeting."[42]
Failure to keep this promise may have been related to the
fact that seminary affiliation problems intervened,[43] but more
probably the thinking of Shields and Pace prevailed: that before extended affiliation could be attempted a complete pedagogical program at the University, including one for the
teaching sisters, was a necessity.[44] This Shahan, Shields,
and Pace set out to provide and brought to a successful conclusion by the fall of 1911. Moreover, once established, the
sisters' summer school and the Catholic Sisters College
served immediately to promote the cause of affiliation in a
most practical way. If there had been any tendency on the
part of the priest-educators at the 1911 CEA convention to
withhold favoring the University as a Catholic standardizing
agency, this was not true of the sisters who attended the University's first summer session in 1911. They expressed
frequently and specifically "their desire for affiliation with
the University in preference to any arrangement that might be
offered by other universities."[45] Thus it seems safe to as-
sume that Shields and Pace, with the encouragement or insti-
gation of the Rector, collaborated on the details of the 1912
plan some time after the Rector's 1910 promise to the Trustees and that probably a great deal of the actual work was
accomplished early in the academic year 1911-1912.[46]

The writings of Shields and Pace during this later period
point rather perceptibly to the forthcoming initiation of a University affiliation plan, although no explicit early announcement was made. Shields, for example, devoted extensive
space in the December, 1911, issue of the Catholic Educational Review to the several points brought out so forcibly at the
1911 CEA meeting and concluded by saying: "The Education
Department of the University should also be in a position to
contribute very materially towards the solution of the many
intricate problems connected with the articulation of Catholic

high schools and colleges."[47]   In February, the Review carried a translation of a recent letter from Pope Pius X to
Cardinal Gibbons as Chancellor of the University,[48] and a
discussion of the letter by Dr. Pace followed. Pace found
significant, and certainly propitious to University affiliation,
the emphasis which the Pope placed on the University as a
center of unification:

> It was never intended that the University should
> be detached from the other elements of our educa-
> tional system or that it should passively and patiently
> await the gradual improvement of the preparatory
> schools as the condition of its own development. On
> the contrary, as Leo XIII repeatedly declared and as
> Pius X now reiterates in the plainest possible terms,
> the University is to be the center and source of
> vitality for all our institutions. Whatever they need
> becomes at once its need and whatever it can accom-
> plish towards the betterment of educational work
> must forthwith turn to their advantage.[49]

Shields followed up this article in the next issue of the
Review, stating that the letter of the Holy Father made it plain
that he expected the Catholic University to use its resources
for the solution of the country's Catholic educational problems, that as the central institution it should be able to assist

> by training teachers of our various educational in-
> stitutions, by standardizing high schools and
> colleges, by suggesting suitable curricula, by
> providing appropriate texts, by developing Catholic
> methods, and by affiliating with itself educational
> institutions of various grades.

> That the Trustees of the University recognize
> the importance of this work is manifest by the fact
> that they have recently developed the Department
> of Education in the University for the training of
> future teachers in the principles and methods of

Catholic education and for the preparation of
diocesan superintendents who will carry these
ideals into the parochial system of the various
dioceses. Finally, in establishing the Sisters
College at the University, they have provided for
the training of members of the various teaching
communities of women to fill positions worthily
in the faculties of the novitiate normal schools,
high schools and colleges. This work has already
produced splendid results in the direction of unification of the Catholic school system of the
country. It is making it possible to bring about
a closer cooperation among our Catholic schools
of every rank.[50]

Dr. Shields could well afford to be this explicit by
March of 1912, since the proposed affiliation plan was then in
the form of a printed brochure. At the Academic Senate meeting of March 16th, the Rector introduced the subject and spoke
of the general desire on the part of other Catholic institutions
to so affiliate.[51] The matter was laid over to the next meeting, which was held less than a week later, and the proposed
plan in printed form was then placed before this body.

In the discussion which ensued, the importance
and desirability of such action was emphasized,
and the consequent necessity of using the utmost
care in the formulation of the plan. It was suggested that some slight addition be made to the
requirements for colleges to ensure that their
curricula be of sufficient breadth. Others were
of the opinion that this was sufficiently covered
by sections 1 and 2 under the heading "Execution
of the Plan." Dr. Shea was of the opinion that
the requirement of 2160 hours of class work in
college was too small. Dr. Aiken desired to
know whether the University was actually comply-
ing with the requirements for the admission of
students which it was proposed to demand of the

colleges.

Passing to the heading "Affiliation of High
Schools," Dr. Pace called attention to the importance of using the same terminology in this
plan as was employed in the Yearbook and other
announcements of the University. Dr. Aiken
raised the question as to whether the requirement
of three units in English was not too much. The
chief discussion was on the relation of the proposed scheme of study to the study of the classics.
Both Drs. Maguire and Bolling were inclined to believe that it should be modified in this respect,
but desired to have further time for the study of
the question before making any definite proposals.

The Rector spoke of the section "Execution of
the Plan of Affiliation," and announced his intention of calling another meeting for a continuation
of the discussion.[52]

Additional discussion by the Academic Senate on the matter
was not recorded, however. The May 8, 1912, minutes of the
Senate noted only that the Board of Trustees at a recent meeting had adopted the plan with the execution of it left to the
Rector and the Academic Senate.[53]

The Visiting Committee, a standing committee of the
Board of Trustees, also studied the proposed affiliation plan
at its meeting of March 26-27, 1912. The deliberations of
this group, chaired by Cardinal Farley and including Bishop
Glennon, Monsignor Harkins, Mr. Walter G. Smith, (all of the
Board), and the Rector, resulted in a recommendation of approval.[54] This endorsement in addition to the enthusiastic
support of the Rector convinced the Trustees.[55] There could
have been little debate or serious objection by the Trustees to
any aspect of the affiliation plan as laid before them at their
April 17, 1912, meeting. The minutes recorded simply:
"The recommendation of plan (Doc. C) of the Right Reverend
Rector for Affiliation of High Schools and Colleges is adopted

by the Board."[56]

There is no evidence that any direct announcement of the new affiliation program was made to individual Catholic institutions, inviting them to seek affiliation with the University. The University did, however, use its two general educational periodicals to bring the plan to the attention of Catholic educators. The Catholic University Bulletin noted the event in its May "University Chronicle" and reprinted the total plan in its June issue.[57] Shields printed the complete plan in the May Catholic Educational Review and also invited Catholic high schools and colleges to make application.[58] Here he stressed the voluntary nature of the program and the benefits to be derived therefrom. Among the latter he listed unity and excellence of the curriculum, superior training of teachers, responsible control of grave defects of method or content in studies, and more searching and thorough examinations.[59] In the next Review he stated that the feasibility of the plan depended on the training of the teachers and then continued: "What the University aims at is not to lessen the autonomy of any institution but rather to secure that autonomy in the right direction, i.e., to make our schools independent of numerous influences which would tie them down to a system and to methods which leave no room for the genuine Catholic spirit."[60] In the October issue, Pace once again defined the University's position as the head of the Catholic educational system of the United States and thus as an integral part of that system. He placed emphasis then on the mutual benefits to be derived from the new affiliation program, with the University itself being "the first to profit by the growing efficiency of the secondary schools, since its own special purposes can be attained the more readily with students who have been duly prepared."[61]

In the meantime, much was being accomplished by way of putting the newly approved plan in good working condition. In mid-summer of 1912, the Rector appointed the first Committee on Affiliation to carry on this work. No list of the members of that Committee, however, could be found, and only three names appeared among the records of the first years of the program's existence: Drs. Pace, Shields, and McCormick. Dr. Pace served as the chairman.[62] His position at the

University in 1912 was that of Director of Studies, and it was probably felt that there was a logical and desirable relationship between that office and the new work of Affiliation. At the same time, however, there is little doubt that the prime mover, the major contributor, and the controlling figure in the development and conduct of the program was Dr. Shields. All the events and records from 1912 until his death in 1921 point to this. The third faculty member whose name was linked early to the work of Affiliation was that of the Reverend Doctor Patrick J. McCormick, who served as the first secretary of the Committee.[63]

The Committee took up its work in earnest immediately following its appointment that summer. How formally or informally it worked is not known, but probably Shields carried the main burden of the work. The only account given was by Ward:

> A Committee on Affiliation was named by the Board of Trustees. During the ten days that elapsed before its first meeting, Doctor Shields talked about affiliation to everyone he met, to men and women, to priests and lay people, to young and old. His whole soul burned with enthusiasm and, as he talked, his own ideas became so clear, so vivid, that he arrived at the meeting with a definite plan worked out in minute detail, which he proposed should be adopted then and there. But this was not the way of the wise and prudent. The other men were ready to consider a plan, to weigh the pros and cons, but were not prepared to act. Yet the tremendous driving power of Dr. Shields prevailed at the meeting; his plan was adopted, only to be held up for future consideration by the Rector. After due delay and when the conventionalities of prudence had been complied with, Doctor Shields' plan was finally adopted in its original form.[64]

The accuracy of this account, however, is open to question. The first statement that the Committee was appointed by the Board of Trustees is not in keeping with University records which show that the Rector made the appointments.[65] There is also obvious confusion between "the plan" and the Committee's duties that summer. The plan which the Trustees had approved the previous April was comparatively complete. College and high school standards were specifically stated therein; two devices for enforcing the standards, the application report and examinations, were specified; and the procedures to be followed were given in some detail. The immediate and pressing needs as far as the Committee was concerned were the preparation of the high school and college application forms and the subject-matter outlines of the approved and required high school courses.

Ward's account probably does reflect the spirit and enthusiasm with which Shields approached the gigantic task ahead and the major role he played. There is no question that a tremendous amount of work was accomplished in a comparatively short time, much of it no doubt by Shields and a few close collaborators, with the final approval being given by the Committee or possibly by the Rector. Shields probably relied heavily on his beloved Sisters College and the help that the sisters in attendance during the summer session of 1912 were able to give him. He stated himself that "an attempt has been made to meet, as far as possible, the actual conditions and needs of the high schools; and for this purpose, consultations have been held during the summer with many teachers representing different institutions and familiar with various systems."[66]

In any case, the first Affiliation brochure or syllabus was ready for distribution early that fall. The nineteen-page booklet, its brief introduction to the course outlines dated September 1, 1912, contained not only the content of the original plan but also the high school course descriptions for four years of religion, English, Latin, and mathematics; one year of history and two years of chemistry.[67] Other course outlines must have been well underway by this time too, for those in other subjects were promised in early autumn.[68] Thus, by September of 1912, one is able to find copies of correspondence by Dr. Shields to various high school authorities in reply to requests for information on the affiliation process. Both the printed booklet and the application form were mentioned as then available and as having been sent. The plan was definitely in working order but much of the pioneering work was yet to follow in the remaining short span of Dr. Shields' life.

FOOTNOTES

[1]Barry, op. cit., p. 257.

[2]Patrick J. McCormick, "Bishop Shahan: American Catholic Educator," CER, XXX (May, 1932), 262-265.

[3]Thomas J. Shahan, "The Catholic University of America (1889-1916)," Catholic World, CIII (June, 1916), 378-379.

[4]"Monsignor Pace: Eminent Educator and Philosopher," CER, XXXVI (June, 1938), 326-336; Patrick J. McCormick, "Tribute to the Memory of Monsignor Pace," CER, XXXIX (November, 1941), 562-564.

[5]Joseph A. Gorham, "Looking Back Fifty Years," CER, LIX (March, 1961), 145.

[6]ACUA, VRF, "The Catholic University of America and the Catholic Sisters College," n.d.

[7]ACUA, Pace Papers, Shields to "My dear Sister," November 1, 1912.

[8]O'Connor, op. cit., p. 33.

[9]George Johnson, eulogy on the occasion of the re-interment of Dr. Shields, cf. "Sisters College Erects Shrine to the Memory of Dr. Shields," Sisters College Messenger, XVII (January, 1929), 3.

[10]Thomas E. Shields, "Notes on Education," CUB, XV (October, 1909), 675-683.

[11]Ibid., (January, 1909), 87.

[12]Ibid., XIV (May, 1908), 468.

[13]Thomas E. Shields, Philosophy of Education (Washington: Catholic Education Press, 1921), p. 395.

[14]As early as 1908, Shields found encouragement in this idea in the then recently established Carnegie Foundation and its success, as a purely private foundation, in standardizing

fifty-five colleges and universities. In so doing, it had set clear lines of demarcation between high school and college, and was reaching down to the content and organization of the high school's curriculum. Similar means, he hoped, could be used for Catholic education; Thomas E. Shields, "Notes on Education," CUB, XIV (June, 1908), 583.

[15]ACUA, BTEM, April 21, 1909, Document K (March 1, 1908).

[16]ACUA, BTEM, April 21, 1909, Shields and Pace, "Some Relations of Catholic to Non-Catholic Schools" (April 18, 1909).

[17]ACUA, MMBT, April 21, 1909, p. 173.

[18]Ibid., November 17, 1909, p. 177. Cf. ACUA, BTEM, November 17, 1909, Document A, "Recommendations of the Committee on Teachers' Institute."

[19]ACUA, RF, Shields to Shahan, June 24, 1909.

[20]Ibid.

[21]O'Connor, op. cit., pp. 82, 106.

[22]Thomas E. Shields, "Notes on Education," CUB, XV (January, 1909), 87-88.

[23]Richard J. Strelecky, "A History of The Catholic Educational Review, 1911-1961" (unpublished Master's dissertation, Department of Education, The Catholic University of America, 1961), p. 95.

[24]Justine Ward, Thomas Edward Shields (New York: Charles Scribner's Sons, 1947), pp. 201, 165-166.

[25]Strelecky, op. cit., pp. 32-34, 39, 95.

[26]See p. 26 of this study.

[27]Thomas J. Shahan, "The Pastor and Education," CEAB, VII (November, 1910), 51.

[28]"Discussion," ibid., 60-61.

[29]Ibid., 62.

[30]Ibid., 63.

[31]Thomas E. Shields, "Survey of the Field," CER, I (January, 1911), 77.

[32]J. P. O'Mahoney, C.S.V., "Number of Units Required and Elective for College Entrance," CEAB, VII (November, 1910), 157-174.

[33]CEAB, VII, 141.

[34]James A. Burns, C.S.C., "Report of the Committee on High Schools," CEAB, VIII (November, 1911), 57.

[35]Ibid., 54.

[36]Ibid., 56.

[37]"Discussion," ibid., 67.

[38]Ibid., 68-70. Also Bishop Schrembs of Toledo and Archbishop Messmer of Milwaukee felt that in some cases affiliation meant merely recognition and that such recognition was expedient because of the demands made by many Catholic parents if their children were to remain even in the elementary schools of the Catholic system (ibid., 183-187).

[39]James F. Green, O.S.A., "Catholic Education Above the Grammar Grades," ibid., 171.

[40]James J. Dean, O.S.A., "The High School: Its Relation to the Elementary School and to the College," ibid., 74-81; Brother Bede, "The Aims and Purpose of Catholic Secondary Education, Cultural and Vocational: What Part Must the High School Take in Their Attainment?" ibid., 87-97.

[41]"College Department: Proceedings," ibid., 114-115.

[42]ACUA, MMBT, November 16, 1910, p. 188.

[43]Although the seminary affiliation plan had been revised in 1907-1908, dissatisfaction over the stringency of the rules continued. Another study was made and further modifications were adopted by the Trustees on April 26, 1911 (ACUA, MMBT, p. 195; ACUA, BTEM, April 26, 1911, Document S, "The Affiliation of Seminaries").

[44]O'Connor, op. cit., pp. 96-98.

[45]Courses of Study for Affiliated High Schools (1912-1913), i. This is a nineteen-page printed booklet on Affiliation, the first of a series of regularly published brochures, which described the 1912 plan, its standards and procedures, and gave the detailed outlines of the courses of study for the affiliated high schools. The first four pages of the 1912-1913 booklet are not paginated. The 1913-1914 and subsequent booklets were entitled Affiliation of High Schools and Colleges and were referred to commonly in the literature of that time as the "Affiliation syllabus." These documents, including the first, will hereafter be noted in abbreviated form as AHSC.

[46]Whether others were closely involved in this phase of

the work is not known.

[47]Thomas E. Shields, "Survey of the Field," CER, II (December, 1911), 925-943.

[48]Pius X Pope to James Cardinal Gibbons, Eve of Ephiphany, 1912, CEA, III (February, 1912), 100-103.

[49]Edward A. Pace, "The Holy Father's Letter," ibid., 107.

[50]Thomas E. Shields, "Survey of the Field," CER, III (March, 1912), 248.

[51]Academic Senate Minutes, III, March 16, 1912, p. 193.

[52]Ibid., March 22, 1912, pp. 195-196.

[53]Ibid., p. 196.

[54]ACUA, BTEM, April 17, 1912, "Report of the Visiting Committee of the Catholic University Corporation, March 26-27, 1912." This report referred to the affiliation plan as "Enclosure A," but this document could not be located. The assumption is, however, that the document was the same printed brochure discussed by the Academic Senate and described later in this study.

[55]McCormick, "Bishop Shahan. . . ," CER, XXX (May, 1932), 264.

[56]ACUA, MMBT, April 17, 1912, p. 199. Document C, mentioned in the Trustees' minutes, could not be fully authen-ticated, although this investigator believes that the printed four-page document referred to by Barry as the "1907 affilia-tion plan" and discussed at length in footnote 76, p. 31, of this study, is the same document submitted for the consideration of the Academic Senate, the Visiting Committee, and the Board of Trustees in the spring of 1912. A second copy of this document was found in the Trustees files for their Novem-ber 19, 1913, meeting (ACUA, BTEM), a fact that would seem to reconfirm the contemporaneity of the document for the 1912 period. The problem of identification of this printed leaflet as the original, proposed 1912 affiliation plan, however, is an academic one, since its content and that of the adopted plan as given in the 1912-1913 Affiliation booklet, Courses of Study for Affiliated High Schools, are practically identical. A com-plete discussion of the substance of the 1912 plan, using the

latter document, is given in the next chapter of this study. Cf. Appendix A.

[57]"University Chronicle," CUB, XVIII (May, 1912), 477; "For the Affiliation of Colleges and High Schools to the University," CUB, XVIII (June, 1912), 550-553.

[58]"For the Affiliation of Colleges and High Schools to the University," CER, III (May, 1912), 445-449; "Current Events," ibid., 459.

[59]Ibid.

[60]"University Degrees for Sisters," CER, IV (June, 1912), 59.

[61]Edward A. Pace, "The University: Its Growth and Its Needs," CER, IV (October, 1912), 357.

[62]Although there seems to have been a popular belief that Shields was the first chairman (cf. O'Connor, op. cit., p. 101), this was not the case. The first official reports on Affiliation to the Academic Senate were signed by Pace as Chairman (Academic Senate Minutes, III, May 14, 1913, p. 211; October 21, 1914, p. 221). At no time from 1912 to 1921 were Affiliation documents or correspondence signed by Shields in that capacity. Moreover, in the Annual Report of the Rector, 1928-1929 (p. 62), recognition was given to Dr. Pace for his service as Chairman of the Committee on Affiliation for a sixteen-year period.

[63]AHSC (1913-1914), p. 26. That there were other Committee members is likely since the work was of a comprehensive nature, especially as it pertained to the various high school courses. A later reference noted that for this reason a policy of representation on the Committee of a variety of University departments had been established (ACUA, VRF, Shahan to Richard J. Purcell, October 20, 1921).

[64]Ward, op. cit., pp. 198-199.

[65]ACUA, RF, Shahan to "My dear Professor," July 31, 1912; this letter read: "It would give me much pleasure if you would act as a member of the Committee to prepare the programme for affiliation of our Catholic colleges, high schools and academies." The minutes of the Academic Senate (III, May 8, 1912, p. 196) also stated explicitly that the execution of the plan adopted by the Trustees was left to the Rector

and the Academic Senate.

[66]AHSC (1912-1913), p. 1.
[67]Ibid., pp. 1-15.
[68]Ibid., p. 1.

CHAPTER III

THE 1912 PROGRAM OF AFFILIATION

As the University's plan of Affiliation of High Schools and Colleges grew out of the existing needs of these same institutions at the beginning of the twentieth century, so too the structure of the plan reflected the then current standardization trends and machinery generally in vogue. Two other factors, however, played important parts in shaping the general nature and the fundamental precepts and policies of the 1912 plan: the founders' understanding of and respect for the traditional independence of religious communities in their educational endeavors and the fullness of Dr. Shields' vision for Catholic education, coupled with a soundness of educational philosophy and psychology that permitted educational progress and enrichment without sacrificing the unchanging principles of true education. The growth that Affiliation was to inspire and support, therefore, was to come from within the affiliate, gradually and naturally rather than disruptively, and from this growth, a unification of the Catholic system without centralization, uniformity without rigidity, so that each modification would contribute vitally to the overall betterment of the matter, method, and product of Catholic education. [1]

The plan submitted to and approved by the Trustees in 1912 showed the influence of all four of these factors. Its original purpose as given in the brief introduction was stated in terms of standardization: ". . .to establish a standard for our colleges and high schools, as well as to secure due recognition for the institutions that are doing good work. . . ." [2] At the same time, however, it was clear from the various writings of Shields and Pace that this was to be no narrow, mechanical goal and that all-important were the far broader results to be achieved through this process of standardization; a unity and excellence of the curriculum and the responsible control of grave defects of method and content within the

programs of studies. Thus standardization was to be the
process, not an end in itself but a practical device to bring
about unity, harmony, and academic excellence within a truly
national system of education that was thoroughly Catholic in
character.[3]

The structure of the original plan was also that of an accrediting agency: a list of standards for colleges and high
schools and the means by which to make these standards effective. A closer examination, however, of each of these
parts of the original plan and of their earliest implementation
shows again that the hoped for results were to extend far beyond that of mere approval and recognition of the Catholic
institution.

The Affiliation of Colleges

The original standards to be met by the Catholic college
applying for University Affiliation were five in number:

1. The College must include at least seven chairs or
   departments and each chair or department must be
   under the separate direction of at least one professor or instructor.
2. Every instructor in the faculty must have at least
   the A.B. degree from a college of recognized standing, and every head of a department must have at
   least an M.A. degree from a college in good standing.
3. The equipment of the college in libraries and laboratories must be sufficient to secure effective work
   in the branches offered.
4. The college must require for entrance the completion of a four years' successful course in an accredited secondary school (high school), or the passing
   of entrance examinations on the subjects required
   in the curriculum of accredited secondary schools.
5. The college course must include 2,160 hours of
   class work distributed over four years. Two hours
   of laboratory work are to be regarded as equivalent

to one hour of class work.[4]

For a period during which the general emphasis in education was on quantitative standards the qualitative character of several of the college standards should be noted. Moreover, all five standards were directly aimed at the existing weaknesses of Catholic colleges and represented a practical attack on fundamental and specific defects. At the same time, the limiting of the standards in number and quantitative scope provided safeguards against the University's usurping functions and policy-making that would encroach on the independence of the affiliated college and against a resulting rigidity that would destroy individual college initiative. The college then would be required to meet and maintain basic quantitative and qualitative standards but would be permitted to continue its own development from within, assisted and encouraged by the University. Cooperation and improved articulation and coordination were to be the key features of Affiliation.

The extent to which the college standards of other educational groups directly influenced the adoption of the five college standards for Affiliation could not be determined. The standards of the Association of American Universities must have carried some weight as the University held a charter membership in that organization. The Association's standards were reflected in those met by the University, and the latter must have been of considerable importance since coordination between the colleges and the University was one of the immediate goals of Affiliation. The deliberations of college standards by the Catholic Educational Association also must have been given full consideration by both Shields and Pace. While the CEA lagged behind Affiliation in positive action on the standardization problem, the debate by this group was getting down to specifics by 1912. It adopted its first college standard that year, namely, the requiring of sixteen high school units for college admissions. In 1913, a second standard was approved: that 128 semester hours of credit should be the minimum requirement for graduation by a standard college; and in 1915 a total of eight standards were finally agreed upon. In addition to the two already mentioned, the others were:

3. a minimum of seven departments and seven full-time professors, with departments of English, history, language, and philosophy prescribed;

4. a college degree or its equivalent to be held by the professors who should also instruct in the department of their special training;

5. a library of at least 5000 volumes;

6. laboratory equipment sufficient to carry on work in physics, chemistry, and general science, this equipment to equal a total value of at least $5000;

7. a required student program of not less than 16 or more than 20 hours a week; and

8. a professor's teaching program not to exceed 16 hours a week.[5]

While in substance there was considerable agreement between the standards of the CEA and those of Affiliation, there were also some important differences. Shields rejected the college admission standard of sixteen high school units in favor of the more general norm of the "completion of a four years' successful course in an accredited secondary school." In practice, however, this actually amounted to a requirement of fifteen high school units since, as will be shown later, the approved course for an affiliated high school was set at a minimum of fifteen one-unit courses in the strictly academic subjects. Other apparent differences were Affiliation's less quantitative approach in its library and laboratory requirements and its greater demands in regard to faculty training. On the other hand, Affiliation made no attempt to regulate through its standards the schedules of either students or professors.

Probably the major difference rested in the CEA's prescription of the departments of English, history, language, and philosophy, since in this its College Department seemed to have thought primarily in terms of the Bachelor of Arts degree only. In the meantime, the University had moved ahead with a then current trend of organizing several programs leading to Bachelor degrees in arts, philosophy, science, and letters. In its 1913-1914 Affiliation syllabus, the courses of study for affiliated Catholic colleges was further delineated by the addition of a paragraph which read:

> The Year-Book of the University announces the
> courses of study leading to the degrees, Bachelor
> of Arts, Bachelor of Philosophy, Bachelor of Science
> and Bachelor of Letters under the different Facul-
> ties. Any course given by an affiliated college in
> conformity with the requirements for the same
> course in the University, will be approved. The
> examinations in each subject shall be based on the
> requirements stated in the Year-Book. An affili-
> ated college offering courses other than those
> given by the University, shall submit its courses
> to the University for approval.[6]

Here it is evident that the University's own degree programs served directly as criteria. This effort toward coordinating other college programs with the University's programs
had been a concern of long standing at the University.[7] Shahan
particularly felt that the attainment of a properly graded sequence of studies throughout the entire Catholic system, eventually permitting the smooth transition of a student from college
to university work, was an important function of the Affiliation
program. This was especially true in the affiliation of colleges
since their affiliation to the University constituted an agreement whereby the University accepted the course work and
diplomas of their graduates in lieu of entrance examinations.
The shaping of the programs of college affiliates, therefore,
would have to be in terms of qualifying their graduates for admission to the University and to Catholic Sisters College, and
the University, in turn, would have to take care to maintain
its advanced studies at a level above the college and appropriate to a university.[8]

This further clarification of the college program was the
only change made in college standards for Affiliation during
Shields' lifetime. In fact, it was not until 1934 that comparatively minor modifications were made and not until 1938 that
major revisions were adopted.

The Affiliation of High Schools

To affiliate a high school with the University only two standards had to be met, but these were comprehensive in terms of the school's program and far-reaching in their implications.

1. The high school must give a course extending over four years and including a total of 15 units, of which at least three must be devoted to English and three to some other one subject.
   Meaning of unit. A subject, e.g., English, pursued four or five hours a week for a school year of from 36 to 40 weeks, constitutes a unit.
2. The subjects required with their respective values are: Religion, 2 units; English, 3 units; some other language, 2 units; mathematics, 2 units; social science (including history), 1 unit; natural science, 1 unit. Four units to be elective. They must be selected in such a way, however, as to give another course of 3 units; i.e., one or more units must be advanced work in one of the subjects, other than English, enumerated above. Where Latin is to be pusued [sic] in college, at least 2 units of Latin must be taken in the high school.
3. Reasons for this curriculum:
   (a) The high school has two functions: one is to give an education to students who will not go beyond the high school, the other is to give a proper preparation to students who will go to college. Hence some subjects are necessary for both classes of students, while other subjects are necessary for only one or the other class. All students need: Religion, English, mathematics, and a second language in addition to English. The student going on to college with a view to theology or law will need Latin, Greek and modern languages, together with social science; if he contemplates the study of medicine he will need more in the line of

natural science, e.g., biology and chemistry. The student who goes no farther than the high school will need more in the way of mathematics, modern languages, economics and the vocational subjects.

(b) The proposed curriculum, by requiring advanced work in at least two subjects, prevents the smattering which gives the student a little of many things and not much of any thing.

(c) At the same time sufficient latitude is allowed to enable the student to determine his vocation and to begin his preparation for it before he leaves the high school.

(d) The curriculum does not prescribe Latin for four years; hence a student, who after one or two years in the high school, may discover a vocation for a career in which Latin is specially required, e.g., the priesthood, can, without loss of time, take up Latin, say in the third and fourth years, and complete his study of that language during his four years at college.[9]

The standards and the reasons given for them need no particular clarification. The goals of broadening Catholic secondary education to include the terminal as well as the college preparatory program, of securing a desired uniformity of curriculums without sacrificing that degree of flexibility necessary to meet local and individual student needs, of maintaining a sound and solid high school program rather than a mere "smattering" of subjects, and of improving articulation between high school and college are clearly evident. Of special interest, however, is the fact that Shields and Pace chose to disagree with the CEA's resolution of 1911 that sixteen high school units constituted an acceptable college preparatory course. Shields felt that too many subjects taught at the same time to the same students, especially without electivism, was highly undesirable; nor should college entrance requirements be such as to prevent the high school from attaining its own specific ends. He found himself in accord with

the report on "Articulation of High School and College," made
by the Committee of Nine, which had been adopted by the
Secondary Department of the National Education Association
in July of 1911.[10]

This report accepted as fundamental principles that the
best preparation for college was a secondary education which
met best the present needs of developing youth and that power
rather than content was primary. The Committee's working
definition of a well-planned high school course accordingly included: (1) a quantitative total requirement of fifteen units,
of which three were in English and one each in social science
and natural science; (2) two majors of three units, one being
English, and one minor of two units, with possible other majors in foreign languages, mathematics, social science, and
natural science; and (3) not less than eleven units to consist
of these fields with the other four units being electives in academic or vocational fields. Shields liked the elasticity permitted by this program and felt that, if religion were added,
it would also meet the needs of the Catholic student.[11]

The importance of religion in the mind of Dr. Shields as
an integral part of the high school program should not be mini-
mized, however, by this self-evident influence by the Committee of Nine. For him religion was the all-important factor.
The synthetic presentation and close organic interrelating of
all items of knowledge presented in the curriculum must for
the Catholic school be done through religious truths as the
center of unified and organized knowledge.[12] And also "the
curriculum in the Catholic school. . .must be so arranged as
to shape life into conformity with Christian standards of conduct and, at the same time, to impart efficiency in earthly
pursuits."[13]

As a well-trained psychologist, Shields also recognized
education to be a developmental process, one in which the
whole man must grow simultaneously.[14] For him then, the
curriculum of the elementary and secondary schools and of the
college must be so adjusted to each other as to avoid any break
in the mental development of the student as he passed from one
level to the next.[15] For this reason it was especially important that the courses of study for the middle institution be

carefully defined, since in so doing goals for the elementary
school could be set as well as a starting point for the work of
the college. This Shields did in the form of content outlines
and statements of appropriate principles for the courses approved for affiliated high schools.

The course outlines given in the first Affiliation syllabus
included four years of religion, English, Latin, and mathematics; one year of history and two years of chemistry.
Each, with the exception of mathematics, was introduced by a
discussion of objectives and general principles, followed by
lists of general or more specific content areas. The exten-
siveness of these materials does not permit full coverage
here, but the following excerpts will serve to illustrate the
nature and purposes of the course outlines as well as wherein
lay some of the greatness of Dr. Shields, the educator:

> The teaching of religion in the high school pre-
> supposes, naturally, the instruction given in the
> grades. It is now taken for granted that the germi-
> nal ideas have been developed to the point where the
> pupil is capable of understanding the fundamentals
> of religion presented in literal, dogmatic, and his-
> torical terms. The basic principle for further
> instruction is that of the Church, a living organism,
> perpetuating on earth the life, teaching, and instruc-
> tion of Jesus Christ, with one supreme purpose of
> leading men to eternal life.
>
> . . . .
>
> The subjoined outline contains many terms
> and topics which might suggest a theological treat-
> ment too advanced for either high school or col-
> lege. It is therefore noted that, in this course,
> only such essential ideas are to be given as will
> serve two purposes: first, the development of
> the ideas already acquired in the grades; second,
> the preparation for the more detailed exposition
> which is given in college.[16]

In proposing a new four years' English course
. . .it will be observed that the required reading
is comparatively small in quantity in each year.
The reason for this arrangement is that experience
shows a few books well read and properly studied
to have more educational and cultural value than
many books read hastily and superficially. . . .

No formal teaching of rhetoric is recommended,
the belief being that such formal teaching properly
belongs to the college, or undergraduate university, course. The rules of rhetoric will have, however, to be constantly in requisition in connection
with the teaching of English prose composition. . . .
In other words, the teacher is expected to supply to
the student in practical form all the rules of
rhetoric as they arise, and to see that they are
properly applied in the various forms of prose
compositions: hence the expression, "Applied
Rhetoric." . . .

Grammar is supposed to have been taught already in the grade school, but the general experience has hitherto been that the minds of younger
students are too immature fully to comprehend
grammar as the science of language. Accordingly,
it will be necessary for the teacher to be insistent,
as occasion arises, on the thorough understanding
and the proper application of grammatical rules:
hence the expression, "Applied Grammar." . . .
It is proposed that in the third year, when the
minds of the students are presumably sufficiently
developed, grammar should be formally taught.
At that stage it ought to prove an excellent mental
discipline. A course in elementary historical
grammar is introduced in the fourth year as a
suitable preparation for college work, and as a
basis for the more advanced studies of those pupils
who, having developed a linguistic taste, may in-
tend later on to specialize in English.[17]

The teaching of Latin should aim, naturally, at developing in the pupil the ability to read Latin. But the chief purpose should be disciplinary, i.e., the training of the powers of observation and reasoning. In addition, it should be remembered that the study of Latin is an excellent means of improving in English, not only by learning the origin of many English words but also by translating into proper English form ideas that have been expressed by great thinkers in perfect language. Finally, the value of Latin for general culture and history should be kept in view; the emphasis should be laid on the fact that Latin is the language employed by the Church in her liturgy and by some of her great teachers.[18]

It is generally recognized that history is not a mere list of names and dates and that the study of history does not consist in storing the mind with unrelated facts. While the memory must be exercised, and the imagination brought into play, the judgment should also be developed, if history is to serve as a practical guide for life and for training in citizenship. . . .
Care should be taken to impress the pupil with the importance of the great movements and institutions which have profoundly influenced the social, political and religious development of mankind. These should be studied not only in their own progress but also in their causes and in their results. As far as practicable, the history topics should be correlated with the work in the other subjects, especially in language and literature.
For Catholic schools it is essential that the pupil be brought to understand the share that the Church has had in shaping the world's history. . . .[19]

The lecture and quiz should cover the field as it is uniformily treated by all standard modern texts on elementary inorganic chemistry.

Besides the knowledge of the sources, proper-
ties, uses, etc., of the common elements, the
pupil should have clear notions of the topics cited
below, which should be crystallized by laboratory
or written exercises tending to show the working
relations between the theory and practice of
chemistry.[20]

While the two quantitative high school standards remained
unchanged from 1912 until the overall reorganization of the
Affiliation plan in 1938 and 1939, the course outlines were
added to and revised with some degree of regularity. The
second syllabus included additional outlines for Greek I-III,
French I-II, German I-II, Physics, Biology I-II, and Logic
(one-half unit).[21] The wide range of approved courses beyond those prescribed, as well as the policy to approve other
elective courses at the request of an affiliate, was further
clarified at that time:

The aim throughout has been to allow to the
high schools the greatest possible freedom con-
sistent with the preparation required for entrance
into higher institutions of learning. . . . Any
given high school, however, may not find itself
equipped for so wide a range of subject-matter
and will very naturally determine the courses
which it is prepared to offer, but such determination in an affiliated high school should conform
to the requirements laid down above [the standards].

On the other hand, it should be understood that
the amount of work indicated above, i.e., fifteen
units, is a minimum requirement, and that the
high school is expected to offer wider opportunities
to more capable pupils.[22]

A table was also included in this syllabus and in subsequent ones to suggest arrangements of courses and to demon-
strate possible variations in emphasis on language, mathe-

matics, social science, and natural science, while meeting at the same time the prescription for each field. The table, reproduced below, gave eleven such variations (I-XI) in terms of the number of high school units that a student might follow in each subject field over a four-year high school program.[23]

COURSES	I	II	III	IV	V	VI	VII	VIII	IX	X	XI
Religion	2	2	2	2	2	2	2	2	2	2	2
English	3	3	3	3	3	3	3	4	4	3	3
Latin	3	3	3	3	3	3	3	4	4	2	2
Greek.........	2			3			2	1			
French		2			3					2	
German			2			3					2
Mathematics..	3	3	3	2	2	2	2	2	2	2	2
Social Science.	1	1	1	1	1	1	2	1	2	3	1
Natural Science	1	1	1	1	1	1	1	1	1	1	3

By the third year of Affiliation, outlines for French III-IV, German III-IV, and History II-IV were approved and published;[24] by 1916, Spanish I-IV had been added,[25] and in 1919, a four-year program for music.[26] These, with a revision of the biology outline from its original two-year sequence to a single unit course in 1916,[27] constituted Shields' contribution to this phase of the developmental work of Affiliation. There were others, no doubt, who assisted him substantially in working out the details of subject content, but Shields' thinking and ideas remained primarily in control and dominated the final product.

Exemplifying the extent of Shields' influence and also portraying the nature of some of the discussions and considerations that went into the formulation of the course outlines was a rather lengthy correspondence carried on by Shields in 1915. From the beginning of the program, the suggestions of affiliated high schools regarding the courses were invited, and this invitation was accepted by Sister Mary Euphrasia, S.N.D., of the Convent of Notre Dame in Dayton, Ohio. The 1914 Affiliation syllabus had completed the outline of the history courses, devoting the first year, which was prescribed, to a

survey of the Christian era up to the Fall of Constantinople;
the second year, to ancient history; the third year, to modern history since the Renaissance; and the fourth year, to
"the history of England with special reference to the influence
of England on American institutions."[28]   Sister Mary
Euphrasia objected to the lack of chronology in the arrangement of these courses and advocated that three years of history be prescribed, one of these being devoted to American
history. To these recommendations, Dr. Shields replied:

> I would not dare accuse a lady of inconsistency,
> so it must be my own tired vision which is respon-
> sible for the fact that it seems inconsistent to me
> that you should insist upon the study of U. S. History
> as a prescribed year's course in our high school
> curriculum while you object to the study of Medieval
> History without a previous study of what preceded it
> in Greek and Roman History.
>   To me Christianity forms the real key, not
> chronology, for the study of human history, hence
> the child begins with Christ and not with Adam,
> and hence, too, I would have our high school pupil
> begin with Christianity and with this as a basis I
> would lead him to understand pagan history and its
> failures. They cannot judge it aright until they
> know the meaning of Christianity first.[29]

He further clarified the position of the Committee on
Affiliation as it had been brought out by its discussion of the
history program, admitting also that he himself had been
largely responsible for the one year of prescribed history.
To maintain an elastic program, he felt, a total of at least
four electives was necessary. It was not possible, therefore, to prescribe more than one year of history at the
secondary level. Furthermore, the Committee felt that for
students who took only the one year, the development and
achievements of Christianity were of greatest importance,
since two years of American history supposedly had already
been received in the grades immediately preceding. If, on

the other hand, ancient history were the prescribed course,
most students would never learn the meaning of Christianity.
Moreover, the principle "from the known to the unknown" was
involved here as well as the positive approach of giving truth
first and then a study of the error.[30]

In a later letter, Dr. Shields made known that he had accepted the one-year history prescription on the recommendation of the Committee of Nine of the NEA because he found
their reasons to be sound. To reduce the Affiliation electives
below four he thought unwise:

> There are many people who have made persistent
> demand that four years of Latin be prescribed in our
> high schools. There are others that demand two
> years of German and two years of French among the
> prescribed studies, and others demand at least
> three years of mathematics, but really none of these
> people have a grievance, since we allow each high
> school to prescribe as it sees fit. Only they must
> allow others who differ from them a like freedom.
> The day of the rigid high school curriculum is really
> passed, as far as the country at large is concerned.
> It may still be maintained by a few institutions who
> prefer to administer only to those who choose to
> follow along the narrow lines of a single groove.[31]

While the number of quantitative standards for the affiliated high school was kept at two, the course outlines
played a major role qualitatively in the standardizing process
by setting instructional goals appropriate for Catholic education. Thus, although such matters as textbooks, teacher
training,[32] and science laboratory equipment were not
spelled out by definitive standards, neither were they left
entirely to the discretion of the affiliate. Shields felt strongly that both good textbooks and the adequacy of the academic
and professional training of the teachers were vital factors
for any effective process of instructional improvements, but
at the same time he hoped to accomplish these things gradually within each affiliate through its own felt needs. To cover

the work of each course adequately in terms of the content, objectives, and pedagogical principles given by Affiliation would require both good textbooks and well-trained teachers. Anything less would become self-evident through the results. It was this appraisal that was to be made possible by the required Affiliation high school testing program. Through an analysis of the test results, the Committee hoped to point up the cases of defective teaching and the causes and to encourage the schools "to move intelligently to remedy the defects discovered."[33]

A somewhat similar approach was taken regarding laboratory equipment. The chemistry outline, for example, listed among its content certain experiments and included among its objectives the acquiring of general laboratory skills.[34] Indirectly this set a requirement of an adequate chemistry laboratory and at least minimum chemicals for any affiliate offering the course. The same was true for physics and biology.[35]

Execution of the Plan of Affiliation

Standardization of educational institutions is not an automatic process once the standards have been set. Shields and Pace realized this and the importance, therefore, of providing practical devices and procedures through which to enforce the standards on a continuing basis. Reports, inspections, and examinations were the commonly applied sanctions within the accreditation movement at that time, and to these methods Affiliation also turned. The last section of the original Affiliation plan, "Execution of the Plan of Affiliation," gave in seven points the working procedures to be used:

1. The school or college applying for affiliation shall submit to the University, on blanks supplied by the University, a detailed statement of its curriculum and equipment and of the qualifications of its professors and instructors.
2. If this statement is satisfactory it shall be verified by personal inspection through some person delegated

by the University for that purpose.

3. Should this report be favorable, the institution in question shall be placed on the list of affiliated institutions.

4. The University shall then send to the institution an assignment of the matter for each subject offered in the curriculum of the institution and, at the end of the year, a set of examination questions sealed and to be opened in the class when assembled for examination. The papers are then to be sealed in the presence of the class and forwarded to the University, where they will be examined and marked according to a certain scale.

5. All students who successfully pass the examinations held during the four years in the high school shall be admitted without further examination to any college affiliated by the University. All students who successfully pass the examinations held during the four years in college shall be admitted, without further examination, into the courses in the University leading to the higher degrees. They must, however, reside in colleges approved by the University.

6. If it should appear, either from the statement submitted or from inspection, that some modification is needed in order to comply with the requirements, the institution shall be placed on the list of tentative affiliation and, when the requirement is fulfilled, the institution shall be placed on the list of permanent affiliation.

7. In all cases, either of permanent or of tentative affiliation, a record, as shown by examination papers, shall be kept by the University of the work done each year by each student in each affiliated institution, and a copy of this record shall be sent to the institution in which the student resides and to the high school or college from which the students graduated. Should it appear from such records that the work of an institution is unsatisfactory, the University shall endeavor to discover the cause of the defect and to indicate the

remedy.[36]

Points 1, 2, 3, and 6, given above, applied to the affiliating process. When it was determined, through the application form and a personal inspection by a representative of Affiliation, that a school or college was able to meet the prescribed standards, approval and listing would follow. Should the Committee's action be unfavorable, "tentative" affiliation would be granted until the institution merited "permanent" affiliation through the proper modifications required. The sanctions of reports and inspections were to be used in the initial step. The third sanction, to which points 4, 5, and 7 referred, was in the form of examinations to assure the continued maintaining of the standards and an acceptable quality level of the educational product of the affiliate. Thus Affiliation was to serve more than as a mere method of approving Catholic institutions. Its machinery, through a combination of all three kinds of sanctions, provided also a means by which the University would guide and assist the affiliate, over an extended period, to strengthen its instructional programs and outcomes.

The exact nature of the first college application form and the evaluation procedures followed by Dr. Shields and the Committee could not be determined, as the only available college form located dated back only to the early 1930's. There seems to be some justification, however, in assuming that its content and format resembled the earlier form used, since the stated standards and procedural regulations for affiliating colleges remained practically unchanged from 1912 to 1938. Moreover, the data requested by the 1930 form corresponded basically to those same areas covered by the standards and those noted in point 1 of the plan given above. If this assumption is correct, the first colleges applying for Affiliation were required to submit the following information: name, location, year established, enrollment, the college departments, heads of departments and other faculty members, their degrees and the granting institutions, whether the college was housed apart from a high school department, number of volumes in the faculty and student libraries, available laboratories, the number of course credits and their distribution by years, the examination schedule and passing grade, entrance requirements, other affiliations or accreditation held, and a copy of the college's yearbook.[37]

That college inspection procedures were developed and used at all during the early period of Affiliation is highly doubtful. There is no record of such visitations until the academic year 1924-1925, at which time the long over-due inspection of affiliates was begun "in a somewhat experimental manner."[38] The possibility that the third sanction of examinations as described in the original plan was applied to the college affiliates is also a remote one. As already mentioned, the 1912-1913 Affiliation syllabus defined the approved college courses in terms of the University's Baccalaureate programs, referring to the description of content as given in the University's Year Book. This same statement included: "The examinations in each subject shall be based on the requirements of the Year-Book."[39] Although this reference to examinations was included in the syllabi until 1938, nowhere in the archival records or in the printed literature on Affiliation was any mention made of college tests or of a testing procedure. Thus, unlike the high school program, it appears that college tests were not made out or corrected by the University but were set by the affiliated college through its own faculty members, who were to be guided by the requirements as stated in the University's Year Book.[40] Whether or not copies of these examinations were sent to the Committee for approval, a process used considerably later for junior colleges and teacher training institutions, could not be verified.

Basically, the process of affiliating a high school was similar to that for a college. The high school form from the 1920's revealed that the following data were probably required of the first high school applicants: name, location, by whom conducted, year established, enrollment, courses offered (optional and prescribed, along with a complete description of the schedule), faculty members with degrees and granting institutions, faculty members without degrees (including years of teaching experience and earned academic credits in specific subjects), laboratory science courses and schedule, and a yearbook describing the high school program.[41] As in the

case of the college, the exact nature of the processing procedures is not known. Standards evidently were strictly applied
since the provision of "tentative" affiliation was used in
twenty-six high school cases in 1912-1913.[42] Some visiting
of high schools was also mentioned[43] but whether these were
genuine inspections and just how they were used sequentially
within the total affiliating process could not be determined.
However, a fairly detailed description of procedures was
made by the Secretary of the Committee on Affiliation in 1924,
and there is reason to believe that those used at that time
were based directly on Shields' earlier methods. This account stated:

> When the high school has sent in its application,
> on the form mentioned above, the Committee con-
> siders the same and approves, as standard high
> schools, the institutions which meet the require-
> ments. Should it appear that the school fails to
> meet all the requirements, it is placed on a list
> known as the Tentative Group; as soon as the de-
> ficiency is remedied, it is listed as a high school
> affiliated with the University. The official list is
> published yearly in the Year-Book of the University.
> The school is notified if its application has been
> approved and if only tentative affiliation is
> granted, a specified time is indicated for the re-
> moval of the deficiency. In those cases where the
> application is not approved a digest of the reasons
> is given and suggestions for the work of bringing
> the institution up to the requirements are also
> forwarded.[44]

From the available evidence, it would seem that in the
early days of Affiliation much was accomplished by way of
raising standards and the general upgrading of the high school
through the application process itself. Many schools desiring
Affiliation made the necessary adjustments and improvements
prior to actively seeking approval and were often successful
as a result. Others, less adequately prepared, were required

to make specific additional adjustments after "tentative" affiliation had been granted.[45] McInerney, in her evaluation
of University Affiliation for a typical Catholic academy, described the process as one of gradual conversion from a
traditional girls' academy in the early 1900's to a full-fledged
high school that was able to meet the changing academic and
vocational needs of the American girl. In 1913, a tentative
attempt was made by the academy to reorganize on a high
school basis; by 1914, the academy had adopted as far as it
could the courses outlined by Affiliation. Departmental work
was introduced and commercial courses were made a part of
the regular program. The final step was the full adoption of
the University's high school curriculum on a first-year basis,
working up through the full four years so that formal application for Affiliation was made in 1919. Because the science
laboratory had not been completed at that time, the academy
was approved tentatively in 1920, with permanent affiliation
granted the next year.[46]
     The examination sanction as described in the original
plan proved to be a very important one for the high schools,
and constituted a major part of the work of Affiliation from
the very beginning. For this reason, a detailed description
of the high school testing program as it was set and as it
evolved over the first several years of the program's existence follows.

The High School Examination Program

     The 1912-1913 Affiliation syllabus called for examinations
to be taken in all the affiliated high schools by the students following any of the approved courses. The examinations were
viewed by Shields as an important standardizing device: they
were not only to keep course standards and student achievement at an acceptable level but also they were to provide a
means of ascertaining teaching defects of method and training
and, in turn, of applying appropriate remedies aimed at the
improvement of instructional outcomes.[47] No time was lost,
therefore, in putting a testing program in operation for the
first affiliated high schools, and in the spring of 1913, thirteen

schools took a total of 1,318 tests. The test fields for that
first year included religion, English, Latin, French, German,
history, mathematics, chemistry, and physics. With each
year the number of schools, tests, and fields grew rapidly.[48]
With the emphasis placed on testing and the resulting rapid
growth in the number of tests taken each spring, it was important that detailed, systematic procedures be established.
While the exact chronological order of each development is
often not known, many of the procedures must have been initiated the first year, with improvements and adjustments
made with each year's additional experience. Through these
stages of procedural development, however, the basic test
plan and the requirements as given in the first Affiliation syllabus remained unchanged.[49]

As the Committee on Affiliation approved a course of
study and outlined its prescribed content in the Affiliation syllabus, a corresponding test was made out annually by the
professors at the University. An affiliate, after the current
year during which its affiliation was obtained, was then required to administer those tests for which courses were included in its curriculum.[50] In an effort to maintain imparti-
ality and reliability of results, detailed regulations for
scheduling and administering the tests were set and enforced.
The form letter, sent out in 1916 to the principals of affiliated
high schools, shows some of the detail involved.

To the Principal:
We are sending you to-day by express the
examination questions ordered by your institution,
those for each subject having a separate envelope.
When the package arrives, open it and see if the
envelopes correspond with your order. Kindly
return the enclosed postal card upon receipt of
the package. If the package does not reach you
by May 16, please notify, by telegraph, Rev. P.
J. McCormick, Ph.D., Secretary, Committee on
Affiliation, so that a duplicate may be forwarded
to you.
The Committee on Affiliation desires that you,

as principal or superior of the school, conduct the
examinations, according to the Regulations for the
Examinations of Affiliated High Schools, a copy of
which is herewith enclosed.

The examinations will be held during the week
of May 22, and in the following order:

Religion,	May 22,	9 A.M.
English,	" 23,	9 A.M.
Latin,	" 24,	9 A.M.
Greek,	" 22,	1 P.M.
French,	" 23,	1 P.M.
German,	" 24,	1 P.M.
History,	" 25,	9 A.M.
Mathematics,	" 26,	9 A.M.
Physics,	" 25,	1 P.M.
Chemistry,	" 25,	1 P.M.
Biology,	" 25,	1 P.M.
Logic,	" 25,	1 P.M.

If you desire to receive early returns of the
marks given your pupils who graduate this year,
please enclose the papers of those pupils in the
separate envelopes which are sent for this purpose. Such envelopes should be plainly marked
"Graduates' Papers." Five extra envelopes are
enclosed in your package; should you need more
please notify us by the return postal card.

THE COMMITTEE ON AFFILIATION[51]

The tests were scheduled at first for early June, but in
1915, at the request of some of the affiliates, choice was permitted between an earlier schedule at the end of April or one
at the end of May or the beginning of June.[52] The earlier
schedule led to the adopting of a policy that the tests were to
cover seven-eighths of the regular course, with the teachers
of the affiliate giving their own tests on the remaining material.[53]

The examinations, which usually required three hours of

working time, were made by members of the University faculty who had been selected by the Committee on Affiliation and
appointed by the Rector.[54] The test questions, of essay type
and some six or seven in number,[55] were drawn from the
prescribed course outlines. The exact principles followed in
correcting the first tests could not be ascertained, but probably the general method used in the early 1920's was employed
from the beginning. A scale or weight for each test item was
affixed by the authors of a test. By having these same individuals also score the test, some uniformity of grading was maintained. Percentage marks were given and the passing score
was set at 70 per cent.[56]

Another important part of the test work was the reporting of the results to the participating schools. The reports
took several forms: the scores earned by each student in
each test taken, class averages and ranks, and a school
rank.[57] Mention was made also of analyses of the test papers
by the correctors. When defects of teaching became evident
from the papers of a given class, the corrector noted these
along with what he deemed to be the chief causes and made
suggestions for their remedy. Specific strengths were simi-
larly noted, and these written impressions were sent to the
respective school.[58]

All of these major aspects of the Affiliation testing program were apparently put into effect before 1918, as Shields
described them in general terms in a Catholic Educational
Review article of that year.[59] Moreover, by this time the
testing program was, in his opinion, functioning well and pro-
ducing the results he had hoped for. A marked improvement
in the work done by the students had been noted with each
year, and student and teacher morale ran high because of the
friendly rivalry promoted by the examinations. The brighter
students were assisting the less talented, and there was even
a diminished eagerness for free days! The teachers were
also aided by the definiteness of the course content as required
by the tests and were less tempted to linger over the better
known or the more agreeable parts of the course.[60]

For Shields then, the 1912 Affiliation plan, as he had
conceived it, was effectively reaching into the classroom, to

both teacher and student, and was well on its way to accomplishing those things which he had envisioned for American Catholic education: unity, system, and strength.

FOOTNOTES

[1]Leo L. McVay, "Dr. Shields and Affiliation," CER, XIX (April, 1921), 273. Cf. McVay, "Catholic High Schools and Affiliation," CER, XX (February, 1922), 84.

[2]AHSC (1912-1913), p. [i]. Cf. Appendix A for the complete 1912 plan.

[3]Shields, Philosophy of Education, pp. 391-394. Cf. Report on Affiliation of High Schools (1920), p. 9.

[4]AHSC (1912-1913), pp. [i-ii].

[5]"Proceedings of the Annual Meeting of the College Department," CEAB, XII (November, 1915), 149-150.

[6]AHSC (1913-1914), p. 26.

[7]See p. 12 of this study.

[8]ACUA, RF, Shahan, "Of Affiliated Colleges and Seminaries," n.d. (handwritten manuscript).

[9]AHSC (1912-1913) pp. [ii-iii].

[10]Thomas E. Shields, "Survey of the Field," CER, II (December, 1911), 925.

[11]Ibid., 932-938.

[12]Ibid., V (May, 1913), 436.

[13]Shields, Philosophy of Education, p. 412. Furthermore, Shields and Pace were greatly concerned about the quality of the religion courses in the schools: the wide chasm between the then current method of teaching religion (memorization of the catechism, Bible, and Church history) and the improved pedagogical techniques used in the other subjects. They believed that religion must be taught as it is embodied in the life of the Church. Cf. Thomas E. Shields, "Notes on Education," CUB, XIV (March, 1908), 289.

[14]Thomas E. Shields, The Education of Our Girls (New York: Benziger Bros., 1907), p. 207.

[15]Shields, Philosophy of Education, p. 412.

[16]AHSC (1912-1913), pp. 1-2.

[17]Ibid., pp. 4-5.

[18]Ibid., pp. 9-10.

[19]Ibid., pp. 11-12.

[20]Ibid., p. 13.

[21]AHSC (1913-1914), pp. 15-16, 19-21, 24-25.

[22]Ibid., p. 5.

[23]Ibid., p. 6.

[24]AHSC (1914), pp. 16-17, 18, 20-21.

[25]AHSC (1916), pp. 19-20.

[26]AHSC (1919), pp. 31-33.

[27]AHSC (1916), pp. 29-30. The reason for the revision was given: "A careful consideration of the ends to be attained by the four years of work in the high school has lead to the conviction that to extend the course in biology over two years is to devote more time to this subject than is necessary" (p. 29).

[28]AHSC (1914), pp. 18-21.

[29]ACUA, CSCF, Shields to Sr. Mary Euphrasia, S.N.D., Dayton, Ohio, October 18, 1915.

[30]Ibid., October 28, 1915.

[31]Ibid., November 12, 1915. A fifth year of history, American History, was approved in the Affiliation syllabus of 1922. The first year of history, however, still remained the prescribed year; AHSC (1922), pp. 30-31.

[32]The Committee on Affiliation did establish a working policy of requiring a minimum of three teachers for a regular, four-year high school, and in 1915 some thought was given to setting a college degree as a minimum standard for high school teachers; ACUA, CSCF, Shields to Sr. Saveria, B.V.M., Fort Dodge, Iowa, October 8, 1915.

[33]Thomas E. Shields, "The Need of the Catholic Sisters College and the Scope of Its Work," CER, XVII (September, 1919), 428. Cf. ibid., CEAB, XVI (November, 1919), 484-485.

[34]AHSC (1912-1913), p. 15.

[35]AHSC (1913-1914), pp. 19-25. In 1922, when a quantitative standard in the form of an approved list of science apparatus was suggested for Affiliation, Dr. Parker, Professor

of Biology at the University, voiced a strong dissent: "If the teacher in any high school is not competent to select her own apparatus in accordance with the needs of the course she is presenting to her pupils and the opportunities provided by her school, no number of approved lists will be of any value to her or her school. In fact such lists will be a menace, for they will simply enable an unscrupulous agent to impose upon her." (ACUA, VRF, J. B. Parker to "Chairman, Committee on Affiliation," November 15, 1922.)

36 AHSC (1912-1913), pp. [iii-iv].

37 ACUA, RF, "Application for Affiliation of. . . College" (mimeographed).

38 ARR, 1924-1925 (October, 1925), p. 59.

39 See p. 64 of this study.

40 This interpretation was further substantiated by interview with Dr. Roy J. Deferrari, June 10, 1963, who could recall no reference to a strictly controlled college examination program during his early association with Affiliation.

41 ACUA, RF, "Application for Affiliation of High School" (mimeographed).

42 Report on Affiliation of High Schools (1920), p. 8.

43 ACUA, CSCF, Shields to Sr. St. Ignatius, January 2, 1914.

44 Leo L. McVay, "The Problems of Affiliation," Catholic School Interests, III (June, 1924), 90.

45 ACUA, CSCF, Shields to Sister Louise, Kansas City, October 12, 1912; ibid., V. Rev. Daniel L. Gorman to Shields, October 29, 1912. Cf. Patrick J. McCormick, "Roman Catholic Parochial Schools," CER, VIII (September, 1914), 147.

46 Sr. St. Thomas McInerney, S.S.J., "A Study of the Educational Outcomes of Affiliation with the Catholic University of America upon a Typical Catholic Academy" (unpublished Master's dissertation, Department of Education, The Catholic University of America, 1934), pp. 24-28.

47 Thomas E. Shields, "The Sisters' College and the High Schools Affiliated with the Catholic University," CER, XV (February, 1918), 100-102.

48 Report on Affiliation of High Schools (1920), p. 9.

[49]See p. 76 of this study.

[50]The tests were on a unit basis, e.g., four tests in English, one each for English I, II, III, and IV.

[51]ACUA, CSCF, May 6, 1916. By 1919, in addition to opening the test envelopes in the presence of the class and re-sealing them in the presence of three witnesses, other detailed rules were added: no further directions other than those given on the tests were to be given to the student; no student was to take more than six tests in a given year; ink and one side only of 8 1/2 x 11 paper were to be used; a test card was to be filled out by the student, identifying the student, school, and examination, and attached to the test paper; and all materials were to be returned within twenty-four hours of the last examination; AHSC (1919), pp. 33-34.

[52]ACUA, CSCF, Shields to Mother F. Borgia, Rock Island, Ill., March 9, 1915.

[53]Shields, "The Sisters' College and the High Schools . . . ," CER, IV (February, 1918), 101-102.

[54]Some of the University's most prominent faculty members contributed to the test work, among them Dr. Pace, heads of departments, and several of the deans; ACUA, CSCF, Shields to the Rector, January 18, 1918.

[55]The only copies of tests located were miscellaneous religion tests for 1921 to 1931. That these tests were fairly typical of the earlier tests in general was concluded by inter-view with Roy J. Deferrari, June 10, 1963. The May, 1921, test for Religion I consisted of the following questions:

1. In what diocese is the School which you now attend, located? Who is the Bishop of that Diocese?
2. Name some of the chief Religious orders. Are they included in the Hierarchy? Explain.
3. What is the difference between the teaching authority and the government of the Church? Answer briefly.
4. What do you understand by the Roman Curia?
5. How many sacraments are there; who instituted them and who can receive them?
6. What is the difference between public and private devotions? Give an example of each. (ACUA, AF.)

[56]ACUA, RF, Leo L. McVay to "My dear Professor,"

February 11, 1923.

[57]ACUA, CSCF, Shields to Father Maladey, Pittsburgh, Pa., January 15, 1916.

[58]Leo L. McVay, "Catholic High Schools and Affiliation," CER, XX (February, 1922), 85.

[59]Shields, "The Sisters' College and the High Schools . . . ," CER, XV (February, 1918), 97-105.

[60]Ibid.

CHAPTER IV

THE PIONEERING YEARS: 1912 - 1921

Early Organization and Growth

In the fall of 1912, the Catholic Sisters College had no building of its own, being temporarily housed near the University in the convent of the Benedictine Sisters in Brookland. Dr. Shields was working out of his house at 1326 Quincy Street, N. E., and it was there, along with all his many other activities, that the first "office" of Affiliation was set up.[1] The work of the very first years must have been centered on organizational and administrative detail as well as on the continued development of the course outlines and the testing program along the lines described in the previous chapter. But another important aspect of getting the program underway was the processing of a steady flow of applications for Affiliation.

The response to the new plan was good and requests for information were numerous.[2] McCormick reported that, among the first applicants, there were some high schools which were ready to comply immediately with the requirements while others found that additional work on their curriculums was necessary for full approval.[3] Because no minutes of the Committee's meetings were available, the procedures followed by the Committee on Affiliation or the channels of authority that functioned are not clear. The Committee did review and act on all the applications, and its recommendations for the affiliation of individual institutions were at first sent to the Academic Senate for final approval. Shields, however, considered this a mere formality, and it is doubtful that more than three lists of recommended applicants were so channeled.[4] By 1916 the action of the Committee was being frankly considered as final.[5]

Three colleges and thirty-three high schools were duly

affiliated by the end of the first academic year. Both the May
issue of the Catholic Educational Review[6] and the June issue
of the Catholic University Bulletin[7] made the announcement
and an official listing of the affiliates appeared that summer
in the University's 1913-1914 Year Book.[8]   Final approval
for a second list of one college and fifteen high schools was
announced the following October, bringing the first year's
total to fifty-two affiliates, all of them conducted by religious
orders of women.[9]   Some of these were given tentative affiliation only and another eight applications were completely rejected.[10]   By the end of the second academic year, the list
had grown to four colleges and seventy high schools.[11]

In September of 1914, when the Catholic Sisters College
moved into its new building on its present site near the University, Dr. Shields as Dean set up his academic offices
there, and the growing work of Affiliation was then largely
transacted from these headquarters. Drs. Pace and
McCormick must have worked closely with Shields in these
early days, McCormick especially being active in the administration of the high school examination program. Sometime
during this period, the Reverend Leo L. McVay also began to
participate in the work of Affiliation and in 1917-1918 took
over the duties of the Secretary for the Committee.[12]

About this time, the general problem of college accreditation received considerable publicity in Catholic educational
circles, and the discussion that took place throws some light
on the lack of interest of the colleges in University Affiliation.
The Catholic Educational Association had finally agreed on
college standards in 1915, but it had not been able to reach a
further agreement on the sanctions to be applied to enforce
these standards. When the matter was tabled at its June,
1916, meeting, an unidentified "Professor" attacked the state
of affairs in an open letter to the Editor of the Ecclesiastical
Review.[13] Shields followed the letter up by an article on the
"Standardization of Catholic Colleges." His main point was
that a Catholic college must be standardized in two ways, regarding the character of its Catholicity and as an academic
program. No mention was made of Affiliation, but his emphasis on the Catholic character of a Catholic college as its

raison d'etre ruled out mere accreditation by secular agencies.[14] While the article did not "raise a row" as he had hoped, the silence that immediately followed, he felt, indicated "consciousness of witness" and perhaps a first step toward amendment.[15]

In March of 1917, the Catholic Educational Review carried another article on Catholic college standardization, this one by the same unknown author of the 1916 letter. The article in substance defended the University's position, as the national pontifical university of the United States and as commissioned by Pope Leo XIII, to assist other Catholic educational institutions through a program of affiliation. In spite of the University's efforts and those of the College Department of the CEA, the "Professor" continued, too many colleges remained colleges in name only, giving no more than a high school course or one or two years of college work. That the cautious efforts of the CEA to set up a standardizing agency were voted down at its last meeting, the "Professor" attributed to the opposition of those very colleges whose standards were most sorely in need of raising. But why, he asked, were Catholic educators groping for a center of united action when The Catholic University of America, sanctioned by the Pope and entrusted to the American hierarchy, had already moved effectively in that direction? Why did the CEA, which had been called into existence by the University, hesitate to turn to her for the standardization of its colleges?[16]

These questions remained unanswered. There was no quickening pace of college affiliations, and during Shields' lifetime the total number of college affiliates never rose above thirteen. This critical attack on the Catholic college may have had an influence, however, on the CEA, as Father Schumacher was able at the next meeting of the Association to get through college accrediting procedures that were to make possible its own list of approved colleges.[17] And it was out of the CEA's overall concern for standardization that the matter of minor seminary affiliation was brought to Dr. Pace's attention.

At the 1919 annual meeting of the CEA, standardization was discussed by its seminary department and the question was raised as to the desirability and possibility of some kind of official recognition of the preparatory seminary or the six-year minor seminary.[18]   Dr. Pace was consulted in November of that year by the Reverend Anthony Volkert, Rector of St. Joseph's Seminary in Grand Rapids, Michigan. Volkert felt that the affiliation of a seminary's high school division only under the regular Affiliation program of the University would be inadequate and doubted that the two-year college division would be approved under the four-year college Affiliation plan. However, if the University were to set a minimum standard curriculum for the minor seminary, he told Dr. Pace, many if not all the seminaries would be willing to adopt it because of their need for greater uniformity and for the general recognition that would ensue. The request was explicitly stated:

> Can provision be made in the near future for affiliation of Preparatory Seminaries as such? They are an institution of the Church and demanded by the Church, an official recognition of the curriculum from our highest center of education will be the most powerful motive for agreeing upon a standardized program.[19]

Both Pace and Shahan were interested. They did not foresee any great problem in regard to the curriculum and were already working on a plan for the affiliation of such seminaries. Any relations established between the University and the seminaries, however, had to be such as to be of a genuine advantage to the latter.[20]   At Pace's request, Volkert studied the matter over the Christmas holidays. His reply was primarily a defense of the preparatory seminary as a college, equating the six-year program to the combined work of a regular four-year high school and a four-year college course. He argued that the seminary student, in following a strong classical program and motivated by his vocational aspirations, gained a more substantial knowledge of ancient languages than the average college student and that in thoroughness and accuracy generally the seminary program was

superior although perhaps less pretentious.[21]   In line with
this thinking, Volkert offered five points for consideration by
the University:

1. The advantages of affiliation ought to accrue to all
    who have successfully completed the entire course,
    including the considerable percentage of students
    who decide to follow another career than that of the
    priesthood, provided they carry the necessary units.
2. Full credit should be given to the students for the
    amount of work after the High School department,
    even in case the work be done during the first four
    years of the Preparatory Seminary curriculum,
    since the Seminary can demand more work than the
    High School at the same time, i.e., at least in sec-
    ondary branches.
3. The studies pursued in the departments of Ancient
    Languages, of English with Elocution and Public
    Speaking, of History and some other secondary
    branches, are in thoroughness and extent not inferior
    to the same kind of work in a full College course,
    cannot the same credits be allowed to them as in
    Colleges?
4. Admission to the university - in certain departments,
    vis. School of Philosophy and Letters - without
    previous examination for admission, might be granted
    to our alumni as to those of complete College courses.
5. If the requirements as announced in the Year Book of
    of the University for degrees of B.A. or B.L. are
    fulfilled at the end of the six-years' course, the same
    degrees conferred by the Preparatory Seminary fac-
    ulty may be approved of.[22]

His sixth, though unnumbered, point implied a reluctance
to accept any kind of sanction through examinations: "When
the University has received sufficient assurance about the
faculty in a Preparatory Seminary, perhaps a larger extent of
confidence may be granted as regards studies and examinations, than in the case of High Schools, especially if the

program excedes the minimum requirements."[23]

Dr. Pace thanked Father Volkert for his valuable suggestions and promised their full consideration by the Committee on Affiliation.[24]   Whether the Committee jointly or Dr. Pace alone was responsible for the "Conditions for Affiliation of Preparatory Seminaries," found in the latter's papers for this period, is not known. The proposed plan combined the already existing college and high school standards, the only adjustments being made in the course requirements and in reducing by half the number of hours originally required of the four-year college. A single classical course was worked out over the full six years of the seminary.[25]   Why this proposed plan received no further positive action by the Committee on Affiliation can only be surmised, but it is probable that the conditions were not entirely acceptable to Father Volkert and the other minor seminary educators, since the six-year program was definitely not equated with a four-year college degree curriculum. In any case, the matter of seminary affiliation was not opened up again for serious consideration until the late 1920's.

Shields also thought in terms of possible extension of Affiliation to cover other kinds of Catholic educational institutions. He had never felt that the Catholic elementary schools should be included but that their unification and upgrading were primarily a matter of local concern. The University's contribution at this level was through its Department of Education by training diocesan superintendents who, in turn, would be able to effect the needed improvements of curriculum and methods in their diocesan schools.[26]   The training of the teaching sisters was, of course, the raison d'etre of the Catholic Sisters College, but Shields realized also that he was reaching a relatively small number of elementary school teachers. Many were being trained in the novitiate normals of their communities, and it was not rare to find elementary school teachers who had less than a full four-year high school course to their credit.[27]

In 1914, the provincial superior of the Sisters of Holy Names of Marylhurst, Oregon, proposed the affiliation of novitiate normals. Shields saw no difficulty regarding the granting

of credits for professional courses and hoped that steps could
be taken in that direction since two such normals had already
applied.[28]   No official action was taken then, however, but in
1919 pending legislation on the certification of teachers made
the matter a pressing one.[29]   While there is no evidence that
Shields or the University authorities sought to set up formal
teacher certification procedures, they saw the possibility of
Affiliation making a practical contribution to the solution of the
problem. McVay surveyed the field to ascertain whether or
not novitiate high schools would accept affiliation based directly on the University's regular high school scheme. The survey letter sent to sister superiors proposed an immediate acceptance of these terms which would result in a tentative listing of a novitiate high school and limited course testing in
August of 1920. Such affiliates would then be given until
August of the next year to make the additional adjustments
needed to meet the full requirements of the plan.[30]   The response must have been favorable. August testing was introduced in the summer of 1920[31] and a list of forty-six novitiate
high schools appeared in the 1921-1922 Year Book of the University.[32]   Thus Affiliation not only provided for the longer-
range effect of bringing the curriculum of these institutions
into line with the other high schools of the Catholic system but
also gave immediate assistance to the elementary school
teachers in meeting minimum certification standards of the
time.

High School Testing and Curriculum Development

Among the regular high schools Affiliation also enjoyed
considerable success during the Shields period. The course
outlines and the testing program were showing the results that
Dr. Shields desired by way of instructional and curricular improvements. An important development within this area was
the introduction of an Affiliation high school "diploma" or
certificate in 1918. The original 1912 plan had specifically
stated that "all students who successfully pass the examinations held during the four years of high school shall be admitted to any college affiliated by the University."[33]   This

was being done, but the Affiliation certificate was to give
added strength to this policy, probably with the hope that non-
affiliates would also recognize it for admission purposes.
The terms for the new certificate were clearly stated:

> A general certificate will be issued to all stu-
> dents of the affiliated high schools who have gained
> by examination, in an affiliated high school, the
> fifteen required units as outlined on page two of
> this syllabus. A yearly certificate will be issued
> to any pupil who requests the same, provided the
> reasons given are deemed sufficient by the Com-
> mittee on Affiliation. This request must be made
> through the principal of the high school. No
> yearly certificate, however, will be sent unless
> the pupil has successfully passed in three subjects.
> The general certificate will be issued only to
> pupils who (a) have attended an affiliated high
> school for at least three years, and (b) have gained,
> before entering the last year in high school, nine or
> more credits through examinations set by the Uni-
> versity.[34]

To earn the general certificate, students were permitted
to make up examinations, if for any reason they had been unable to take them in a previous year.[35] Those unsuccessful
in passing all the required tests were issued a special certificate, a practice which evolved out of the "yearly certificate"
referred to above. The first year 179 general certificates
and 263 special certificates were issued, and in 1919, 272
general and 113 special. The continued increase in the number of certificates issued in the next several years was viewed
as further evidence of internal progress within the schools
and of improved articulation between the high schools and
colleges.[36]

The number of high school tests given also grew with
each year of the Shields' period. In 1913, 13 schools had
taken a total of 1,318 tests set for 27 different courses. In
1919, 146 schools took 26,479 tests in 45 different courses.[37]

While Dr. Shields was definitely pleased with the results, there were problems and the first signs of troubles to come. He had been worried about the amount of correcting work involved as early as 1914, when the total number of test papers was still under 5,000.[38]   The difficulties involved in scoring accurately over 25,000 essay-type tests must have been enormous. From the affiliates' point of view, the expense at a set fee of fifty cents for each test was not always easy to meet, and there were cases when the test requirements and costs were direct obstacles to promoting Affiliation among non-affiliates.[39]   Moreover, from 1913 through 1919, twenty-four affiliated high schools were dropped from the official list "chiefly because they failed to stand the yearly tests set by the University."[40]   In February of 1919, Dr. Pace received a formal complaint regarding the examinations:

> . . . should not a personel [sic] composed largely of the University's own graduates be evidence enough of a secondary school's fitness for affiliation? We think it should, and so, since, upon the teaching staff of St. Joseph's Academy three Bachelors degrees and one Masters are represented, we feel justly entitled to an honorable place upon the University's affiliated list without having to inflict upon delicate, nervous girlhood the hardship of extraneous examinations. Could not the University's ruling in this matter be so modified as to exempt from examinations schools vouched for by even one of its own graduates? in fact might not such graduates -- Doctors or Masters or even Bachelors -- be appointed unpaid visitors of affiliated schools in their respective districts and so do away with such examinations entirely?[41]

Dr. Pace replied:

> It has been suggested more than once that the tests required of the Affiliated schools should be modified or entirely rearranged; and no doubt in

any plan of reconstruction due consideration would
be given to both of your suggestions.

There are many phases in the work of the University itself, which call for modification on the
part of the authorities; but for the time being, we
live in the midst of uncertainty, and I doubt very
much whether the Trustees would favor any movement directed toward a radical change, either in the
University itself or in its relations to other schools.
They would probably say that it is risky to adopt a
new scheme until we see clearly how the issue of the
War is going to affect the country at large and, in
particular, our Catholic Education.[42]

Thus the problems of testing were tabled for the time being,
but they were to become of serious concern at a later date.

Dr. Shields continued also the curriculum work, completing the course outlines for the traditional academic
courses[43] and giving further consideration to courses in do-
mestic science,[44] physiography,[45] music, and business.
While the first two never reached a state of approval, a four-
year program in music did so in 1918-1919. When the music
courses were being considered as possible free electives,[46]
Shields became interested in the Progressive Series of Piano
Lessons published by the Art Publication Society. The formal
adoption of this series, which was the first and only adoption
of a particular textbook for an Affiliation course, constituted a
two-part music course for each of the four years of high
school, one part devoted to theory and the other to practice.[47]
On February 11, 1918, Shields wrote the Rector, then Bishop
Shahan, describing the planning steps that had gone into the
final decision regarding these courses:

I have devoted several years of careful study of the
problem of securing academic credit for work in
music. The Board of Studies and Discipline and the
Academic Senate gave very careful consideration to
all the facts in the case before adopting the present
plan.

. . . .

. . .Before credit could be given for music work in the high schools, it was necessary to adopt some standard course which would be uniform throughout the country. Two chief reasons called for this uniformity. First, as in all the other subjects in affiliated schools, the same program must be followed in each course pursued, and the same set of examinations at the end of the year used. . . . I see no way where this can be avoided for Music, any more than for any other branch. We are not claiming that a course which we adopt is the only one available or necessarily the best one. It is the best and most suitable in our judgment. When a pupil passes from one affiliated high school or academy to another, she drops into a place in the new school without any disturbance, since the matter is identical. This should be so in Music as in other branches.

Prior to the organization of the work by the Art Publication Society, there was no single music course enjoying wide adoption in the country. It was difficult to get at the system that was being followed. In the summer of 1915, my attention was called to the Progressive Series of Piano Lessons. I obtained all the literature on the subject, and a copy of their course, and sought the advice of a number of eminent musicians in the matter. It was pointed out to me that the editors of this system were among the leading pianists of the world. . . . This was sufficient guarantee for the musical excellence of the work. I examined it carefully from the pedagogical point of view, and found that it followed in a wonderful way the fundamental pedagogical principles, the acceptance of which we have been laborin [sic] so strenuously in the other departments of education. Mrs. Ward, . . .took the matter up with a number of eminent musicians in New York and Boston, and found practically a unanimous approval of the plan.

Our next step was to write a letter of inquiry to the Mother Superiors of the Communities who were most widely concerned, as shown by the attendance of their members at the Sisters College. In reply, I received letters of enthusiastic endorsement from every one of the communities addressed, without a single adverse criticism. . . .

It was decided then, to invite Mr. Henneman, the head of the School Department, of the Music course in question, to deliver a series of lectures on the course at the Washington and Dubuque Summer Sessions of 1916. I attended these lectures as frequently as possible, and the musicians who were there, both students and instructors, were quite enthusiasitic [sic] about the course. . . .
. . . .
We have no binding contract with anybody in this matter, and when any other definite course in music presents to us claims, which in our judgment would render it more suitable for adoption in our affiliated high schools and the Sisters College, than is the Progressive Series of Piano Lessons, I am sure the Board and the Senate will give their attention to the matter and their award from unbiased judgments.[48]

Business courses too were accepted by Shields as having a legitimate place in Catholic high schools. His reply to a letter seeking his advice on the desirability of more electives and lighter work for students not desiring a full academic program or even a full four-year course[49] reveals his usual thorough consideration and broad approach to a complex problem:

I am still somewhat at a loss to answer you. There are so many things to be considered. Your letter, it is true, states the case very plainly, but there are many other things to be taken into

account. Now, as an affiliated high school your
pupils are required to take Religion (2 units),
English (3 units), Mathematics (2 units), Latin (2
units) or some other language in its stead (2 units),
one Physical Science and one History. Now, your
program presents an extra unit in Mathematics,
an extra unit in Latin, and 3 units in Greek that
are not called for. Of course, Latin, Mathematics,
or some other course must be lifted to 3 units to
meet our requirements. There is no question of
the desirability of offering a good number of electives if the school can afford to do so. Spanish is
undoubtedly a desirable elective; while Greek is
of a very high cultural value, still it is question-
able whether we have the right to force this on un-
willing pupils; and the same may be said of Latin.
Pupils who contemplate going into business, engin-
eering, etc., can get along without Latin, and a
modern language is a great asset. For pupils who
contemplate going into the teaching profession,
Biology is even more desirable than either Physics
or Chemistry. Pupils who contemplate an engineer-
ing course will want 3 units of mathematics, and
probably both Physics and Chemistry, and 2 units
of each if possible; while to those who contemplate
going into the learned professions in a classical
college Latin is indispensable and Greek invaluable;
whereas those who contemplate a business career
might want more than a unit of History, and perhaps
two modern languages with some commercial
courses thrown in.

There is an increasing number of pupils of
high school age who want a business course, and
it would be highly desirable to offer such of them
as cannot take the four years' course a two years'
business course. The business course doesn't
yet come under the scope of our affiliation work.
But I am quite convinced that we ought to do some-
thing in the matter.[50]

While the courses in commercial arithmetic, bookkeeping, commercial geography, and economics were not added until the year following Dr. Shields' death, and business law and stenography and typing not until 1926 and 1928, respectively, Dr. Shields' thinking, if not his direct contribution to the outlines, was influential in bringing them about.

The textbook problem was another area to which Shields devoted considerable time during the first years of Affiliation. His correspondence, after 1915 especially, referred repeatedly to this textbook work in the fields of educational philosophy, music, and religion. Dr. Pace also felt strongly about the need for better religion books for the high schools "based on the fundamental principles of Education and in part, on our experience with the affiliated schools" and was devoting efforts in this direction in 1918.[51]   Both Shields and Pace gave personal advice on textbooks to the individual affiliate but at the same time continued to emphasize their policy that each school was "free to use such texts as they might deem best in following the outline for each year."[52]   In the fall of 1920, textbook assistance for affiliates was put on a somewhat more systematic basis. The various academic departments of the University were requested to prepare lists of textbooks which they could recommend for use by the affiliated high schools in those courses which fell under the supervision of each department.[53] These lists were kept on file and copies were sent to affiliates on request.[54]

Early Recognition, Benefits, and Evaluations

While an evaluation of the effects of Affiliation does not fall within the scope of this study and any conclusive appraisal is not possible from the evidence on hand, yet there were specific instances in the early records of Affiliation which indicate that the pioneering work of Shields and Pace received some recognition as a process of standardization. O'Dowd, in his 1935 study of the influence of standardization on Catholic secondary schools, stated that Affiliation "is not an accrediting agency in the strict sense of the term and it does not enjoy reciprocity with the regional and state agencies of standardization," but at the same time he credited it as an effective "coordinating agency."[55] This, of course, was true; yet there were results of the program which may be classified as "accreditation," a term which was used interchangeably with "affiliation" by University authorities in the early days. The original plan had promised to the graduates of affiliated colleges admission, without further examinations, to University courses leading to higher degrees. Admission to Catholic Sisters College was included in this exemption, and advanced standing was also granted on this basis.[56]

The general reputation of the University as a charter member of the Association of American Universities also carried weight with the professional educators, so that frequently the opinion of the University in rating other Catholic colleges was sought. In replying, Affiliation was used as one of the criteria for a satisfactory rating.[57] At the same time, it was made clear that Affiliation was not to be interpreted as giving an affiliated college the right to grant an academic degree, this right being reserved to the state in which the college was located.[58] It was here that the distinction between the University's two affiliation plans, the earlier one for theological curricula and the 1912 plan for other Catholic colleges, rested. In the former, Dr. Pace explained,

. . .the University confers the S.T.B. degree for work done in the Seminary and completed with examination.

For the degrees Bachelor of Arts and Master of Arts, the University had not, thus far, made arrangements with any other institution that would correspond to the above-named provisions for the S.T.B. We have a system by which colleges are affiliated to the University and students who successfully pass the examinations held during the four years in college are admitted without further examination to the courses in the University leading to the higher degrees. In such cases, the student's work in the college is regarded as equivalent to an A.B. degree, but the degree itself is not formally conferred by the University.

The University, of course, will be very glad to
offer suggestions for the arrangement of courses
leading to the A.B. degree and I think we all realize the need of greater uniformity in this matter.
But I also feel that the degree should be conferred
by the institution which has given the student his
training. The authorities and teachers of that institution have had an opportunity of acquainting
themselves with the student's ability and character;
and since it is on their judgment and recommendation that the degree must be conferred, it seems
to me that they are the proper agencies to confer
it.[59]

In the case of the affiliated high schools, their graduates
benefited from Affiliation in much the same way as they would
benefit from state or regional accreditation. The original
agreement was confined, however, to affiliated colleges and
to the University, which was willing to admit to its undergraduate schools, without further examinations, those young men
who were graduated by an affiliated high school and who presented the proper Affiliation test records.[60]   There were also
several instances of requests made by secular colleges for information and advice concerning the nature of Affiliation and
of the Affiliation examinations, in order to interpret the
records of applying graduates of affiliated high schools and to
make decisions regarding the acceptance of these examinations
in lieu of their own entrance examinations.[61] The final decisions made in these cases, however, are not known.

Within University circles, a general enthusiasm for the
new program, because of its early accomplishments and its
promise of even greater benefits to Catholic education, was
clearly evident. A student of the 1912 summer session of
Catholic Sisters College wrote of it as the fulfillment of the
University as the cornerstone of American Catholic education;[62]
the Alumni Association congratulated the University on its
nationwide influence through Affiliation;[63] and the undergraduate student body took note of it as an opportunity to unify,

systematize, and perfect "the wonderful Catholic educational organization of the U. S."[64]   At the 1914 commencement exercises of the University, the Very Reverend George A. Dougherty, then Vice Rector, spoke of the mutual benefits to be derived from Affiliation by turning people of all sections of the country toward Catholic University and by building up a body of undergraduate students to meet University standards.[65] The editors of the Catholic University Bulletin wrote that "the first fruits of the Sisters College may be seen in the movement for Affiliation with the University of high schools and colleges," the benefits of which could hardly be over-estimated.[66] On the occasion of several University functions in 1915 and 1916, James Cardinal Gibbons had warm words of praise[67] and expounded these also to others outside the immediate University family in his pastoral letter of 1919.[68]

Dr. Shields too was generally satisfied with the early accomplishments of the program. In his visits to affiliates he found a new spirit and renewed energy among teachers and pupils.[69] He noted also a marked improvement each year in the results of the testing program, a gradual building up of unity and system, added strength from less isolation, and a smoother transition of high school students to the standard Catholic college.[70] While Shields was the first to admit that much still remained to be done before the full unification and strength of Catholic education would be realized, he was also sensitive to criticism, even implied. Perhaps his sensitivity was reserved primarily for the CEA, since one of his disappointments in Affiliation was the lack of support received from schools and colleges conducted by the religious orders of men, these being also in large part the constituents of the CEA.[71] In any case, when Father Burns, a prominent leader in the high school movement within the Association, published his new book, Catholic Education: A Study of Conditions,[72] in 1917, Shields was upset by what he thought was a complete ignoring of the contribution made by University Affiliation and the inadequate treatment given the Catholic Sisters College. Taking the author to task in the February, 1918, issue of the Catholic Educational Review, Shields defended Catholic University's large scale accomplishments as compared to the

"futile attempt" made by the CEA to bring about some kind of
an affiliation scheme.[73] Burns replied by a letter to the editor in the next issue of the Review, quoting a single sentence
reference to Affiliation as it appeared on page ninety-two of
his book: "The University has been quick to recognize the opportunity that this condition [need of high schools for recogni-
tion] offers, as is shown by its long list of accredited high
schools."[74]

For his error, Shields apologized profusely, stating
that he was not ungrateful for the "meager" reference, even
though it was not in proportion to the importance of Affiliation.
He further objected that the cited passage had been placed in
the chapter on high schools for boys, since the University Affiliation program had been primarily effective among the high
schools for girls.[75]

The following year the Committee on Affiliation made its
first attempt to estimate its own accomplishments through a
statistical survey report. Each affiliated high school was requested to submit current data on teachers, enrollment,
courses, and graduates.[76] The response was good, and with
the permission of the Rector the report was printed in 1920
and distributed to all affiliates. Quantitatively, Affiliation's
first seven-year span showed considerable growth in tests and
in the number of high school affiliates.[77] A total of 207 high
school applications had met with approval within that period
while 36 had been rejected, although some of the latter had
since been able to meet the requirements.[78] Equally inter-
esting were the statistics on the students and graduates of the
affiliated high schools for the year 1919. The total enrollment
for the high schools that year was 12,700, of which 11,287
were girls and 1,415 were boys.[79] The two tables, [80] which
follow, were given on the 1919 graduates:

TABLE II. -- Number of Graduates of 1919 at College

	Catholic	State	Non-Catholic
Boys........	20	6	2
Girls	187	97	89

TABLE III. -- <u>Number of Graduates of 1919 in other Institutions of Learning</u>

	Boys	Girls
Normal Schools	3	74
Business School	5	95
Technical Schools	6	38
Special Courses	--	89
Total	14	296

The general conclusions which McVay drew from the 1920 report were highly favorable: the constantly increasing number of affiliates showed in a forceful manner the faith and interest that the high schools had in the University and its influence,[81] and the growth in the testing process exhibited a recognition of the Affiliation tests "as a means of unifying, standardizing and adjusting courses and methods to meet the demands of the constantly changing requirements of our rapidly developing American life."[82] "On the other hand," he wrote the Rector, "a comparison of these encouraging and hopeful elements with the figures as found in the general tables of our national educational strength alone is sufficient to impress us with the truth that much yet remains to be done through this important factor of University life."[83]

Internal Problems and Dr. Shields' Death

But while growth in the number of affiliates and the general development of the program were moving ahead most satisfactorily, there were problems other than the amount of work still to be done. In 1916 Dr. Shields' health broke down. He had developed valvular heart trouble and was told by his doctor to cut down his work. This was difficult for him to do, and the heart attacks reoccured.[84] In 1918, after suffering a severe one, he wrote to an old friend: "The Sisters College, affiliation of high schools, and general movement for integrating and uplifting Catholic education is well on its way, and I believe it will get along very well without me, even should I be unable to take a very active part in the future."[85]

In March of the same year he limited his work somewhat, with
Father McVay taking over his duties at the University and
Trinity College.[86]   By the end of the year, he reported that
he was recovering slowly, but this was only temporary. Writing to one of his former students in the spring of 1919, he expressed a strong desire to complete his textbooks and manuals
of methods for the elementary school as well as the organization of an art course.

> I will be 57 years old in a few days, and I realize
> more and more every day that I cannot solve all the
> problems in the educational field. Many of them will
> have to be faced by my pupils. I am anxious to finish
> out before it is too late some of the things I have on
> hand.[87]

His correspondence during 1919 and 1920 referred to a series
of set-backs and partial recoveries, but by the end of 1919 he
was giving all his Affiliation mail to Father McVay for answering.[88]

There were troubles also among the several personali-
ties involved in the work of Affiliation. Ward in her biography
of Shields referred frequently to the close friendship between
Shields and Pace, resulting in their working together on many
University projects. There was, however, in the years just
before Dr. Shields' death, a definite break between them.
Just how this affected Affiliation was not possible to determine, but there were differences of opinion. Dr. Pace
seemed to have been less satisfied with the testing program
as a method of standardization.[89]   By 1919 he felt that there
was an urgent need for modification of the Affiliation sanctions.
In an undated memorandum, written after "seven years upon
which to base our estimate of the results," which would date
the document about 1919 or 1920, Dr. Pace brought out what
he considered several major defects of Affiliation. He made
it clear first that much good had already been accomplished
by it and that the system should be maintained. Thus, he
wrote:

Among the satisfactory results, I would mention: the larger interest aroused in the work of the University, the stimulation given to teachers and pupils, greater uniformity in courses of study and requirements for completing the same: in a word, a practical standardization of the schools that have been affiliated. On the side of the University, it is safe to say that the professors who take an active part in the work have gained a better insight into the operation of our Catholic high schools and into the relative efficiency, of the various teaching communities.

On the other hand, we have to regret that the benefits of affiliates have not been shared by a larger number of our institutions. The list of colleges includes only--- [sic] and that of the high schools, though here we have a better showing, is less than one-half the total number of Catholic high schools in the United States. Each year, also, while some new institutions are added, some others are stricken from the list.

It is also to be regretted that we have reached so few of the institutions for boys. One result is that the number of students coming from the high schools and colleges, to the University is not sufficient to afford us a personal acquaintance with the products of our affiliated institutions, though such an acquaintance would undoubtedly supply the surest basis of judging the work of each institution. Concerning the girls who complete the high school course and receive our certificate, we have but meagre information as to their later career, Trinity College being our chief, and perhaps only, source.

There are minor difficulties which would call for mention in a complete report. Some of these have been removed by changes in our regulations, others still confront us and come up regularly at the meetings of the Committee on Affiliation. Perhaps the most serious is found in the tendency of many Catholic schools to seek affiliation with non-Catholic

institutions such as state universities, Boards of
Regents and other agencies whose influence is
considered useful or even necessary to our schools.
The problems which thus arise are not new; but
they come home to us with special force now that
we realize more fully what affiliation implies.

In my judgment, it is possible to improve our
system and now is the time to do so. Reorganization is needed and it must be based on the acceptance
of the principle that the schools are affiliated to the
University. This was the original intention and it
was the understanding of the institutions that applied
for affiliation. But an impression had gone abroad
that affiliation is to the Catholic Sisters College,
and whether founded or not, it is doing harm. The
situation has become more complicated since 1914,
when Sisters College was organized as an independent corporation separate and distinct from the
University, but affiliated to it. The schools certainly do not seek affiliation with one of the affiliated
colleges, but with the University as such. It is
necessary, therefore, and in the best interest of all
concerned, that the entire system of affiliation, in
its academic, administrative and financial aspects,
be so readjusted as to make it both in reality and in
name, affiliation to the University. With that end
in view, I submit the following recommendations:

1. The Committee on Affiliation to include the
   present members and such additional members as may be needed to secure representation from each of the Schools of Philosophy,
   Letters, and Sciences.

2. The administrative office to be located in
   McMahon Hall or Caldwell Hall, as circumstances permit and to be in charge of the
   Secretary. All records and equipment now
   used for affiliation to be transferred to this
   office.

3. All accounts with the affiliated institutions

to be kept by the Secretary. Bills for examinations and other expenses to be made out in
the name of the University and payment of the
same, whether by cheque or otherwise to be
made to the University.

4. Proper compensation to be made to the Secretary and an allowance for such clerical assistance as the Committee may decide to be
necessary. These salaries as well as the fee
for examining papers to be paid by the University out of the moneys received from the institutions.

5. The surplus of such moneys after all expenses
have been deducted will, if the University sees
fit, be handed over as a contribution, to Sisters College, and receipted for, and the
amount duly entered on the books of the University as balancing each year the account of
the Committee on Affiliation.

6. At least twice a year the Committee on Affiliation shall hold a meeting to which all instructors taking part in the work of Affiliation shall
be invited. Each shall be requested to give
his criticism and suggestion for the improvement of the work.

7. A system to be desired for securing more
accurate information regarding the work of
the affiliated schools, for getting their view
of the plan of affiliation; for following up
students who receive our certificate and for
extending affiliation to a larger number of
male institutions. It will also be necessary,
as the number of examination papers increases,
to enlist the services of additional examiners
and a fair distribution of this work will bring
the University into more general notice and
secure friendly cooperation throughout the
country.[90]

All of Dr. Pace's recommendations were eventually carried out in some form or other. The Committee was enlarged in the early 1920's and the test work was coordinated better through meetings of all those working in each test field, but these changes came after Dr. Shields' death. Following more immediately was the 1920 survey report on the high schools, which was probably a result of Pace's last recommendation. Also in the summer of 1920, the break between Affiliation and Catholic Sisters College was made. It would seem only natural that the Affiliation program under Shields as the driving force would have become closely linked with the Sisters College, since the work was carried on there in his office quarters. Moreover, his own personal conviction that the training of the teachers and the standardization process were necessary complements was reflected throughout his writings and often, for an uncritical reader, seemed blended into a single movement. Yet Shields himself clearly made the distinction:

> Catholic University, through its Department of Education, is putting forth every possible effort to uplift and unify our Catholic school system throughout the entire country. We are endeavoring to build up a curriculum, text-books, manuals of methods, etc. for our elementary schools, and you know what we are trying to do to standardize our high schools and colleges.[91]

However, when he wrote on the achievements of the Sisters College, which was frequently, he usually made mention also of the accomplishments of Affiliation,[92] and the early Year Books of the Catholic Sisters College and several issues of the Sisters College Messenger carried descriptions of the Affiliation plan and the list of affiliates.[93]

There were also other complications which brought the matter to a head. The sharing of office quarters and staff at the Catholic Sisters College with the Secretary of the Committee on Affiliation was proving by this time not to be the best of arrangements. The financial accounting for Affiliation, of which there was considerable in connection with the test orders and the correctors' fees, had been made a part of the accounting system of the Sisters College, any surplus evidently accruing to the College.[94]   The complications which arose out of this situation, caused by McVay's absence from the University over the summer months and the resulting delayed billing, as well as office staff friction arising out of conflicting directions from Shields and McVay, led Dr. Shields to make a formal complaint to the Rector. In spite of his poor health, he suggested as the solution that he be made Secretary of the Committee.[95]   The Rector, however, solved the problem by following Dr. Pace's earlier advice. The office was moved to the campus-proper of the University sometime in the summer of 1920 and all direct connection with the Sisters College was severed at that time.[96]

Dr. Shields continued his Sisters College work up to almost the very end of his life, although under great physical difficulty. He died on February 15, 1921.[97]   Thus within a period of about nine years, he had brought the University's long-awaited Affiliation plan into existence and had accomplished the pioneering work of its organization and administration. He had seen it grow and achieve in a substantial way the desired improvements in the unification and standardization of the Catholic educational system of the country. His had been an all-encompassing vision, and, as Dr. Pace said in his eulogy, Dr. Shields' life had been the gradual unfolding of a plan for Catholic education, step by step, building a unified, coordinated system from the elementary grades through the University:

> . . . if our schools have been raised to a higher
> degree of efficiency, these results are due chiefly
> to the movement in which Dr. Shields was a pioneer
> and a leader.[98]

> With the same end in view, he took an active
> part in the affiliation, or accrediting, of Catholic
> high schools and colleges to the University. He
> regarded affiliation as the best means of raising
> the standards of education and of securing such

uniformity as was desirable. It would also bring
about a solidarity of thought and purpose among
our teachers and stimulate them to constant improvements.[99]

FOOTNOTES

[1]ACUA, CSCF, Registrar, Catholic Sisters College, to
Sr. Mary Edmond, Sinsinawa, Wis., September 24, 1912.

[2]Ibid., Shields' correspondence for 1912 and 1913.

[3]Patrick J. McCormick, "Roman Catholic Parochial
Schools," CER, VIII (September, 1914), 147.

[4]Academic Senate Minutes, III, May 14, 1913, p. 211;
ibid., October 21, 1914, p. 221; ibid., February 10, 1915,
p. 241. Even when the list of recommended affiliates was
sent to the Academic Senate, the announcement of favorable
action by the Committee was made before the final approval
was given by the Senate; ACUA, CSCF, Shields to Rev.
Albert Lohmann, San Antonio, Texas, May 3, 1913. The
complete file of Academic Senate minutes, however, was not
made available to this investigator. Thus the part that the
Senate played in matters pertaining to Affiliation in general
could not be determined.

[5]ACUA, CSCF, Shields to Mother Aloysius, April 11,
1916.

[6]"Colleges and High Schools Affiliated With the University," CER, V (May, 1913), 417-418.

[7]"University Chronicle," CUB, XIX (June, 1913), 430-
432.

[8]Year-Book of the Catholic University of America, 1913-
1914 (Washington, 1913), pp. 220-223. The Year Books continued to be used for the official listing of affiliates and the
general membership statistics for this study have been drawn
from these annual issues; cf. Appendix C. The Year Book
lists do not usually agree with the statistical reports made by
the Committee on Affiliation. This does not necessarily reflect inaccuracy of either source since the specific cut-off
dates were not given and probably varied considerably; e.g.,

the Year Book lists would tend to include only those institutions affiliated as of the end of the previous academic year while the Committee's reports might have used any current cut-off date.

[9]"Colleges and High Schools Affiliated with the University," CER, VI (September, 1913), 181-182.

[10]Report on the Affiliation of High Schools (1920), pp. 8, 10. This document reported a total of fifty-six high schools for 1913, twenty-eight of which were only tentatively affiliated.

[11]Year Book of the Catholic University of America, 1914-1915 (Washington, 1914), pp. 234-238.

[12]ACUA, CSCF, Shields to McVay, October 6, 1919. McVay, from Providence, R. I., had taught in the 1912 Summer School and at the Catholic Sisters College since 1913. In the fall of 1915, he had been made an instructor in the Department of Education of the University; CER, X (November, 1915), 359.

[13]Professor, "Standardization of Catholic Colleges," Ecclesiastical Review, LV (September, 1916), 302-303.

[14]Thomas E. Shields, "Standardization of Catholic Colleges," CER, XII (October, 1916), 193-203.

[15]ACUA, CSCF, Shields to Rev. D. J. Maladey, Pittsburgh, Pa., November 9, 1916.

[16]Professor, "Standardization of Catholic Colleges," CER, XIII (March, 1917), 193-199.

[17]"College Department, Proceedings," CEAB, XIV (November, 1917), 89-90.

[18]ACUA, VRF, Rev. Anthony Volkert to Pace, November 29, 1919.

[19]Ibid.

[20]Ibid., Pace to Volkert, December 6, 1919.

[21]Ibid., Volkert to Pace, January 4, 1920.

[22]Ibid.

[23]Ibid.

[24]Ibid., Pace to Volkert, January 7, 1920.

[25]Ibid., "Conditions for Affiliation of Preparatory Seminaries," n.d.

[26]ACUA, CSCF, Shields to Sr. Regina, Cincinnati, August 11, 1915. Cf. "Editor's Note" to J. B. Culemans' article, "A Plea for Diocesan School Superintendents," CER,

XI (January, 1916), 40.

27George Johnson, "A Plan of Teacher Certification," CER, XIX (September, 1921), 450.

28ACUA, CSCF, Sr. Flavia to Shields, May 16, 1914; Shields to Sr. Flavia, Marylhurst, Ore., May 31, 1914.

29ACUA, VRF, McVay to "My dear Professor," January 29, 1920. Catholic educators feared that state laws on teacher certification would involve further state supervision of private schools. The need for improving the qualifications of parochial school teachers, however, was acknowledged and the minimum standard of a high school training was generally acceptable. To forestall state interference, therefore, some centralized system through the CEA or Catholic University for the certification of Catholic school teachers seemed desirable; cf. George Johnson, "A Plan of Teacher Certification," CER, XIX (September, 1921), 450-451; George Johnson, "Fundamentals of Catholic Teacher Training," CER, XXI (October, 1923), 449-460.

30ACUA, VRF, McVay to the Sister Superior, n.d. By offering an August examination program, the sisters already teaching in the field, as well as the novices, were able to return to the motherhouse in the summer and take the examinations. An additional concession was made for those who had already completed studies equivalent to the high school course by permitting a maximum of eight examinations the first year. This maximum was to be reduced by one in each of the succeeding years until it automatically ceased when the regular limit of five was reached. This final limitation of five examinations would permit the novice to obtain a high school certificate in three or at most four years, but exemptions from these regulations might be granted by the Committee on Affiliation in cases of grave necessity.

31ACUA, VRF, McVay to "My dear Professor," January 29, 1920.

32Year Book of the Catholic University of America, 1921-1922 (Washington, 1921), p. 231.

33AHSC (1912-1913), p. [iv].

34AHSC (1919), pp. 3-4.

35Shields, "The Sisters College and the High Schools. . . ,"

CER, XV (February, 1918), 100.

[36]ARR, 1924-1925 (Washington: 1925), pp. 57-58.

[37]Report of Affiliation of High Schools (1920), pp. 8-9.

[38]ACUA, CSCF, Shields to Sr. St. Ignatius, Villa Maria, January 2, 1914.

[39]ACUA, VRF, unsigned letter to Shahan, October 15, 1915; Brother Richard to Pace, December 19, 1916.

[40]Report on Affiliation of High Schools (1920), p. 10.

[41]ACUA, VRF, Sr. Evelyn O'Neill to Pace, April 1, 1918.

[42]Ibid., Pace to Sr. Evelyn O'Neill, St. Louis, Mo., April 1, 1918.

[43]See pp. 71-74 of this study.

[44]Shields, "The Sisters College and the High Schools. . . ," CER, XV (February, 1918), 101.

[45]Ibid.

[46]See p. 124 of this study for explanation of "free electives."

[47]Credit for music was not given for theory without practice. The University set the examination in theory and the music teacher provided the practice examination and reported the grade (ACUA, RF, Shields to "Dear Sister," July 31, 1919). Cf. Thomas E. Shields, "Syllabus for Music in Affiliated Schools," CER, XV (February, 1918), 106-108.

[48]ACUA, CSCF, Shields to Shahan, February 11, 1918.

[49]Ibid., Sr. Paulinus to Shields, March 22, 1919.

[50]Ibid., Shields to Sr. Paulinus, Pittsburgh, Pa., April 11, 1919.

[51]ACUA, VRF, Pace to Sr. Josephine Mary, S.N.D., Cincinnati, March 8, 1918.

[52]Ibid., Pace to "Gentlemen," St. Procopius College, Lisle, Ill., February 26, 1918.

[53]Ibid., McVay to "My dear Professor," September 6, 1920.

[54]Leo L. McVay, "The Problems of Affiliation," Catholic School Interests, III (June, 1924), 90.

[55]O'Dowd, op. cit., p. 27.

[56]ACUA, CSCF, Shields to Sr. M. Ignatius, New Rochelle, N. Y., November 23, 1914, and May 6, 1915. Colleges that were members of the Association of American Universities

were granted the same exemption. A college might also establish itself through its graduates who had been admitted by examination, but if none of these qualifications had been met, examinations were required and the college in question was usually invited to standardize through the University's program of Affiliation.

[57]ACUA, VRF, Pace to Walter A. Payne, Examiner, University of Chicago, March 4, 1918; Shahan to C. D. Koch, Director, Professional Credentials Bureau, Department of Public Instruction, Harrisburg, Pa., June 30, 1923.

[58]Ibid., Pace to Rev. M. F. McEvoy, St. Francis, Wis., May 25, 1917.

[59]Ibid., Pace to Rev. Dr. Joseph Oeh, Columbus, Ohio, May 3, 1919.

[60]Announcements of the School of Sciences, 1913-1914 (Washington: 1913), p. 33.

[61]ACUA, VRF, Pace to Miss Katharine S. Doty, Barnard College, Columbia University, New York City, July 16, 1915; Pace to Walter A. Payne, Examiner, University of Chicago, January 14, 1918.

[62]A Sister of the Congregation de Notre Dame, "The Second Summer Session of Sisters College," CER, IV (September, 1912), 153.

[63]Bernard A. McKenna, "The Alumni Association," CER, V (May, 1913), 415.

[64]Rayson E. Roche, "The Sisters College: The Summer School -- Affiliation of Schools and Colleges," The University Symposium, V (April, 1915), 360.

[65]"Commencement Exercises, 1914," CUB, XX (October, 1914), 564.

[66]CUB, XXI (January, 1915), 26-27.

[67]"Cardinal Gibbons' Sermon on the Occasion of the Silver Jubilee of the Catholic University of America," CER, IX (May, 1915), 394; James Cardinal Gibbons, "The Anthony Nicholas Brady Memorial," CER, XII (June, 1916), 5.

[68]"Pastoral Letter of the Archbishops and Bishops of the U.S.," CER, XVIII (May, 1920), 258. The letter was dated September 26, 1919, and was signed by Cardinal Gibbons in the name of the hierarchy. It pointed out that the process of

Affiliation was in keeping with the aims of the University
founders, that the University existed for the good and the
service of all Catholic schools.

[69]ACUA, CSCF, Shields to Sr. St. Ignatius, January 2,
1914.

[70]Thomas E. Shields, "Home and School," CER, VI
(December, 1913), 447; Shields, "The Sisters' College and
the High Schools. . . ," CER, XV (February, 1918), 102.

[71]The only recognition the CEA gave to Affiliation in its
annual proceedings, as far as this investigator could discover,
was a reference made by its Advisory Board in 1915. In urging individual colleges to affiliate qualified Catholic high
schools, it noted that Catholic University had seen the opportunity and "has already a respectable list of accredited high
schools and the list appears to be lengthening out annually";
"The Condition of Catholic Secondary Education in the U. S.,
Report of the Advisory Board to the Executive Board of the
C.E.A.," CER, X (October, 1915), 211.

[72]Rev. James A. Burns, C.S.C., Catholic Education: A
Study of Conditions (New York: Longmans, Green and Co.,
1917).

[73]Shields, "The Sisters' College and the High Schools. . . ,"
CER, XV (February, 1918), 98-100.

[74]James A. Burns, C.S.C., "A Letter to the Editor and a
Reply," CER, XV (March, 1918), 205.

[75]Ibid., 206-207.

[76]ACUA, VRF, McVay to the Principal, n.d.

[77]Cf. Appendix C and Appendix D of this study.

[78]Report on Affiliation of High Schools (1920), p. 10.

[79]Ibid., p. 15.

[80]Ibid.

[81]Ibid., p. 8.

[82]Ibid., p. 9.

[83]ACUA, RF, McVay to the Rector, n.d. This letter
accompanied the typescript of the 1920 report.

[84]Ward, op. cit., pp. 270-271.

[85]ACUA, CSCF, Shields to Sr. Leo, Sinsinawa, Wis.,
March 5, 1918.

[86]Ibid., Shields to Sr. M. Ruth, Sinsinawa, Wis., March

21, 1918.

[87]Ibid., April 20, 1919.

[88]Ibid., Shields to Fr. Fitzgerald, December 16, 1919.

[89]See p. 97 of this study.

[90]ACUA, VRF, "Memorandum on Affiliation," n.d.

[91]ACUA, CSCF, Shields to Sr. Flavia, Marylhurst, Ore., May 31, 1914.

[92]An example of this is his article, "The Catholic Sisters College," CER, XII (June, 1916), 10-17. After calling attention to the contribution which the College had made to the standardization, cohesion, and unification of the Catholic system, he stated: "The most striking illustration of this is to be seen in the movement for affiliation of our Catholic secondary schools and colleges to the University" [underscoring mine] ; p. 14.

[93]The Catholic Sisters College at the Catholic University of America, 1914-1915 (Washington: 1914), pp. 68-69; ibid., 1917-1918, pp. 8-14; ibid., 1918-1919, pp. 8-14; Sisters College Messenger, I (April, 1915), 10-15; ibid., II (April, 1916), 8-14.

[94]The first record of Affiliation as University expense and income was given in the ARR, 1921, pp. 27 and 59.

[95]ACUA, CSCF, Shields to Bishop Shahan, October 6, 1919. Cf. ibid., Shields to McVay, October 6, 1919.

[96]Ibid., Shields to the Rector, January 17, 1920.

[97]Ward, op. cit., p. 279.

[98]"Thomas Edward Shields: Illness -- Death -- Funeral," CER, XIX (April, 1921), 196.

[99]Ibid., 221.

CHAPTER V

THE STATIC YEARS: 1921 - 1937

The Affiliation years from 1921 until the complete re-organization of the plan in 1938 and 1939 appeared in some respects to be cautiously progressive; yet by 1938 the revitalization of the entire program was definitely over-due. Whatever progress was made in those intervening years was evidently not sufficient to keep up with the rapidly changing educational picture of the country and of the Catholic school system.

The Program of Affiliation from 1921-1927

From Dr. Shields' death in 1921 and through the remainder of Bishop Shahan's rectorship, which ended in September of 1927, there still was a momentum from the first success of Affiliation that carried the program forward. Dr. Pace remained Chairman of the Committee during that period, with Father McVay continuing in his capacity as Secretary and Dr. McCormick as a member of the Committee. Their names, along with those of Dr. Richard J. Purcell of the Department of History, Dr. Audrey E. Landry of Mathematics, and Dr. Roy J. Deferrari of Greek and Latin, were listed as the current Committee in 1923-1924.[1] Regular monthly meetings were held "to act on new applications and other matters within the scope of the Committee,"[2] but again, because no minutes of the Committee meetings could be located, the details of its work are not known.

The Affiliation office was located on the third floor of McMahon Hall,[3] and Father McVay with a small office staff handled the growing detail which was centered primarily on the high school examinations and on a bulky correspondence. In addition, he continued to teach in the Department of Education at the University and at the Catholic Sisters College and in the summer at the University's Pacific Coast Summer Session.[4]   An office assistant was placed in charge of the test work over the summer months so that the process could be carried on without interruption during his absence.[5]

Under this arrangement, the program held its own fairly well quantitatively. The 1921 list of affiliates included 15 colleges, 177 high schools, and 46 novitiate high schools.[6] By the end of 1927-1928, the college list had increased to 25,[7] setting a pattern of slow but steady growth for the college affiliates, one which was to continue throughout the 1930's. The high schools showed a more substantial increase over these same years, reaching a peak of 229 schools by 1928.[8]   The peak in novitiate high schools was reached in 1923,[9] with 60 that year, but the number declined to 54 by 1928.[10]

Quantitatively, the number of high school examinations was also increasing until 1926. In 1921, 37,359 tests were administered;[11] in 1925, the total was 61,746;[12] but small decreases came with each of the next two years and a considerable drop was suffered in 1928, bringing the test total down to 53,880.[13]   The certificates followed much the same trend as the tests: from 179 certificates in 1921, to 2,065 in 1926, and back down to 1,897 in 1927.[14]   In 1928 there was another big drop to 1,644, with the loss being sustained almost entirely in the general certificates.[15]   The significance of these losses is further emphasized by the fact that the potential for increased test and certificate participation had been widened during this very period by a still growing number of affiliates and by the adding of commercial courses, thus permitting students following business programs to earn certificates.[16]

From the affiliate's point of view, the only changes in testing procedures in the 1920's were the addition of tests in the commercial subjects and the expansion of the diagnostic reports to any teacher so requesting.[17]   The Committee, however, was concerned about the correcting problem and efforts were made to ease the situation by enlarging the test subcommittee to provide for a more equitable distribution of the test papers. The new members were also to sit in officially at the meetings at which the test questions were made out, in the hope that an infusion of new ideas would result as well as

a more uniform system of marking.[18] To encourage the latter, each sub-committee was also instructed to limit each
three-hour test to seven questions, six of which were to be
answered by the student. A value scale for the test questions
was set, and each test group was to work out and adopt for itself a common and uniform method of marking.[19]

Some feeling had grown among the University departments that the Affiliation tests in their departmental subjects
were under the direction of the department and the allotting of
the work involved was therefore up to the head of the department. It was common University knowledge at the time that
the stipends for the correcting of the papers entered into the
desire on the part of some to keep the sub-committees relatively small,[20] and McVay foresaw that there would be objections to the new plan.[21] He was right. At least one formal
complaint was made, but both the Rector and Dr. Pace stood
firm on the new regulations.[22]

A more progressive outlook was evident in the Committee's continued work on the course outlines. Commercial
arithmetic, commercial geography, bookkeeping, and economics were adopted in the fall of 1921,[23] and a course in business
law was added in 1925,[24] as well as a two-year course in
stenography-typewriting in 1928.[25] Other subjects were given
consideration by the Committee with a view to adoption:
Polish, civics, general science, art, Italian, and drawing.[26]
Both the needs of the affiliates and the resources of the University were prime factors in these considerations and not all
subjects were finally approved. Polish I-IV courses were
brought to a favorable conclusion in 1924-1925 in an effort to
meet the needs of a number of large Polish schools.[27] Italian
I-IV were approved in 1927-1928,[28] and civics was also eventually adopted in 1934.[29] The available syllabi for the 1920's
also showed some revision of the older course outlines. While
minor revisions were made each year, more substantial
changes were made in 1922 in the fields of Latin, Greek, and
history;[30] in 1924, in Latin IV;[31] and in 1928, in English,
Latin, mathematics, and music.[32]

With the advent of the four new commercial courses in
1922, the term "free electives" appeared for the first time

in the syllabus. In addition to the commercial courses, music
and logic were also grouped under that heading.[33]   A distinction was made from that time on between "limited electives"
and "free electives."   A student was required first to offer
for credit the eleven prescribed courses as given in the original standards[34] plus four electives of his choice. One or two
of these electives had to be selected from the same subject
areas as the prescribed courses in order to present a second
major in addition to the prescribed English major; these were
designated as "limited electives." The remaining electives
could be chosen from either the "limited" or "free" electives.
Commercial arithmetic could be offered as the third unit in
mathematics to form a second major for a student following
a commercial program. In this case, however, the other
three "electives" had to be the three other commercial courses,
so that, in fact, the commercial students had no free electives.[35]   In 1928, the two-year course in stenography-typewriting was also listed under the "free electives, " but since
sixteen high school units were then required of the commercial student for college admissions, he still, in the strict
sense, had no choice of free electives.

The process of affiliating an applying institution remained basically unchanged although attention was given by
1924-1925 to Dr. Pace's earlier concern for the lack of personal contact between the University and its affiliates.

> For a long time the Committee has felt the
> need of some sort of inspection of the schools and
> the actual work they are doing. The reasons for
> this are obvious. Realizing the labor, cost, and
> other features of such a step we have acted cau-
> tiously and perhaps very slowly. This year we
> began the work in a somewhat experimental man-
> ner. During the recess between Summer School
> and the opening of the Fall term the Secretary of
> the Committee made a tour of the States of
> Michigan, Indiana, Illinois, and Wisconsin. He
> visited most of the schools in these states and his
> report proved that the step was in the right direc-

tion. The local authorities and the heads of the
teaching communities, without exception, expressed great satisfaction and interest in this
action of the Committee. The experiment was
such a success that we decided to repeat it during
the recess at Christmas time. The schools located in the States of Tennessee, Alabama,
Arkansas, Mississippi, Texas, and Louisiana
were selected for this visit. The trip was carefully planned both to save time and expense. All
the schools and Motherhouses located in these
States and affiliated with the University were
visited. In every instance the pleasure and satisfaction shown by the principals and the teachers
plainly evidenced to us that some well organized
plan must be adopted, whereby each affiliated
school be visited at least once every three years.
In our opinion nothing will do more to keep active
that needed intimacy and relationship which must
exist between the University and the affiliated institutions, if the primary aim of the process of
affiliation, as laid down by the founder of the University in his Apostolic letter, "Magni Nobis
Gaudii," is to be realized.

On the above visit the Secretary covered about
4,500 miles, spending 15 out of 18 nights on the
trains. By this mode of travel he was able to devote his days to the schools and their inspections.
Twenty-six high schools, 2 Colleges and 6 Motherhouses were visited. The Secretary addressed the
pupils of each school and in some cases met the
parents who had been invited by the local authorities. The Bishop of each diocese visited extended
a most cordial welcome and in some instances in-
sisted that his house be the headquarters of the
Secretary while in the Episcopal city. All showed
a paternal interest in the work and warmly approved
the plan of inspection.

During the Easter recess the Secretary visited

some of the schools in Connecticut and during
the year made short trips to the schools located
in Virginia, Maryland, and Pennsylvania. In
these as in all the other cases, the results have
shown that there are great possibilities in the
plan, which the future will unfold.[36]

The next fall, McVay visited the schools located in Oregon, Washington, the Dakotas, upper Minnesota, Wisconsin,
and Illinois, and in December, those in West Virginia, Ohio,
and again in Illinois. At mid-term he spent his time visiting
in the Providence-Boston area and at Easter time, in Washington and Baltimore. Conferences between the teachers and
visitor were often held for the discussion of educational problems and the exchange of opinions. "In other cases the visit
took the form of a meeting of the visitor and the pupils, with
an informal talk by the visitor."[37]   Extensive visiting was
also reported for 1926-1927[38] but not in subsequent years,
although announcements of visits and speaking engagements
by Drs. Pace and McCormick as well as by Father McVay
were scattered through the Catholic Educational Review issues from 1923 to 1927. From Father McVay's own descriptions, as given above, the visits appear to have been on an informal basis. At the same time, however, it must be
remembered that these were days well before the Evaluative
Criteria, and accrediting procedures in general had not been
developed into any kind of scientific technique.
     Textbook work immediately following Shields' death was
confined primarily, if not entirely, to the maintaining of an
approved textbook list for affiliates. The selection of the
books was done by the University departmental faculties, with
subject aims, correct method, and sound pedagogics all being
considered as well as the content. The list was strictly a
general service to affiliates, as textbooks remained, except
for music, unprescribed.[39]   The revised music outlines of
1928 also eliminated any required textbooks for music.[40]
     To reach affiliates regularly and more systematically
and to bring them into a closer relationship with the University had been recognized as a need for some time. Through

the Catholic Educational Review a new method was introduced
in 1923. In the November issue of that periodical, the first
"Affiliated High School and College Section" appeared and was
carried regularly thereafter until February of 1928. The
material covered generally fell into one of four classifications:
discussions of the underlying principles or regulations of Affiliation, official announcements of the program, news items,
and suggestions to affiliates. Under the first category, a
good deal of space was devoted to the high school curriculum:
reasons and explanations of the changes which appeared in the
annual syllabus, specific methods, and the meeting of individual differences. Other articles in this category covered the
gamut of Affiliation and general educational principles: testing, the diagnostic reports, textbooks, student loads, promotion of students, the school diploma and Catholic University
certification, supervised study, staff conferences, and the
school paper. The official announcements of Affiliation, the
second category of items, were so labeled and usually tied in
directly with a new regulation or a current problem. Thus
such subjects as free electives, reading lists for Polish and
suggested grammars, the business law course, revised
mathematics courses, and the stenography-typing courses
were formally announced through the "Section." News items,
the third kind of material covered, included mostly activities
of the affiliates, ranging from bazaars, fires, sports, new
buildings, to deaths, jubilees, scholarship awards, and other
personal items concerning students and teachers. Some of
the activities were enlarged upon sufficiently that the "know-
how" was shared with other affiliates, and the cooperative
potential of Affiliation was thus emphasized. This kind of
item overlapped with the fourth category which included such
suggestions to affiliates as how to conduct a successful alumni drive, the making of school visits to other affiliates, a
medical inspection plan, and an experimental course in religion.[41]   The response to this new feature in the Review was
good, and the cooperation of affiliates in supplying items was
ample.[42]

    Two other innovations were introduced about this same
time. A first attempt at studying the needs of affiliated high

schools through the Master's dissertation was made in 1925-
1926. Two were completed that year, one a "Comparative
Study of the Requirements for English in Our High Schools"
and the other a study along the same lines for biology.[43]
Promise of further cooperation from faculty members of the
University made this plan for increasing the needed Catholic
educational literature appear both practical and extremely
worthwhile. In the summer of 1926, another line of direct
communication between the University and its affiliates was
opened. Through the Catholic Sisters College, the Committee
on Affiliation held a series of conferences for the teachers of
affiliated high schools who were attending the summer session.
These "Round Table" discussions were announced in the May
Review, proposing to cover questions pertaining directly to
Affiliation, analyzing and clarifying problems as the need required.[44] Seven meetings were held and were attended by
representatives of about thirty high schools and twenty teaching communities. Cooperation, unification, and the practical
aspects of the following topics were treated: the annual Affiliation examinations, use of school time after the examination
period to the close of school, school publications, modifications of the religion course, athletics, dramatics, faculty
meetings, pupil loads, promotion and graduation, teaching
Latin and mathematics, English course requirements, and
attitudes toward visitors. This "Round Table" may well have
been a forerunner of the workshop technique for the idea and
the resulting esprit de corps were enthusiastically described
by McVay. It was further suggested that the "Round Table"
be made a regular, annual affair of Affiliation with extensions
of it conducted in various sections of the country for both high
schools and colleges.[45]

There is no further evidence that the "Round Table" was
repeated in other summer sessions, but in the academic year
1928-1929, a series of round table discussions were held by
Father McVay for the faculties of the affiliated high schools
of the District of Columbia. These were monthly sessions
centered on the needs, objectives, and standards of secondary
education in direct application to the affiliates. McVay
recorded only a single comment on the results: all those

attending "were unanimous in their opinion that the sessions were productive of much personal improvement and constructive criticism."[46]

There is little or no evidence of any further development of the college Affiliation plan during the 1920's. The annual report of the Rector noted only the number of affiliated colleges each year and their slow but steady increase.[47] A proposed plan for college entrance examinations, to be activated in the spring of 1924, was presented to the affiliated colleges for acceptance, but from the purpose and nature of the plan, it would seem that the Committee had the needs of the high schools primarily in mind. The idea was to provide an additional opportunity for the seniors of affiliated high schools, whose admission to college was already endorsed by a specific college, to secure through Affiliation tests such entrance credits as they might still need. The tests, which were to be administered at centers located in designated affiliated high schools, were to be more comprehensive in nature than the regular Affiliation tests so that more than one unit of credit could be acquired through a single test. Although details of eligibility, registration, administration, costs, and reports were all worked out in the original document,[48] no mention was made of its acceptance by the colleges or its actual initiation. It can only be assumed that active support by the affiliated colleges was not forthcoming.

During these last years of Bishop Shahan's administration, one broader aspect of University development touched directly on Affiliation and showed again an awareness of a concern for what must have been a growing critical response to the high school examinations. In September of 1922, Cardinal Bisleti, Prefect of the Sacred Congregation of Seminaries and Universities, wrote to Archbishop Curley, the Chancellor of the University, commending the University on its work and its influence on the Catholicity of the United States. It was the desire of Pope Pius XI that the University exert an ever-increasing efficiency in this regard by the appointment of new faculties for the teaching of pontifical and public ecclesiastical law and that a program be so drawn up by the American hierarchy. Archbishop Curley felt that a complete survey of the

activities of the University by a committee of bishops would
be highly beneficial.[49] A committee of six archbishops and
six bishops was appointed that fall, "to make a full inquiry
into the internal status of the University and to present a program to the Holy See as soon as possible."[50] A sub-committee chaired by Archbishop Curley and consisting of Bishops
Turner, Schrembs, McDevitt and O'Connell, met at the University for a three-day session of interviewing and study.
The Rector and Dr. Pace, who served as secretary for the
sub-committee, were also present.[51] The Affiliation of High
Schools and Colleges was a part of the agenda, and evidently
the matter of the tests and their expense to the schools was
discussed. In February of 1923, Pace wrote to the Archbishop:

> It might perhaps be stated in the Report going
> up to the Full Committee, that the present system
> of Affiliation, including annual examination, was
> prescribed by the Trustees in April 1912 -- as is
> plain from the Circular which I am sending you
> under separate cover. The plan is worked out in
> considerable detail, but no mention is made of a
> fee for the examination.[52]

The printed report of the sub-committee, which was
presented to the Trustees at their April meeting of that year,
called attention first to the general success of Affiliation in
terms of the number of affiliated schools and colleges. It
also stated briefly that the plan, as prescribed by the Trustees, required annual tests for which a fee was charged. The
sub-committee recommended that this method be abandoned
and that a different method, such as inspection, be adopted.[53]
The final report to Cardinal Bisleti, however, made no mention of Affiliation, and no action was taken on the sub-committee's recommendation.
       The overall study of the status of the University did
point up the need for some revision of the Constitutions, and
a committee of the Board of Trustees was appointed in 1924
for this purpose.[54] The new Constitutions, approved by the
Holy See in 1926, left the original article dealing with affilia-

tion basically unchanged, [55] but other changes made apparent
the need for a new University charter. The petition for a
supplementary and amendatory Act of Incorporation was made
to Congress and was passed and approved by the President of
the United States on April 3, 1928. Section 3 of that document read:

> Sec. 3: That said University may enter into
> affiliated agreements with any institutions of learn-
> ing outside the District of Columbia, for the pur-
> pose of giving students of such institutions the
> educational facilities of said University, upon such
> terms as are mutually agreed upon by the said
> University and the affiliated institutions. [56]

While neither the revised Constitutions or the amended charter effected any change in the status or methods of Affiliation,
both did serve to reconfirm affiliation as a proper function of
the University and to clarify its legality.

The Program of Affiliation from 1928-1937

Bishop Shahan resigned as Rector on September 13,
1927. Then seventy years old, he had decided against another
term, wanting a few years of quiet and rest away from the
pressing responsibilities of the office. [57]   Monsignor James
Hugh Ryan was accordingly appointed the fifth Rector of the
University and took over in the summer of 1928. Monsignor
Pace had been made Vice Rector under Shahan in 1925 and
continued in that capacity under the new Rector. Probably
because of the growing demands of this office and his delicate
health, he relinquished in 1928 the chairmanship of the Committee on Affiliation. Monsignor Ryan appointed Dr. Roy J.
Deferrari to the post. Dr. Deferrari had come to the University in 1918 as an Instructor of Greek and Latin and had
been serving as a member of the Committee on Affiliation at
least since 1923-1924. Those who had served with him at
that time remained unchanged in 1928: McVay as Secretary
and Drs. McCormick, Landry, and Purcell. [58]

Evidently the problems of Affiliation were of some concern to University authorities, since the first meeting of the
Committee on October 12, 1928, was devoted to procedures
and a classification of the three major areas demanding their
attention. The problems to be attacked first were:

> I. Plans to secure greater uniformity in methods of
> marking the papers which are received from the affili-
> ated high schools.
> II. The question of preparing a statement of the
> standards and other conditions for the affiliation of
> Preparatory Seminaries, Junior College and Novitiates
> to the University was then presented.
> III. The problem of devising ways and means for the
> inspection of the colleges which have been or are to be
> affiliated was also proposed.[59]

The Committee seems to have been responsible at first
to Dr. Pace; at least a report of this first meeting was sent to
him and later in the fall his advice was sought on the extent of
the Committee's power to act,

> whether or not our present Committee is a contin-
> uance of the former Committee on Affiliation
> appointed by the Trustees with power to act. . . .
> As a Committee we felt it best to have the Vice
> Rector attend the next meeting of the Committee
> on Affiliation and instruct us as to our status,
> authority and functions.[60]

The question raised referred to the power of the Committee
to take final action on the applications for Affiliation without
official reference to the Academic Senate. As far as could
be determined, however, no change seems to have been made
at that time, and the Committee continued to function autono-
mously as it had in the past. Nor did the new Chairman take
over the direct supervision of the program; Father McVay,
as Secretary, continued to play a major part in the handling
of the details and the general implementation of the program.[61]

Just how much discussion or what long-range reorganizational plans were made by the Committee at this time and through the first half of the 1930's is difficult to estimate from the available records, since positive action along these lines were slow and cautious. Ryan urged a comprehensive attack on the problems of Affiliation and a proposed survey was drawn up by the Committee probably during the academic year 1928-1929. The survey was to include the following points:

1. Purpose of Affiliation.
2. Advantages of Affiliation.
3. To What Extent Affiliation Has Fulfilled Its Purpose.
4. Statistical Record, Year by Year, of the Number of Schools Affiliated, and the Number of Students Affected; showing number of schools added and dropped each year.
5. Method of Affiliation.
6. Organization.
   a. Committee on Affiliation; duties, powers.
   b. Secretary of Committee; duties, powers.
   c. Office of Committee on Affiliation.
7. How "Affiliation" Is Carried On.
   Examinations.
   a. How made out.
   b. How papers are distributed.
   c. How papers are corrected.
   d. How the reading of the papers is controlled.
8. What Personal Inspection Exists at Present.
9. Budget of Affiliation.
   a. Cost to Schools.
   b. Cost to the University.
   c. Disposal of Surplus.

Recommendations

It is proposed that the consideration of recommendations proceed according to the following outline.
1. Enlargement of Actual Scope.

      a. Affiliation of Junior Colleges.
      b. Affiliation of Junior Seminaries.
      c. Affiliation as Means of College Entrance.
2. Improvement of Present Method of Conducting Examinations.
      a. Improvement in Drawing up of Examinations.
      b. Improvement in Conduct of Examinations in Schools.
      c. Improvement in Distribution and Correcting of Papers.
3. Improvement in Conspectus of Courses.
4. Wider Personal Inspection of Schools, Colleges, etc.
5. Active Program for Securing Wider Recognition for our Affiliated Schools in Non-Catholic Circles.
6. Possible Improvements in Organization.
7. Possible Modifications in Cost of Affiliation.
      a. To the School.
      b. To the University.
8. Recommendations Regarding Disposal of Surplus.
9. Means of Procuring Greater Publicity Among Catholic Educational Circles.[62]

Whether a comprehensive survey and study were made in the years immediately following this 1928 proposal is doubtful, but several points of the survey were followed up in the early 1930's. Among these was the recommendation for the enlargement of the actual scope of Affiliation. Consideration had been given to the affiliating of both the preparatory seminary and the normal school by Shields and Pace, and as early as 1924-1925 the Committee had plans under advisement. The Committee had felt, however, that careful study was required and that the details should be worked out slowly.[63] Thus in 1926-1927, the matter was still "under advisement," although the work preparatory to issuing the standards, course of studies, and other requirements for the affiliation of minor seminaries was reported as practically completed. The annual report of that year stated: "Working in cooperation with a Committee appointed by our School of Sacred Sciences, our Committee has endeavored to secure proper articulation of its

work in this matter with the demands that will be made by the
School of Sacred Sciences of the applicants to its recently approved course of undergraduate clerical students."[64]   But in
1927-1928, there was further delay and only a renewed promise that a special committee would present a completed plan by
the end of the next academic year.[65]   The following year's
report to the Rector, the first to Monsignor Ryan, made no
mention of this seminary plan but noted that the final draft of
a junior college plan, requirements and form, would be ready
by July of 1929.[66]   Neither plan received further mention until
1930-1931, when it was announced that one junior college, two
normal schools, and one preparatory seminary had been added
to the list of affiliates.[67]   These must have been temporary
or "experimental" affiliations, however, as the Annual Report
of the Rector announced at the same time that the conditions
for the affiliation of junior colleges and of seminaries and the
application forms would be ready for distribution by the opening of the school year of 1931-1932.[68]

These specific plans and forms could not be located. As
far as could be ascertained, the preparatory seminaries were
classified among the regular high schools and probably the
regular plan of Affiliation was generally applied. In the case
of the junior colleges and teacher training schools, these
seemed to have functioned on a post-secondary school level
only in the summer time and were housed in an already affiliated novitiate high school. There is evidence that a modified
college plan was used and that the following regulations were
enforced:

1. Every student shall be a graduate of a standard high
    school.
2. No student shall be permitted to follow more than
    three credit courses, that is, six semester hours of
    class work during the summer school.
3. That a typewritten copy of the questions set for each
    examination and a schedule of the dates on which
    these examinations are to be held be submitted to
    the Committee on Affiliation two weeks before the
    opening date of the examinations.

4. At the close of the summer school a record of the
   marks given to each student will likewise be submitted.
5. If the Committee requests the papers of the pupils
   for any one course, they shall be sent for inspection
   at any time before January 1st, . . . The examination papers written by all the student must therefore
   be held for six months after the dates of the examinations.[69]

It is doubtful that any official announcement of the acceptance of seminaries, junior colleges, or normal schools was
made or that any systematic promotional work in this regard
was carried on. The number of affiliates in these categories
remained small until the 1938-1939 reorganized plan of Affiliation made these kinds of institutions a regular part of the
Affiliation program. But the supervision of examinations as
described above was made effective by the Committee, so that
in 1931-1932 a total of 390 examinations taken by students in
affiliated normal and junior colleges were submitted.[70]   A
peak of 1,991 such examinations was reached in the summer
of 1935,[71] but no other activities were recorded.
    The Committee on Affiliation also gave attention in the
1930's to the four-year general college. The debate on college
standardization had been continued in educational circles
throughout the 1920's, with the American Council on Education
and the Catholic Educational Association pushing successfully
toward the adoption of higher standards.[72]   Affiliation during
this time had maintained its original college standards but in
1934 several significant changes were made. The degree requirements for the college instructor were raised from a
Bachelor's to a Master's degree and from a Master's to a doc-
torate in the case of a head of a department. Also the college
course requirement, which had originally been stated in terms
of hours of class work, namely, 2,160 class hours over the
four years of college, was restated in terms of semester
hours: 120 semester hours of class work over the four
years.[73]   These changes were more in keeping with the standards set by other groups. About this same time, the Com-

mittee devised a plan for the visitation of college applicants
for Affiliation. The desire was to introduce greater flexibility
in dealing with college affiliates and to improve articulation
between these institutions and the University. The stimulation
of the affiliate toward self-improvement was made the major
objective of the visitation, this achievement to be attained
through a detailed survey report made by the inspector and
sent to the affiliate after its review and approval by the Committee.[74] The affiliated colleges in Texas, Louisiana, Pennsylvania, Kentucky, Michigan, New York, and Illinois were
inspected in 1935-1936, and the policy was then enlarged to include re-inspection of affiliated colleges every three or four
years, thus providing the servicing of the colleges on a closer
and continuing basis.[75]

These several new trends within the college Affiliation
procedures, while slow in coming, reflected a definitely new
spirit and approach on the part of Affiliation. The individual-
izing of the services and the seeking of a continuing developmental process through the cooperation of the affiliate and the
University were important innovations for Affiliation, innovations, however, which were not at all alien to the Shields'
concept of affiliation and which were to become the heart of the
reorganized 1938-1939 Affiliation plan. But at the high school
level there was less progress. In spite of what seems to have
been a mounting dissatisfaction with the high school testing
program among the affiliates and University authorities, no
sweeping changes were made. The problem of uniform grading
of the test papers continued to plague the Committee and no
solutions were found.[76] Testing rules and procedures remained the same.

Nor were there any major, far-reaching revisions of the
high school course outlines in the 1930's. In 1933, the one-
half unit course in logic was dropped and in 1934 civics was
added as a free elective.[77] Latin and English were revised
substantially but some of the other course outlines in effect
dated back to 1912 or to the first years of Affiliation.[78] Dr.
Deferrari was well aware of this situation and sought to remedy
the matter. As Head of the Greek and Latin Department also,
he centered the 1933 Latin revisions on meeting what he con-

sidered the legitimate requests of affiliates: that there be greater correlation between the Affiliation Latin requirements and those of the College Entrance Examination Board. The Latin sub-committee agreed with the latter in that the emphasis should be placed on the power to translate, and the revisions were made accordingly.[79] However, the material submitted by the sub-committee defining this approach was not used in the revised outline as it appeared in the 1933 syllabus.[80]

Also a special sub-committee of five was appointed in 1937-1938 to revise the religion outline. Work on the first three years was completed with the fourth year to be ready by Christmas of the next academic year. Other outlines were also reported as under study by the Committee.[81] Because syllabi for 1937 and 1938 could not be located (and may not have been printed), it is not known if the resulting revisions were actually made effective at that time or whether or not the results of this work were absorbed later by the extensive reorganization of the program in 1938 and 1939.

Only one minor change was made in the affiliation standards for high schools during this period. In 1930, the recommended maximum load for a high school student was increased from twenty hours of class work per week to twenty-two.[82] Procedures too seem to have remained the same, although there was no evidence of any extensive visiting or "inspecting" of the high schools as McVay had done in the earlier 1920's. Approved textbook lists were kept up-to-date,[83] and considerable emphasis was placed on the development and success of the diagnostic test report as a means to improved instruction.[84]

There was one other important, although somewhat subtle, change within the total Affiliation program, which while probably evolving gradually became evident in the 1930's. In 1912 and during the early years of Affiliation, the program had been viewed as a standardizing device primarily but with major qualitative benefits accruing both to the affiliate and to the Catholic educational system in general. The terms "accreditation" and "accredited" had been used interchangeably with those of "affiliation" and "affiliated." In 1923, after the plan had been operating for some ten years, standardization and unification still received major emphasis:

> The purpose of affiliation is primarily to provide a standard for our colleges and high schools and to secure due recognition for those institutions that are doing good work. . . . Cooperation rather than prescription is its guiding spirit. It aims to secure uniformity of standards, courses, and methods in order that the local needs of the affiliated schools will be strengthened and adapted to wider application, losing nothing however of their individuality, their freedom and the special purposes for the pupils they serve. . . . As a process of motivation, that is sound and effective, affiliation has, in the educational history of our country, few parallels.[85]

By the 1930's, however, there was little or no use in the written records of Affiliation of the term "accreditation" as synonymous with "affiliation," and a new emphasis had appeared. The primary aims of Affiliation were then stated as follows:

1. To preserve the autonomy of each institution.
2. To secure growth from within.
3. To maintain a supervisory control of the work of teachers and pupils.
4. To set up standards in courses and methods.
5. To test each school by the work of its pupils.[86]

The higher ranking position of "growth from within" over the setting and maintaining of standards foreshadowed the official reversal of these aims in 1938 and 1939, when the continued development of the affiliate through a cooperative program of services and professional consultation was made the prime objective, and standards and testing were recognized as merely two of the several means available.

In the meantime, however, the nature of the dissatisfaction among affiliated high schools was becoming more clear.

The number of examinations required of a student was felt to
be a great imposition since the resulting benefits to the student, it was claimed, were small. The cost of the tests was
another factor which in the eyes of the affiliate appeared to be
unjust taxation. A more or less typical reaction to the testing
problem was voiced strongly by an affiliate as early as 1928:

> They [the faculty] think that after all these years
> some other and more scholastic method of affilia-
> tion should be adopted.
>
> If it is impossible for you to engage a high school
> visitor, as most state universities do, we suggest
> that each school be taxed a reasonable fee for affili-
> ation, and be required to submit an annual report
> along such lines as you would suggest in a form
> drafted for that purpose. If such an arrangement
> as we suggest cannot be effected, we ask that each
> year the members of our Senior class, only, be
> required to take but one examination.
>
> Our school is a member of the North Central
> Association, and is also affiliated with our state
> university. We wish to show our loyalty to the
> Catholic University, and to recognize and respect
> it for what it stands; but aside from this, affiliation
> does not mean any more to us.
>
> We know that we are not alone in the attitude we
> take in this regard. We hope that the committee
> will give this question due consideration, and that
> it will decide upon a more suitable and satisfactory
> method of conducting its affiliation.[87]

Apart from the scattered individual complaints of principals, parents, and one bishop, perhaps the most objective
evidence of an unhappy situation existed in the comparatively
rapid and continuing decrease in the number of tests administered over these years. A peak of more than 61,000 tests had
been reached in 1925, but with each subsequent year a decrease ranging between 2,000 and 7,500 tests was sustained.[88]
By 1937, just before the inauguration of the new examination

scheme, the annual total, including June and August examinations, had dropped to 17, 304. Correspondingly, the number
of certificates issued fell with each year, from a peak of
2, 065 in 1926 to 582 in 1936.[89]
     The number of affiliated high schools was on a similar
downward trend. A high of 229 schools was reached in 1928,
but the following years' lists showed a steady decline. By
1938, there were only 131 affiliated regular high schools and
academies. The number of novitiate high schools also de-
creased over these same years, but the rate of decline was
less serious. In 1928, there were 54 such high schools while
for 1938, 44 were listed.[90] The significance of these decreases was further emphasized by the fact that the 1915 to
1928 period represented a 67 per cent growth in the number of
Catholic high schools throughout the United States.[91] Thus
while the potential had been enlarged considerably, the affiliating of high schools by the University was deteriorating quantitatively at a rapid pace.
     The slowness of University authorities to act on the situa-
tion was not due to a lack of concern. Dr. Pace had seen the
need for reorganization in 1919, and Bishop Shahan and the
sub-committee of bishops in 1923 had called the matter at that
time to the attention of the Trustees. When Monsignor Ryan
became Rector, he too was acutely aware of the problem and
gave almost immediate consideration to it. The University
records, located by this investigator, do not show definitely
why more forceful action was not taken sooner, but there are
clues among these materials. First, the organization of the
high school Affiliation plan, within which most of the difficulties rested, was a complex one involving curriculum, methods,
and general operating procedures for a relatively large number
of schools. There was little real agreement among educators
at this time concerning these very areas.[92] An overall, sound
revision required another Shields, with vision and energy and,
equally important, freedom to effect the reforms necessary.
     The problem of finances from the University's point of
view was also not a small one. The financial conditions of the
University had never been good, and the University was in no
position to place Affiliation on a non-paying basis. The program

had to maintain itself. Some consideration had been given in
1912 to the setting of a general fee which would cover all expenses, [93] but evidently the final decision had favored a charge
for the high school tests only. This was set at fifty cents for
each examination. As far as could be ascertained, this meant
that the affiliated high schools supported the complete program
and that the only cost to the affiliated colleges was in connection with the visitations which became effective only in the
1930's. [94] The income so furnished by the sale of the examinations was more than ample to meet the costs of maintaining
the program and whatever surplus accrued was a great boon
to the University in helping to solve its other constant financial
problems. [95] Thus the substituting of a scheme of inspections,
as was so frequently suggested, for the financially sound testing program[96] was no easy decision to make. Moreover,
there was also an academic problem involved. The securing
of a sufficient number of qualified high school and college inspectors to carry on any comprehensive program of inspections would be difficult, and the effectiveness of such a program depended largely on this one resource.

In spite of these complexities, Bishop Ryan felt in 1934
that adequate ground work had been laid by Dr. Deferrari and
his Committee to make feasible more direct action. On
February 28 of that year he appointed a special committee to
investigate all branches of the University's affiliation work.
Dr. Deferrari, then Dean of the Graduate School of Arts and
Sciences as well as Chairman of the Committee on Affiliation
of schools and colleges, was made the chairman. Serving
with him were the Reverend James M. Campbell, Reverend
Edward B. Jordan, Reverend Leo L. McVay, Right Reverend
John A. Ryan, Reverend Valentine Schaaf, and Reverend
Nicholas A. Weber. [97] The committee attacked first the nature and status of the affiliated theological institutions and the
neighboring houses of studies. A thorough study and report
were made, the latter going to the Rector and the Academic
Senate on April 27, 1934, with a promise that a second report
on those affiliated institutions under the supervision of the
University's Committee on Affiliation would be made at a later
date. [98] It is highly doubtful that this second report was

carried to completion. None was located and the following year Ryan again brought the matter up: he wrote to Deferrari that "His Excellency, the Most Reverend William Turner, Bishop of Buffalo, moved specifically that the Board of Trustees authorize the Rector and the Deans to make a complete study of a sound method of affiliation of high schools, and to report thereon at the November meeting."[99] From this request did come a report, dated November 12, 1935:

In general the committee on affiliation feels that the present scheme of affiliating high schools should be modified only as to the nature and frequency of the examinations, and that in addition, some form of inspection be inaugurated upon which in the main will depend the actual affiliation of the institution. The committee proposed the following general proposals:

I. Plan for granting affiliation:
   (a) Present standards and general requirements as set forth in the syllabus should be maintained.
   (b) Personal inspection under the direction of the Committee on Affiliation should be made for all high schools that apply.
   (c) Careful survey of all high schools now affiliated should be made by
      1. Securing a report from each school as to its present condition.
      2. A personal inspection under the direction of the Committee on Affiliation.

II. Plan for maintaining affiliation:
   (a) Each high school should file names and degrees of faculty members each year.
   (b) Each high school should file changes in curriculum in September of each year.
   (c) Personal inspection of those schools where reports a & b above seem to demand it.
   (d) Present system of examinations should be maintained for all schools except those schools which maintain an excellent standard.

These latter should conduct their own examinations and should submit for approval by the
Committee on Affiliation the questions for
each course and later the grades given to
each pupil.

(e) University is to continue to issue certificates.

(f) Each high school should file names of graduates entering college and names of the colleges at which they matriculate.

(g) Careful supervision of the marking of the
examinations by the Committee on Affiliation.

(h) By means of diagnostic reports the work of
both the inspectors and readers of the examinations should aim to assist the high schools
to improve so as better to meet their own
local needs as well as the general needs of
Catholic high school education.[100]

It is not surprising that there is no evidence of direct
and immediate action stemming from this report. On August
6, 1935, Ryan had been made Bishop of Omaha, and was named
Rector Emeritus on November 12, 1935, the same day as the
date of the report. It was accordingly left to his succesor,
Monsignor M. Corrigan, to bring the matter to a successful
conclusion several years later.

While it has been shown that Affiliation during the 1920's
and early 1930's had lost much of its first vitality and progressive spirit, this period of its history should not be written off
as one of mere deterioration or even of complete stagnation.
The continued development and expansion of the program for
institutions of higher education, though slow and cautious in
coming, was sound and laid a foundation of experience upon
which to build a comprehensive reorganization of the college
plan in 1938 and 1939, within a comparatively short space of
time. At the high school level the problems were considerably more serious and complex. The maintaining of a testing
program of the kind and scope that had been acceptable in the
1910's, under the inspiration and careful supervision of Dr.
Shields, through and well past a time when both the mammoth

correcting problems and the developments of scientific testing
cast a heavy shadow of doubt over the reliability of the tests
themselves and their value to students and affiliates, can only
be viewed as a breakdown of the high school affiliation plan.[101]
Even here, however, the early 1930's were fruitful as a practical and necessary stage of study leading to the later reform.

There is another aspect of high school Affiliation during
the period after Shields' death that merits at least brief recognition.   When the standardization of schools had been effected
in the earlier years of Affiliation, the need to modify the original plan to meet the new needs of these affiliates grew with
each passing year.   Yet there were others that faced the standardization problem at a later date, and for these Affiliation
still served as a valuable guide and aid.   McInerney, in her
study of the influence of Affiliation on a typical Catholic academy in the 1920's, concluded that her

> research would indicate that along all the major
> phases of secondary education there has been
> definite and measurable advantage and that the
> affiliation continues to be a source of inestima-
> ble assistance with educational problems of
> administration and organization. As examples
> of specific outcomes of the affiliation we might
> cite, -
>   Curriculum adjustment through standardization.
>   Differentiation of curriculum for the several
> levels of ability.
>   Establishment of norms of achievement through
> regular examinations by the Catholic University.
>   Improved school administration through the
> faculty's having shared in the formulation of school
> policies at the time of the affiliation.
>   Improved program of vocational guidance.
>   Solution of problems of articulation within the
> school and with institutions of higher education.
>   Fine school spirit through enjoyment of reason-
> able surety of the educational and vocational
> outcomes of the affiliation system of education.

Impetus to the staff to improve its cultural and professional preparation.[102]

McInerney further stated that when the academy found it advisable to seek accreditation by the state of Pennsylvania in 1927 it was successful with comparatively little adjustment. The state representatives visiting the academy recommended that its affiliation with the Catholic University be continued:

> The suggestion from experienced secular school-men of high intellectual caliber that affiliation with the Catholic University be retained in a state accred-ited Catholic High School is pregnant with matter for serious consideration. The suggestion in conjunc-tion with the State's commendation of our high standards of work seems to carry with it the recog-nition of the fact that these standards are due to the protection, support and guidance of the affiliating institution, and that a withdrawal of this element of support from the school would be tantamount to a lowering of its standard.[103]

While McInerney's study was highly favorable to Affilia-tion as it existed from 1920 to 1934, it is with some insight that the following observation was made at the end of that period:

> The institution of the affiliation system with its potential possibilities for unification and support through standardization served vital purpose when the Catholic secondary school was looking for authoritative organization. . . .
> . . .The infiltration of the Catholic High School with the potential power of its Catholic standards and principles must inevitably affect society and the slow moving state school systems, and it is safe to assume that we can trust the affiliation sys-tem and all it represents of wisdom centuries old, to meet the growing needs, sanely, safely, and

purposefully as they met a different but as urgent
a need in 1912.[104]

FOOTNOTES

[1]ARR, 1923-1924, (October, 1924), p. 82. Since Dr.
Purcell was appointed to the Committee in 1921 (ACUA, VRF,
Rector to Richard J. Purcell, October 20, 1921), it may be
that both Drs. Landry and Deferrari joined the Committee then
also.
[2]ARR, 1923-1924, p. 82.
[3]By interview with Roy J. Deferrari, August 24, 1963.
[4]ARR, 1923-1924, p. 83.
[5]ACUA, VRF, McVay to Pace, May 28, 1923.
[6]Year Book of the Catholic University of America, 1921-
1922 (Washington: 1921), pp. 243-252.
[7]Ibid., 1928-1929 (Washington: 1928), pp. 147-149.
[8]Ibid., pp. 149-156.
[9]Ibid., 1923-1924 (Washington: 1923), pp. 148-149.
[10]Ibid., 1928-1929, pp. 156-158.
[11]ARR, 1923-1924, p. 82.
[12]ARR, 1925-1926 (September, 1926), p. 60.
[13]ARR, 1926-1927 (September, 1927), p. 68; ARR, 1927-
1928 (September, 1928), p. 56; ARR, 1928-1929 (October,
1929), p. 61.
[14]ARR, 1924-1925 (October, 1925), p. 58; ARR, 1926-
1927, p. 68; ARR, 1927-1928, p. 57.
[15]ARR, 1928-1929, p. 61.
[16]AHSC (1924), p. 4.
[17]"Affiliated High School and College Section," CER,
XXII (May, 1924), 304. Until this time, the test reports point-
ing out defects in teaching and suggesting remedies must have
been limited to the teachers most in need of improvement.
McVay emphasized at this time the opening of this service to
other teachers as well.
[18]ACUA, VRF, McVay to Shahan, n.d. The content of
the letter would set the date of the letter in late January or
early February, 1923.
[19]Ibid., Secretary, Committee on Affiliation, to "My

dear Professor," February 11, 1923.

20By interview with Roy J. Deferrari,August 24, 1963. The correctors were paid twenty-five cents per test paper (ACUA, CSCF, Shields to J. J. Griffin, February 19, 1915).

21ACUA, VRF, McVay to Shahan, n.d.

22Ibid., P. J. Lennox to Pace, February 19, 1923; Pace to Lennox, February 21, 1923.

23ACUA, RF, typed report on Affiliation, January 23, 1923. Cf. AHSC (1922), pp. 32-33, 41-45; Leo L. McVay, "Educational Notes," CER, XX (February, 1922), 112-115.

24ACUA, VRF, McVay to "Dear Professor," October 24, 1925. Cf. AHSC (1926), pp. 49-51.

25AHSC (1928), pp. 49-50.

26Cf. ARR, 1924-1925, p. 58; ARR, 1926-1927, p. 70; ARR, 1927-1928, p. 57.

27ARR, 1924-1925, p. 58.

28ARR, 1927-1928, p. 57.

29AHSC (1934), pp. 54-55.

30AHSC (1922), pp. 17-19, 30-31. A fifth year of history, American history, was added.

31AHSC (1924), p. 18.

32AHSC (1928), pp. 15-21, 35, 54-57. In ARR, 1927-1928, p. 58, McVay reported that the revision work was done by special sub-committees with "careful consideration of the needs, objectives, and standards of secondary education from a Catholic viewpoint," reflecting thus the Committee's fundamental purpose to be constructive.

33AHSC (1922), pp. 41ff.

34See p. 65 of this study.

35"Affiliated High School and College Section," CER, XXII (January, 1924), 49-51.

36ARR, 1924-1925, pp. 59-60.

37ARR, 1925-1926, p. 63.

38ARR, 1926-1927, pp. 68-69.

39"Affiliated High School and College Section," CER, XXII (June, 1924), 373.

40AHSC (1928), pp. 54-57.

41The "Section" appeared in each issue of the Catholic Educational Review, XXI (November, 1923) through XXVI (February, 1928).

[42]ARR, 1924-1925, p. 58; ARR, 1925-1926, p. 62; ARR, 1926-1927, p. 69.

[43]ARR, 1925-1926, p. 62.

[44]"Affiliated High School and College Section," CER, XXIV (May, 1926), 301.

[45]Ibid., (September, 1926), 423-425.

[46]ARR, 1928-1929, pp. 61-62.

[47]The first Annual Report of the Rector to mention Affiliation was the 1922-1923 report in which Pace as Director of Studies mentioned the number of affiliates (p. 12). Starting with the 1923-1924 report, Pace as Chairman of the Committee on Affiliation made a separate report on Affiliation and, thereafter, McVay as Secretary gave a detailed report each year through 1936-1937. These reports were devoted almost entirely to high school activities.

[48]ACUA, RF, "Outline of the Proposed Plan for College Entrance Examinations," n.d. Testing dates of June 16-21, 1924, were specifically mentioned in the document.

[49]ACUA, MMBT, September 26, 1922, p. 286.

[50]ACUA, BTEM, April 11, 1923, "Report of the Sub-Committee on The Catholic University of America."

[51]Ibid.

[52]ACUA, VRF, Pace to Michael J. Curley, Baltimore, Maryland, February 26, 1923.

[53]ACUA, BTEM, April 11, 1923.

[54]Ibid., September 23, 1924.

[55]Ibid., April 14, 1926, "Schema for Revision of the Constitution Approved by the Board of Trustees"; ACUA, MMBT, September 14, 1926, p. 324.

[56]ACUA, BTEM, April 27, 1927, "Supplementary and Amendatory Act of Incorporation of the Catholic University'; ACUA, MMBT, April 18, 1928, pp. 356-357.

[57]Ibid., September 13, 1927, p. 346.

[58]The Catholic University of America: General Information, 1929-1930 (January, 1929), p. 16.

[59]ACUA, VRF, McVay to Pace, October 15, 1928.

[60]Ibid., Deferrari to Pace, December 12, 1928.

[61]By interview with Roy J. Deferrari, August 24, 1963.

[62]ACUA, VRF, "Proposed Survey of 'Affiliation' by the

Committee on Affiliation of Schools and Colleges," n.d.
While this document was not dated, it seems reasonable to
conclude that it dates back to 1928-1929. In the Rector's
first report to the Trustees, November 13, 1928, he questioned the academic and financial situation of the "affiliated"
neighboring houses of studies (ACUA, BTEM, November 13,
1928). He appointed the Rev. Thomas V. Moore chairman of
a committee to study this matter in the fall of 1928. The survey document cited above was clipped to a letter from Moore
to the Chairman of the Committee on Committees, December
13, 1929, in which Father Moore made a brief report on the
organization of his new committee. Moreover, on January
12, 1929, Ryan wrote to an affiliated high school that "this
matter of affiliation is one that we are examining at the present moment"(ACUA, RF, Ryan to Sr. Mary Henry, St. Louis,
Mo., January 12, 1929). This general sequence of events was
also verified by interview with Roy J. Deferrari, August 24,
1963.

[63]ARR, 1924-1925, p. 60.

[64]ARR, 1926-1927, p. 70.

[65]ARR, 1927-1928, pp. 57-58.

[66]ARR, 1928-1929, p. 61.

[67]ARR, 1930-1931 (October, 1931), p. 78.

[68]Ibid., p. 79. While the number of affiliates under
these three new classifications grew slightly each year until
in 1936-1937 seven junior colleges, seven normal schools,
and three preparatory seminaries were so reported (ARR,
1936-1937, p. 79), no separate listings of these classifications were made in the General Information catalogues of the
University, in which the annual official lists of affiliates were
appearing at that time.

[69]ACUA, RF, McVay to Pace, March 18, 1930. McVay
stated that these terms were set as of May 1, 1929, for St.
Cecilia Normal School, Nashville, Tennessee, the first summer session normal school to be affiliated.

[70]ARR, 1931-1932 (October, 1932), p. 73.

[71]ARR, 1935-1936 (October 15, 1936), p. 78.

[72]Daniel J. Murphy, "The National Catholic Educational
Association and Standardization" (unpublished Master's dis-

sertation, Department of Education, The Catholic University
of America, 1930), pp. 30-42. Cf. a series of articles by
Edward B. Jordan, "Some Problems of the Catholic College,"
CER, XXII (March, 1924), 129-140; ibid. (November, 1924),
513-522; ibid., XXIV (February, 1926), 65-75.

[73]AHSC (1934), pp. 3-4.

[74]ARR, 1934-1935 (October 31, 1935), pp. 83-84.

[75]ARR, 1935-1936, pp. 79-80.

[76]ACUA, AF, McVay to "My dear Professor," February
1, 1929; McVay to Deferrari, February 4, 1932.

[77]AHSC (1934), pp. 54-55.

[78]A comparison of the Affiliation syllabi from 1912-1913
through 1936 showed that the outlines for the four years of religion and two years of chemistry remained the same throughout the entire period. With the exception of only minor
changes, French, German, Spanish, the first four years of
history, physics, and biology outlines dated back to various
years before 1920 and, with the exception of French and
biology, to original outlines as first approved by the Committee.

[79]ACUA, AF, Deferrari to McVay, April 26, 1933.

[80]Ibid., "Latin."

[81]ARR, 1937-1938 (October 31, 1938), p. 80.

[82]AHSC (1930), p. 5.

[83]ARR, 1929-1930 (October, 1930), p. 70; ACUA, AF,
McVay to Deferrari, May 10, 1933.

[84]Cf. ARR, 1933-1934 (October 31, 1934), p. 75; ARR,
1934-1935, p. 83; ARR, 1935-1936, p. 79; ARR, 1936-1937,
p. 80.

[85]ACUA, RF, January 23, 1923; an unsigned memorandum
from the Office of the Secretary, Committee on Affiliation.

[86]ARR, 1931-1932, p. 74.

[87]ACUA, RF, Sr. Mary Henry to McVay, December 1,
1928. Deferrari gave three reasons for dissatisfaction with
the tests: high costs, unreliability of the scoring, and the
fact that the scientific advancements in the test field were not
reflected by the Affiliation tests (Deferrari, Memoirs. . . ,
pp. 191-192).

[88]Cf. Appendix D. These statistics were collected from

the annual issues of the Report of the Rector, 1923 to 1938.

[89]Cf. Appendix D. These statistics were collected from the annual issues of the Report of the Rector, 1923 to 1938.

[90]Cf. Appendix C. These statistics were collected from the annual issues of the Year Book of the Catholic University of America, 1913 to 1923, and the General Information Announcements, 1923 to 1938. By way of contrast, however, the number of college affiliates grew from 25 in 1928 to 40 in 1938.

[91]James E. Cummings, "Pertinent Facts on Catholic Secondary Education," CER, XXVIII (October, 1930), 447.

[92]ARR, 1937-1938, p. 83. This was the first report to the Rector on Affiliation made by Deferrari; previous ones had been made by McVay as Secretary.

[93]ACUA, CSCF, Shields to Sisters of Notre Dame, Hamilton, Ohio, November 27, 1912.

[94]By interview with Roy J. Deferrari, August 24, 1963.

[95]Pace implied this strongly in his 1918-1919 document in which he recommended the removal of Affiliation headquarters from the Catholic Sisters College to the University campus, providing at the same time that any surplus be returned to the then financially struggling Sisters College (see pp. 109-111 of this study). Deferrari, in his Memoirs. . . , stated that during the Shahan administration the University "lived truly a hand-to-mouth existence" (p. 398) and that "Bishop Ryan found the financial condition of the University in a serious state" (p. 405). This interpretation by the present investigator that finances played a major role in delaying the reform of the Affiliation testing program was further substantiated by Roy J. Deferrari by interview, August 24, 1963.

[96]ARR, 1928-1929, p. 119. The receipts for the academic year 1928-1929, one of the better years for examination sales, amounted to $28,541.26 as compared to Affiliation expenses for that year amounting to $18,529.12.

[97]ACUA, RF, "Committee Investigating Affiliation of Schools and Seminaries with the Catholic University of America," February 28, 1934.

[98]Ibid., "To the Most Reverend Rector and the Academic Senate," April 27, 1934.

[99] Ibid., Ryan to Deferrari, June 7, 1935.
[100] Ibid., Deferrari to Ryan, November 12, 1935.
[101] Cf. Deferrari, Memoirs. . . , pp. 190-192.
[102] McInerney, op. cit., p. 43.
[103] Ibid., pp. 32-33.
[104] Ibid., pp. 34-35.

CHAPTER VI

THE REORGANIZATION YEARS: 1938 AND 1939.

A New Committee on Affiliation and Extension

Dr. Roy J. Deferrari had come to the Catholic University from Princeton in 1918, to teach in and head the Department of Greek and Latin. He replaced Dr. Pace as chairman of the Committee on Affiliation early in the Ryan rectorship, but like Pace before him, he had been unable to effect immediately any overall reform of the program. The work of Affiliation continued directly in the hands of Father McVay, a staunch disciple of Dr. Shields. McVay, close to the day-by-day detail of the work, failed to see the need for a thorough over-hauling. Added to this stalemate were the financial problems of the University faced by both Rectors Shahan and Ryan. And just about the time that Ryan felt that he could bring the matter to a head, he was appointed Bishop of Omaha.

Early in the academic year 1930-1931, Monsignor Ryan had appointed Deferrari Acting Dean of the Graduate School of Arts and Sciences and Dean the following year. With this turn to administration, Deferrari became active also in a variety of educational associations, among them the National Catholic Educational Association, the Association of American Universities, and the Middle States Association of Colleges and Secondary Schools.[1] Thus he became familiar not only with the internal activities of the University but also with the general American educational scene. Moreover, his appointment as Director of the University's Summer Session in 1929 led to many very successful relationships with the various religious teaching communities and to a sympathetic understanding of their educational problems and those of Catholic education in general.

It was not surprising then that Monsignor Joseph M. Corrigan, the new Rector in 1936, selected Deferrari as his

Secretary General and so appointed him in 1937, nor that he sought his help in the thorny Affiliation problem. It became apparent to him that nothing short of a complete reorganization could save Affiliation. The matter, as he saw it, required a new committee that would be empowered to study the problem and work out solutions unhampered by ill-placed loyalty to the old plan. In consultation with Dr. Deferrari in the fall of 1937, the attack, dealing with fundamentals, was set up: a new committee, a re-definition of affiliation and its purposes, and a thorough study of procedures and costs. The then current needs of Catholic education were to serve as the guide lines in formulating a new plan.[2]

A second matter was also given attention at that time. Extension or off-campus courses had never been generally encouraged at the University. Before a full pedagogical program had been offered by the Department of Education and before the Catholic Sisters College had been founded, Drs. Shields and Pace had conducted a series of correspondence courses and summer institutes in an effort to meet the immediate needs of teachers in the Catholic schools. These were abandoned, however, when academic and professional programs for the teaching sisters were provided more adequately by other sources. In 1902, the University undertook one venture in extension work in the form of the New York School of Pedagogy, with Drs. Shahan and Pace actively involved in its establishment and maintenance. But its very success, as well as the inherent difficulties of maintaining staff and standards, had led to the approval of a department of education and an "on-campus" program in education.[3]

The popular extension movement of the early 1900's and the practice of some religious teaching communities to invite non-Catholic instructors from state universities and colleges to conduct summer institutes for their sisters had been viewed with alarm by Shields and Pace. The dangers to and the implications for Catholic education resulting from such extension courses had been closely linked to the secular affiliation problem in the mind of these two professors and had been offered in their 1909 document as a strong reason why the University should extend and strengthen its own program

within the Department of Education and through a Catholic sisters college.[4]

The University, however, was not without requests for
extension courses. In 1929, the question was brought to the
attention of the Trustees, but this was a time of extensive University reorganization, and the Trustees felt that no "Extension
Division" could be recommended until the reorganization of the
faculties had been completed and all was in good running order.[5] The need and demand for extension work did not abate,
and the fact that not infrequently the needs were being met by
the non-Catholic institutions prompted both Corrigan and
Deferrari to consider the possibility of tieing in extension work
with Affiliation.[6] Such an arrangement was not illogical in
concept or practice. Philosophically, both Affiliation and a
program of extension courses had a common objective: the
general strengthening of Catholic education.   Practically, it
was desirable that the administration of extension courses
should not fall under any one particular dean, since the extension work was envisioned as cutting across the several schools
of the University as specific requests would require.[7]   The
Office of the Secretary General met this specification, and
since Dr. Deferrari was serving both as Secretary General
and as Chairman of the Committee on Affiliation, the Committee on Affiliation presented a ready-made academic body
through which to supervise the extension work.

With this dual goal of initiating new programs of affilia-
tion and extension, the Rector assembled in his office on
February 25, 1938, the members of the new Committee on
Affiliation and Extension and made his official appointments.
In addition to the Rector and Vice Rector serving ex officio and
to Deferrari as Chairman, the Committee included the Right
Reverend Edward B. Jordan, Associate Professor of Education
and Dean of Sisters College; Reverend George B. Johnson,
Associate Professor of Education; Very Reverend James Mar-
shall Campbell, Dean of the College of Arts and Sciences; Dr.
Arthur J. Harriman, University Registrar; and Father McVay,
who was given the new title of Recording Secretary.[8]

The meeting, conducted by the Rector, was used to lay
down basic principles and directives.   The minutes recorded

these as follows:

Definition of Terms "Affiliation" and "Extension"

1. By "Affiliation" is not meant "Accreditation." An institution of learning will be required to meet only a very minimum in the way of tangible requirements. The most important prerequisite will be an earnest desire on the part of the authorities to improve as a Catholic institution under the guidance of the University Committee on Affiliation and Extension.

2. By "Extension" is meant courses offered by the University authorities off the campus of the University.

Purpose: The purpose of affiliation is to assist Catholic institutions of learning through the facilities of the University to attain their aims and purpose in the most effective Catholic way, without in any degree losing their autonomy. The statutes of the University recently approved by the Holy See, read in part as follows on this point:

Art. 2. The University must look to the welfare not only of the students enrolled but also of all the Faithful in the United States of America and hence it should be of help and assistance to Schools, Colleges and Seminaries. . . .

Art. 6. The University is empowered to affiliate other Institutions for the purpose of conferring Academic Degrees, according to the requirements of Art. 71.

Art. 71,2. Colleges, Seminaries and other Catholic Institutions may, without prejudice to their autonomy, be affiliated to the University by the authority of the Rector and Academic Senate upon fulfillment of the conditions to be prescribed by said Rector and Senate.

It is hoped that some definite form of regular service for affiliated institutions will be developed. I have in mind at this moment a bulletin of general information on pertinent topics.

2. The purpose of extension work is to offer to Catholics necessary courses under Catholic auspices

which they can not otherwise so obtain.

General Principles of Affiliation

1. By no means will any institution be allowed to lose any of its autonomy.

2. In the case of secondary schools a scheme of inspection and comprehensive examinations at the close of the senior year only may be considered. The details of procedure and items of cost could be worked out later.

3. In the case of colleges periodic inspections with frequent information on progress would be sufficient.

4. As other kinds of institutions of higher learning are considered for affiliation, the appropriate Dean at the University would be consulted, by the Committee, for that particular work and be made a member of the Committee.

General Principles of Extension Work:

1. It is hoped that the University will be able to carry on extension work in such a manner as will not make it necessary or desirable for a Catholic institution to invite a non-Catholic institution of learning to enter its walls to offer courses, so often directly prejudicial to Catholic principles.

2. For all instances the appropriate Dean at the University will be consulted for the establishment of any extension work.[9]

Reorganizational Work: The College Plan

Dr. Deferrari and his new Committee lost no time. Weekly meetings were begun at once. Conducted by Deferrari, they were held on Thursday mornings at 9:00 a.m. in the Affiliation quarters, located then in Room 20 of the Mullen Library.[10] The Chairman went directly to the heart of the matter, proposing that, pending study and action by the Committee, the requirements of the then current Affiliation syllabus be continued until the end of the academic year. During this time, the future Program of Affiliation would be considered under two main topics: the college plan and the high school plan. To start the discussion relative to the first area,

he had prepared three Affiliation documents concerning institutions of higher education. These were given to each member
at the March 4, 1938, meeting, the first meeting after the one
with the Rector present, and the request was made that these
"be carefully studied and amended according to the experiences
and views of each member; all this as a preparation for later
discussions on this phase of affiliation."[11]

The remainder of that meeting was then devoted to the
general problem of the high school. The views given were
varied but the majority opinion was that the old plan of examinations had to be eliminated. The minutes not only summarized the discussion but also brought into relief the promise of
a thoroughly professional and comprehensive approach to the
problems of Affiliation by the new Committee:

> The Committee, at this point, turned to a dis-
> cussion of the affiliation of high schools and espe-
> cially the present examination system. Msgr.
> Jordan opposed the present examination plan be-
> cause it is too expensive, too traditional, abandoned
> by all agencies except the Regents of New York. He
> considers inspection, with some plan for follow up
> attached, a better method. Dr. Johnson not in favor
> of the examination system. His reasons are that
> they are no longer used by others except the Regents
> of New York State. Dr. Deferrari not in favor of
> present system of examinations. He suggested a
> sort of comprehensive examination system at the
> end of the Fourth Year. Father McVay stated that
> he felt from his experiences with affiliation that it
> would be unwise to abandon the plan of yearly
> examinations completely. Many of our high school
> faculties are accustomed to this method and to no
> other; this is especially true of those who have
> come recently from European systems of Education.
> It is a tangible method whereby the work and the in-
> fluence of the University through affiliation comes
> into personal contact with the pupils of our affiliated
> high schools. Inspection without some system of

examinations is not adequate as a concrete means of carrying out the basic aim of affiliation which is an endeavor on the part of the Catholic University to help to make and keep the Catholic High Schools not only autonomous but conscious of their part in rounding out, building up and maintaining the ideal and standards of Catholic secondary education. Dr. Harriman agreed with this last point.

Monsignor Jordan then took up the discussion and pointed out that Catholic high schools were, because of actual local conditions, really forced to be conscious of the ideals, requirements and standards set up by the several states, and thus grew to follow them.

Dr. Deferrari here pointed out that from his experiences many of the Catholic high schools were willing but found themselves unable to follow both our requirements and those of the State and had dropped out. Dr. Deferrari here suggested that a rather detailed questionnaire be prepared for the high schools so as to get at this and several other phases of the question of high school affiliation. He promised to present a tentative draft of such a questionnaire at the next meeting.

Dr. Johnson here took up the discussion and asked the members of the Committee if they thought it not best if we restricted our present endeavors to build up a curriculum for that group of our Catholic secondary schools which devote their activities to preparing pupils for college. He felt it wise for us to do this because the other phases of education on the secondary level are at present in a state of flux. He promised to secure for each member of the Committee copies of Douglass' "Study of the Development of American Secondary School" and Eel's "Cooperative Study of Accrediting Secondary Schools."[12]

At the next meeting, officially the third for the new

Committee, the discussion was centered on the three college
documents which each member had received at the previous
meeting. In drawing up these documents, Dr. Deferrari had
worked from his vast experience as a member of the Commission on Higher Education of the Middle States Association.
This aligning of college Affiliation with a regional accrediting
group had been done with full deliberation. While the distinction between Affiliation and accreditation was to be sharply
drawn in the reorganized program, the need for both was
recognized as was also the potential within Affiliation for encouraging and assisting affiliates to seek state and regional
accreditation. Because Deferrari felt that the developments
within the Middle States Association were progressive and
generally sound and that a pattern of procedures similar to
those of that Association would serve to make the process of
Affiliation in itself a preparatory device leading to accreditation, he had taken his own ideas directly to Mr. Frank Bowles,
then Executive Secretary of the Commission on Higher Education of the Middle States group. They had met at the annual
meeting of the Association in Atlantic City in November of 1937
and had discussed at some length the principles of institutional
evaluation as applicable to Catholic colleges. By that time,
the idea (initiated by Dr. George F. Zook, United States Com-
missioner of Education, and accepted now as the basic principle of all educational evaluation) that the determining of the
quality of any educational program must be in direct relationship to the stated objectives of the program had taken root
among the educators. Bowles felt too that this criterion led
logically to an examination of the institution's outcomes and
that the available resources and how effectively these were being used to attain the stated objectives were clearly the connecting links between the objectives and the outcomes in any evaluative process.[13]

It was this broad outline that Deferrari and Bowles had
discussed as well as ways and means for implementing it. Dr.
Deferrari's idea was to use the evaluation process as a practical Affiliation tool for the development and improvement of
Catholic educational institutions apart from any function of
accreditation:

The process through which an institution must
pass when seeking affiliation is admittedly similar
to the procedure required by the accrediting agencies.
It is so, however, only because by such a process the
University seeks to know an institution, especially its
problems, thoroughly, so that it may be in a better
position to assist its affiliates. It should be stated
also that the University is on the constant lookout to
improve the Catholic element in such institutions. . . .

Affiliation with the Catholic University, then, rep-
resents a systematic effort on the part of the University to assist Catholic academic institutions of all
kinds to achieve the objectives which they have set
up for themselves, without in any way interfering
with their autonomy.[14]

Thus, Affiliation's primary purpose was to be of service to affiliates through inspections or visitation, this concept replac-
ing entirely the old plan's standardization or accrediting aim.[15]

The first of the three documents taken up by the Committee, "Principles and Standards for Affiliating Institutions of
Higher Education," defined Affiliation negatively as not being
the equivalent of accreditation and positively as assistance to
Catholic institutions in the achievement of their general and
special objectives.

In the affiliation of an institution, attention will
be centered on the manner in which the institution
as a Catholic institution performs its task of instruction as a whole. Consideration of course must be
given to matters which have an important bearing on
instructional efficiency such as the financial resources; building and grounds; the organization of
the curriculum; the administration; the library,
laboratories; admission policy, graduation requirements; student activities and faculty competence.[16]

Following this introductory statement were fifteen principles and standards, each dealing with a single major aspect

of the Catholic college: (1) purpose, (2) admissions, (3) faculty, (4) instruction, (5) curriculum, (6) library, (7) laboratories, (8) graduation, (9) catalogue, (10) professional courses, (11) graduate work, (12) student activities, (13) administration, (14) finances, and (15) buildings and grounds. A sixteenth principle was given but referred only to the junior college, stating that those already outlined were applicable also to the junior college with "allowance being made for the shorter curriculum and the more elementary nature of its program."[17] Taken as a whole, these standards represented a considerably broader approach to college evaluation than had the original 1912 standards. They were for the most part of a general and qualitative nature, lending themselves to the desired flexibility of application and the preservation of each affiliate's special objectives. Quantitative and specific criteria were set only in relation to the graduation requirements (no less than 120 or more than 136 semester hours of work for the Bachelor's degree) and the minimum prescribed content of the college's published catalogue. It was further understood that the principles and standards were not to be applied rigidly or in their totality but were also to serve as goals for the individual college affiliate whose overall efficiency had been rated satisfactory at least to a minimal degree. The capabilities and the willingness of the administrators of each college to work systematically toward higher levels of achievement carried considerable weight also.[18]

The Committee's reaction to the proposed document on college principles was favorable. The contents of the entire paper, with only minor modifications in phraseology, were approved and recommended to the Rector for formal acceptance at the Committee's third meeting on March 10th.[19] At its next meeting on March 17th the second document, "Questionnaire for Colleges," was reviewed and also recommended to the Rector for final approval.[20]

The questionnaire application form was a six-page outline of the major aspects of a college program presented usually in question form. The first fifteen sections covered the same fifteen areas which constituted the list of standards in the first document. Section XVI pertained only to the junior college

and Section XVII, only to the teacher training college, and were
to be answered by those institutions in addition to the other
sections of the questionnaire. The purpose of the form was
given on its cover page:

> First, it [the Committee] wishes to obtain informa-
> tion which will determine an institution's placement
> or continuance on the affiliated list. Second, it
> wishes to encourage the institution to undertake
> periodically a critical examination of itself. It be-
> lieves that such an examination will be made easier
> by use of this questionnaire.[21]

The information requested by the questionnaire was frequently of a quantitative nature, but the questions asked were
basic and probing. It was Deferrari's thinking, and the Committee agreed, that factual data would have to be the starting
point for an Affiliation evaluation and that the more qualitative
judgments should be left to the evaluator after he had familiar-
ized himself more thoroughly, through a visitation, with the
college's procedural details and the less tangible outcomes.[22]

The third and last college document was a "Guide for Inspectors of Colleges." This was barely a three-page affair,
covering briefly the same previously mentioned fifteen educational areas of a college and adding two new ones, record
keeping and honorary degrees. The points raised were for
the most part broad, avoiding any recognition or forcing of a
single pattern. Under "Purposes," for example, there was
one question: "Is the college realizing its purposes?" Under
"Faculty," four items were listed for checking: training,
ratio of faculty to number of students, teaching loads, and interest in research. It was understood that the inspector would
also have the questionnaire data, with the inspector's "Guide"
leading him to place the desired emphasis on qualitative standards according to their relative importance to total efficiency
rather than on miscellaneous detail.[23] This document was
approved by the Committee on March 24th, at its fifth meeting.[24]

During this same period of intensive work on college

Affiliation, the Committee also came to an agreement on fees for the colleges. An application fee of $15.00 and a continuing annual fee of $10.00 were set. A college undergoing an inspection was subject to a fee of $50.00, one-half of which was to serve as a stipend for the inspector, whose travel expenses were also to be charged to the affiliate.[25]

Thus by the end of the fifth meeting and one month after the first meeting called by the Rector, a basic foundation had been laid for a new scheme of college Affiliation, and the Committee was ready to concentrate on the high school problem. About this same time, Father McVay withdrew from the Committee because of illness,[26] and Dr. Harriman, the University Registrar, was elected Recording Secretary.[27] To facilitate further the work of Affiliation, its headquarters were moved from the Library to the Secretary General's Office in McMahon Hall and the meetings continued there.[28]

Reorganizational Work: The High School Plan

The high school problem was in many ways the most difficult one faced by the Committee. Dr. Deferrari felt that the chief basis for the affiliating of a high school should be, as it was for the college, the personal inspection and that renewals also based on inspection would prevent the school from descending below the minimum standards. By this method, a framework would be provided the Committee through which it could assist the affiliate systematically and regularly toward maximal academic development. To achieve this goal, however, the inspectors would have to be experienced and well qualified educators, working along specific guide lines established by the Committee. If any part of the examination program were to be retained, the control of the marking of the papers had to remain directly in the hands of the Committee.[29] Deferrari recommended accordingly objective type testing which would make this possible and felt that a complete revision of the course outlines was also necessary.[30]

The Committee's discussion of these and other aspects of high school Affiliation continued throughout the spring of

1938. Not only did it become evident that more time would be
needed to bring a new plan to a satisfactory conclusion but also
that additional, specialized help was needed. In spite of this,
however, several major steps were taken before the last meeting of that academic year. As early as May 5th, Deferrari was
able to submit to the Committee a high school document very
similar in structure to that on the college principles and standards. The same introductory statement defining the nature
and purpose of Affiliation was used, followed by high school
standards on (1) organization and administration, (2) preparation of teachers, (3) teaching loads, (4) curriculum, and (5)
physical equipment. While certain quantitative requirements
were set (e.g., definition of a unit, maximum daily teaching
load of 150 pupil-periods, 30 as maximum number of pupils
per class, etc.), the standards allowed for variations and ex-
ceptions through an emphasis on quality outcomes and general,
overall efficiency as evidenced by the total program. The application questionnaire and inspection were to be the devices
used by the Committee to determine this combined effect. The
document proposed also to issue a certificate of Affiliation to
the affiliated schools and a secondary school diploma to students
taking comprehensive, written examinations, the details concerning which would be announced later. Fees for the high
school included an initial application-annual fee of $10.00 and
a continuing fee thereafter of $5.00 a year. An inspector's
travel expenses and a stipend of $15.00 were to be charged at
the time of a visitation.[31]
     Not only was this first document approved early in May
by the Committee, but three other high school documents were
put into final form and approved on June 2nd. These included
the application form, a teacher's schedule form, and an annual
report form.[32] A copy of the application form only could be
located. This four-page questionnaire consisted of five sections, corresponding roughly to the five standards or principles
of the earlier document but with one section devoted entirely to
the school library. Under "Organization and Administration"
were included such factors as grading, guidance, records,
testing, scheduling, graduation requirements, admission of
graduates to college, and the accreditations held. The data on

teachers required information on both training and experience, and the curriculum section asked for enrollments and student activities as well as program offerings. The physical plant was covered only briefly in terms of the number of buildings, number and size of classrooms, and estimated value of the science laboratories. The placing of special emphasis on the importance of a good school library was made evident by a total of ten questions pertaining to the collections, organization, schedule, training of librarian, and the library budget.[33]

While the acceptance of these fundamental documents set up a working plan for the affiliating of high schools, probably the most difficult job remained for completion the next year: the revision of the course outlines, the reorganization of the testing program, and the construction of the new tests themselves. But even here some positive action was taken that first year of reconstruction. First, the Committee agreed that the testing program must be placed strictly on a voluntary basis, to be used by an affiliate as it desired, and that it should be limited to the major college preparatory fields. Even more important for the continued success of the high school plan was the securing of the services of a specialist in secondary education. When it became apparent that much depended on such a step, Dr. Deferrari, with the approval of the Rector, approached Mother Lucy of the Benedictine Sisters of Atchison. His friend of many years did not disappoint him. The minutes of the May 12th meeting recorded:

Sister Immaculata has been permitted by Mother Lucy to accept the University's offer of appointment to Instructor in Education. She is to teach no more than four hours per week and to devote the rest of the time to inaugurating testing work of the Committee. In response to her inquiry as to whether she should do any preliminary work before coming to the University it was decided to ask her to summarize all testing in high schools at present, especially state tests in Iowa and Wisconsin, and, if she has time to study the N.C.W.C. collection of 1937 Secondary School courses.[34]

Procedural and Promotional Work

February to June of 1938 was productive for the Committee also in terms of setting up procedures for its more routine business. College applications initiated before the appointment of the new Committee were still pending, and while the Committee felt that new policies and procedures could not be applied completely during this transitional period, the required Committee action did permit the discussion of practical procedural problems and some experimentation. In several cases previously made inspections were honored and in others inspections were made either by Drs. Deferrari or Campbell, who reported back to the Committee. These reports seem to have been detailed and thorough, covering faculty training, teaching loads, research and membership in professional associations, the library, entrance and degree requirements, instruction, the curriculum, and the science laboratories. Precedents were set on such matters as a requirement of a written constitution; the granting of initial Affiliation usually for a two-year period when action was favorable; the requiring that an applicant carry out specific recommendations when Affiliation was postponed; and the sending of the full report, with the Committee's suggestions, to the applying institution.[35]

The work on the summer normal programs was heavy throughout that spring. The specific programs for the coming summer were submitted by each of these affiliates for the approval of the Committee. In so doing, additional criteria were established. The summer course had to be of a full six-weeks duration; teachers had to hold at least a Master's degree from a recognized graduate school, with a major or minor in the subject to be taught; and student loads could not exceed six semester hours of credit. The nature and the frequency of the problems involved with this type of institution led the Committee to conclude that the scheme for the affiliating of normal schools was not well organized and that a review of the facts and further study should be placed on the agenda of a future meeting.[36]

From the Office of the Secretary General, Dr. Deferrari continued to make other developmental plans and to implement

those already approved by the Committee. It was within this
early period of reorganization that the affiliation of schools of
nursing was first given serious consideration. The University's own School of Nursing Education had been approved by
the Board of Trustees only in 1933, [37] and Sister M. Olivia
Gowan, O.S.B., of the Benedictine Sisters of Duluth, Minnesota, had been named its first Dean. It was with Sister M.
Olivia that Dr. Deferrari worked, preparing materials to be
presented to the Committee on Affiliation and Extension early
the next fall. [38] Both felt that much pioneering work in this
field remained to be done and that the Catholic hospital and
collegiate schools of nursing could benefit greatly by a systematic program of improvement under qualified professional
advisement. The approach to alleviate existing weaknesses
was to be a double one: affiliation and extension. The opening of an extension center in the field of nursing had been
effected as early as the first semester of 1937-1938, before
the new Affiliation Committee had been appointed. It and two
others were put into operation the second semester, with Dr.
Deferrari and Sister M. Olivia working in close cooperation
in setting up the courses and securing the teachers. Two
basic criteria were applied to extension requests: that a genuine need would be so met and that the work could be carried
on effectively with due regard for academic standards. [39]
Formal approval of the accomplished work was given by the
Committee at its March 31, 1938, meeting, [40] and this procedure of retroactive approval was followed in the years to
come.

The summer of 1938 was also productive for Affiliation,
even though the Committee did not function as a unit over
those months. Since the new college plan had been fully approved in June, a two-page form letter to Catholic colleges
went out over the Rector's signature in August. The abandon-
ment of accreditation as a major function of Affiliation and its
replacement by a concept of service was emphasized and the
reason for the change was given:

> In the twenty-five years which have passed since
> Affiliation was established, the Catholic colleges,

novitiates and secondary schools have needed less
and less the accrediting services of the Committee.
As national, regional, and state accrediting agencies have clarified their aims and perfected their
procedures, however, Catholic institutions have
looked more and more to the University for guidance
on how to become recognized by one and another of
these agencies, how to maintain recognition already
secured, how to meet specifically Catholic problems
presented by the processes of obtaining and maintaining non-Catholic accreditation.[41]

The services or benefits to be derived from Affiliation, in
an attempt to meet these contemporary needs, were then summarized:

I. The Benefits Common to All Affiliates
   1. The strength that would naturally come to all affili-
      ates from a union for a common purpose. (This
      has weight with non-Catholic educational groups.)
   2. Facility in cooperating on investigations of com-
      mon interest to affiliates.
   3. The University as a source of information on aca-
      demic matters.
   4. The University as a medium of inquiry and of ex-
      change of information on matters of common inter-
      est not only through correspondence but through
      special institutes and meetings.
II. Some Benefits Special to Affiliated Colleges
   1. The University as a source of advice for the devel-
      opment of a college.
   2. The University as a practical source of assistance
      to the college in the development of the faculty,
      e.g.: (1) in helping to procure new members for
      the faculty; (2) by advising on the training of old
      members of the faculty.
   3. The University as a source of information on move-
      ments of special interest to colleges, v.g. text-
      books, grants-in-aid, comprehensive examinations,

honor systems.

4. The University as a help to a college when seeking any form of accreditation deemed necessary for a college of national influence.

5. The University as an aid to a college in placing students in institutions of higher learning, especially when the college in question does not enjoy all forms of accreditation.

6. The affiliated college as a possible center of a University activity deemed necessary in the region of the affiliated college.[42]

The response to the Rector's letter, which closed with an invitation to the colleges to seek Affiliation under the new plan, was good. The requests for further information were frequent and support was generally forthcoming. One response, that grew into a rather lengthy correspondence between the writer and Dr. Deferrari, showed some skepticism as to the potential values of the plan. The Very Reverend Anselm M. Keefe, O. Praem., Dean of St. Norbert College, West de Pere, Wisconsin, wrote for "concrete information. . . wherein the University could better perform the functions now so ably carried out by the North Central Association, and so inspiringly by the Catholic Educational Association. . . ."[43] Deferrari felt that Father Keefe had misunderstood the whole purpose of Affiliation. He replied that the University was not trying to duplicate the work being done by these other agencies and that while some standard must be exacted of the affiliate,

this standard as far as we are concerned consists mainly in an upward looking policy on the part of the administration of a college, and a very definite understanding on their part of what they are aiming to accomplish.

. . . .I want to say further that affiliation with the Catholic University certainly does not mean further restrictions. It would mean a slight expenditure of funds, . . . and very little expense thereafter, just the annual fee of ten dollars.[44]

Father Keefe was still not entirely favorably impressed. He wrote again:

> We are not at all sure that either we as an insti-
> tution or the Catholic University itself will have much
> to gain by affiliation with a group of institutions fifty-
> two percent of which have absolutely no educational
> standing with the various reputable accrediting agen-
> cies throughout the United States.
>
> It is undoubtedly a labor of love actuated by the
> highest spirit of Christian charity for the Catholic
> University of America to gather under its wings a
> mixed brood (some of which are educational ugly
> ducklings). For those colleges, however, which
> have managed through long and painful endeavors to
> reach the standards set by the rest of the educational
> world, it is to be doubted whether such an affiliation
> will be an honor to which they can point with pride.[45]

Dr. Deferrari made one last effort to clarify the nature and the spirit of the new Affiliation plan for Father Keefe:

> As I told a member of the Committee on Classi-
> fication of Institutions of the Association of American
> Universities, affiliation with the University does not
> mean anything very specific as to the academic stan-
> dards of that particular institution. It does, however,
> very definitely mean that the University considers
> such an institution as in the hands of good administra-
> tive officers and very definitely in the process of im-
> provement. Such an institution we are interested in
> affiliating for the sole purpose of helping such an in-
> stitution to obtain the accreditation of other bodies
> and to help it in any way possible to make it a better
> Catholic college. This, of course, accounts for a
> great many discrepancies in the actual standards
> already achieved by the various colleges on the af-
> filiated list. . . . We are distinctly an advisory
> group and do not in any way wish to interfere with

the autonomy of any institution.[46]

It was not easy to separate the old idea of accreditation
from the new plan. The Committee was well aware of this and
continued to feature prominently this distinction in all of its
literature.[47]   But probably more important in counteracting
the old concept were the actions taken by the Committee. At
one of the earlier meetings of this group, the list of college
affiliates had been reviewed to ascertain the accreditation
status of each institution.[48]   As shown by the minutes of the
meetings which followed, the policies adopted included the
direct encouragement of non-accredited affiliates to seek such
recognition, the offering of assistance for such a step, and the
avoidance of the duplication of effort by accepting a recent regional evaluation in lieu of an immediate Affiliation inspection.
The value of this approach as well as the general soundness of
the overall Affiliation plan showed early signs of favorable
recognition by the accrediting groups themselves. Not only
did Dr. Deferrari's personal friends in the Middle States Association respect the plan but others too saw its worth: before
the end of 1939, the Committee was informed that the state of
New Mexico was relying heavily on the process of University
Affiliation to guide one of its Catholic teacher training institutions to meet state standards, [49] and with each year this function of the plan grew.

The High School Testing Program and Course Outlines

When the Committee on Affiliation and Extension resumed
its regular meetings in the fall of 1938, two new members were
present: Sister M. Olivia and Sister M. Immaculata. The
former was to assist the Committee primarily in matters pertaining to the proposed nursing plan, while Sister M. Immaculata was to serve as a special consultant in the field of secondary education. Thus the work in both of these fields was able
to move ahead rapidly, with each of these sisters playing major
roles in her respective area of specialization.
Since the basic structure and the standards for high school

Affiliation had been approved in the spring, the Committee took up at once the problems of testing and the course outlines. The old testing program had been kept in effect for May of 1938 and a total of over 15,000 tests had been taken by the affiliates.[50]   But this was definitely to be the last of the old plan and much still remained to be accomplished. The first discussion of the Committee that fall was centered on the high school diploma or certificate. It was agreed that the diploma should be retained but on a strictly optional basis. The suggestion was made that four comprehensive examinations, issued and corrected by the Committee, should be required in the senior year along with graduation by the affiliated high school. The examinations would be in religion, mathematics and the natural sciences, English and a foreign language, and the social sciences.[51]   The final requirements were somewhat modified to cover the same fields but by a total of six distinct tests, which would be taken by a diploma candidate over the full four years of high school and whenever the study of the appropriate subjects had been completed. The tests were to be of an objective type and semi-comprehensive in nature. English and religion would cover the entire four years of study and were thus restricted to senior students; the foreign language and mathematics tests would require two years of study and could be taken as early as the end of the sophomore year. Mathematics would be comprised of algebra and plane geometry, but in the foreign languages, the student would have a choice of Latin, French, German or Spanish. The tests in the natural and social sciences were to be on a single unit basis, but here also freedom to elect was made possible by the Committee's approval of unit tests in biology, chemistry, physics, American history, world history, and social civics. The time allowance for each test was set generously at ninety minutes, with double that amount of time for the two-part mathematics test.[52]

Other changes were made. The test period was reduced to three full days and costs to twenty-five cents for each examination. Regulations for administering the tests were considerably simplified, but the confidentiality of the tests was still to be maintained through sealed test packets, and

booklets were to be returned to the Committee for scoring.[53]
More important, however, was the new viewpoint taken on the
value of the test results: "to facilitate comparisons among
individual classes with norms of attainment for each of the
subjects by treating the scores of all students in the group as
though they had been made by one large class."[54] To achieve
this end, namely, the comparison of the work of an affiliate
with that of other schools of the same general character as a
means to study the success of its teaching, an annual descriptive and analytical report of the test results was to be made
and disseminated in addition to the earned scores of all the
students. It was hoped that, with these general reforms and
the maintaining of the calibre of the tests at a high level both
in regard to content and testing techniques, the value of outside testing under Catholic auspices would be sufficiently great
to the schools to invite their participation without prescription.[55]

The correcting problem, which had loomed so large in
eventually defeating the old test plan, was eliminated by the
objective nature of the tests. Subjective judgments were to
be required no longer and all grading was to be done within
the Affiliation office. But one other very large problem did
still remain: the revision of the course outlines.

From the beginning of the reorganization period, the
Committee had been in agreement that there should be no prescribed curriculum, textbooks, or methods for the affiliated
high schools. While the Shields' curriculum had been carefully planned on these same principles and the elective device
had been introduced as a result, yet the requiring of University examinations had tended to fix the content of the courses.
This at a time when there was little uniformity or articulation
among the Catholic schools was exactly what Dr. Shields had
hoped to accomplish, but as the situation improved the unre-
vised plan became open to criticism as prescribing a fixed and
comparatively rigid curriculum. Conflicts arose between
Affiliation and diocesan and state groups that had developed
their own curricular requirements.[56] Any repetition of this
kind of difficulty the new Committee was determined to avoid.
At the same time the Committee realized that in some instances

reliable guides for improving curriculums would be needed and requested by the affiliates themselves. The validity of the tests also demanded some agreement on an outline of the major content areas and objectives for the courses to be tested.

To fill all these conditions, Sister M. Immaculata immediately took on the task of revising the syllabus under the Committee's policy that the outlines be kept concise and confined to the common essentials of each course so that they would permit the use of "any well balanced, complete, and thoroughly Catholic program which may be in force in any Community."[57]   The work was arduous, but Sister M. Immaculata had prepared for it over the summer months and tackled the'job with enthusiasm. A good collection of high school syllabi was available to her through the National Catholic Welfare Conference, and she was already well acquainted with textbooks and other curriculum aids. She solicited at once the assistance of others: the various subject-matter departments of the University, successful secondary school teachers within her own Benedictine community, and University graduate students who had considerable teaching experience. Course outline revisions started in the last years of the 1912 program were probably also of some help to her.

In any case, as early as November of 1938, the Committee was given tentative outlines for two years of high school Latin, French, German, and Spanish and one-year outlines for physics, chemistry, biology, world history, American history, social civics, algebra, and plane geometry. At the December 2nd meeting, all of these were approved.[58]   The four-year course outline for English was considered and approved a week later.[59]   While no mention was made of similar action on the religion courses, these must also have been under study, for time was running out if the new booklet, Program of Affiliation, was to be printed and distributed well before the end of that academic year in order to permit the initiation of the new testing program in May.

The course outlines in general included objectives and content, with the final arrangement of the content and the method of presentation left to the affiliate. There were variations from course to course in the amount of detail given.

English, for example, dealt with grammar and rhetoric only in a very general way but the required readings for the third and fourth year were fairly numerous and specific. Physics and chemistry also used the more explicit approach. The religion outline, an eight-page exposition, included the principles of good teaching and educational psychology applied to the religion program, and the fine hand of Monsignor John M. Cooper, of the University's Anthropology Department, can be seen throughout it. The Committee made no claim to perfection for the course outlines as a whole. They recognized not only that the normal changes and developments within the high school curriculum would make revisions necessary but also that with a further study of the results improvements might well be required.[60]

Another item discussed during this period was the high school inspection form. The end product, like the college form, provided the inspector with the barest outline, comprehensive only in the areas it covered: buildings and grounds, organization and administration, child accounting, staff, instruction, equipment, laboratories, curriculum, student activities, and the library. The form allowed for an overall rating of the school at one of three levels: poor, average and very good.[61]

Perhaps as a final touch and to increase the prestige factor of the new program, the Committee also approved a special certificate of Affiliation, obtainable by an affiliate upon request and on payment of a two-dollar fee.[62]

The Initiation of New Services

Another major achievement of the Committee in the second year of its existence was the initiation of the nursing school plan. Since Dr. Deferrari and Sister M. Olivia had been working on the principles and standards throughout 1937-1938, they were able to submit these materials to the Committee at its October meeting in 1938. The first document pertaining to hospital schools of nursing was accepted after some revision was made to bring out those principles which were

strictly Catholic in character, [63] and a second document for
collegiate schools of nursing was acted on before Christmas.[64]
The general approach, introduction, and topics covered by
both documents followed along the same lines as the equivalent
college document. Adaptions, of course, were made to provide adequately for the professional aspects of the field in keeping with the requirements and standards of State Boards of
Nurse Examiners and the National League of Nursing Education. Catholic aims were fully recognized as influencing the
whole curriculum and especially such courses as psychology,
sociology, history of nursing, ethics, and religion.[65]

There was no record of discussions of new procedures and requirements for the Affiliation of junior colleges and
teacher training institutions. These were definitely thought of
as a part of the college plan, but at some point the adapting of
the college plan to fit these two kinds of institutions must have
been given consideration by the Committee. Mention had been
made in the early meetings of the Committee that changes were
needed, and the final product of their work, the 1939 Program
of Affiliation, showed that revisions were effected. Thus in
addition to principles, standards, and procedures for the four-
year college, the high school, and the school of nursing, a separate section of the Program was devoted to the junior college
and the normal school. The junior college was defined as a
two-year collegiate program equivalent in prerequisites,
methods, and thoroughness to the first two years of an accredited four-year college; a teacher training institution was subject to the same definition but offered "in addition professional
courses to satisfy the needs of student-teachers who desire to
meet the requirements for Normal Diplomas or State Teachers'
Certificates."[66] It was understood that the general college
principles and standards applied to these affiliates also, but
modifications were made as were necessitated by the nature
of their programs and by a realistic understanding of their
then current developmental problems. Thus the standard for
faculty training was set somewhat lower and other standards
(size of class, library, schedules, etc.) were spelled out
quantitatively. The laboratory school and regulations govern-
ing practice teaching were described in some detail for the

normal school.[67]

Nor was any further mention made in the minutes of the Committee's meetings regarding a preparatory seminary plan. It was felt that under the flexibility of the new 1939 schemes, seminary high schools, junior colleges, and the philosophy divisions of major seminaries (upper division of a seminary college) could be classified according to the regular academic classifications already provided and that the full benefits of Affiliation would accrue to the seminary affiliate under these plans.[68]

Thus the approval of the new nursing plan in December, 1938, marked a definite milestone in the Committee's work. The basic work of reorganization had been completed. Moreover, the literature that had been produced in the study of the college, high school, and nursing plans provided in large part the necessary copy for the new Affiliation booklet which was to announce the new plans. Discussion of the manuscript of the Program of Affiliation took place at the January 20th meeting,[69] and a committee of the Academic Senate approved final copy in early February.[70] Sometime in March of 1939 the booklet was printed and its distribution was underway.[71]

With the newly printed Program available it became highly desirable that the promotion of the new plan be carried forward as rapidly as possible. In fact, Dr. Deferrari had not waited for the printed literature. In January of 1939 he had sent a form letter over the Rector's signature to some five hundred secondary schools and another letter to about the same number of nursing institutions. In the former letter, the problems of the previous high school plan were frankly stated, and emphasis was placed on the direct benefits to be derived from the new plan through a series of services: bulletins, special institutes, aid in dealing with accrediting agencies, comprehensive educational guidance, and such other services as would be developed as the need for them became clear.[72] The same emphasis on services appeared in the nursing school letter, and thirteen benefits were enumerated: advice on all aspects of nursing education, securing and exchange of faculty members, help on accreditation problems, institutes and extension courses, faculty development, sponsoring of graduates in securing post-graduate instruction, development of curriculum and courses of study, scholarship information, and information on movements and trends in the field and on research and legislative matters.[73]

A third letter, also signed by the Rector, was sent to high school principals in February in answer to "persistent inquiries,"[74] but the nature of the contents is not known. Toward the end of February, Deferrari contacted the diocesan superintendents. To them he described Affiliation "as a unifying agency for Catholic institutions above the elementary level," such as non-Catholic agencies which have used their unity and strength to exert pressure and shape opinion when desired. Again the services of Affiliation were emphasized, and the superintendents were invited to seek further information on the reorganized plan.[75]

Only scattered responses to the several letters were located. If those answering the high school and nursing school letters were any sampling of the replies received, the general reaction from these two sources was highly favorable. The superintendents, however, seemed generally cool to the idea of Affiliation. Several felt that state and regional accreditation were of first importance to their high schools, but would not oppose Affiliation for any individual school under their jurisdiction.[76] The old idea of Affiliation as "accreditation" was not easy to shake, nor was the general ineffectiveness of the old plan in its later years. One superintendent wrote:

> Previous experience with Catholic University affiliation will discourage some high schools from accepting any plan. From comments I have heard, I have formed the opinion that a number who dropped the affiliation in past years felt that it was of no value to them. . . . Perhaps your office may be able to convince them of the value of C. U. Affiliation.[77]

Another found value in the proposed inspection method but objected to annual examinations since "the objections to the old affiliation were precisely these annual examinations."[78]

Others were noncommital but interested, with a few sending the names and addresses of their principals for direct mailing of the literature and promising encouragement if their advice was sought. One of the available replies, however, was enthu-siastic:

> You will recall that I have waited at least two years for this plan and had very definite objectives for setting it up in our diocese. I think that it can still be a great force in our schools and will discuss the matter with you when I am in Washington attending the Convention.[79]

Balancing out this highly favorable letter was a curt res-ponse from the Secretary of the New York State Council of Catholic School Superintendents:

> The affiliation of the Catholic secondary schools of the state with the plan being inaugurated by the Catholic University of America was not deemed of sufficient educational interest to the Superintendents to warrant further investigation. All Catholic secondary schools are registered with the Univer-sity of the State of New York and there seems no great advantage in being additionally affiliated with the agency proposed.[80]

This general lack of enthusiasm among the superinten-dents could have been of no great disappointment to Deferrari and his Committee. Not only were they aware that the effec-tiveness of the new plan would have to be demonstrated if old disillusionments were to be erased but also that it would take a little time to develop the program to its full potential. Thus the matter of setting up regular services for affiliates became of prime importance once the structure of the new plan was under control. At that very first meeting of the Committee at which the Rector had presided, a "bulletin of general informa-tion" had been suggested. Following this up, Deferrari pro-posed to the Committee in October of 1938 that three such

bulletins be issued at least three times annually, one each for
the colleges, the high schools, and the schools of nursing.[81]
This was acceptable, and it was further agreed that the bulletins would be devoted to summaries of the most important
articles appearing in the technical journals of the educational
field, thus keeping Catholic teachers and school administrators
informed of current educational thought and encouraging at the
same time a wider reading of such literature. Editorial comment, original articles, and Affiliation announcements would
maintain the bulletins as a direct means of communication between the University and its affiliates.[82]

The editors of various Catholic and secular educational
journals were contacted and permission to abstract articles
was secured. Dr. Deferrari and Sister M. Immaculata worked
on the summaries for the first issues of the college and secondary school bulletins, and Father Campbell prepared a brief
editorial on the subject of "Affiliation vs Accreditation." The
material was ready for the inauguration of the Bulletin for
Institutions of Higher Learning and the Bulletin for Secondary
Schools in January of 1939, and both were followed by March
and May issues. The Bulletin for Schools of Nursing, under
the supervision of Sister M. Olivia, had only a March issue
that year, but all three bulletins were soon developed as a
regular quarterly service to affiliates without additional cost
to them.[83]

The high school service that received considerable attention throughout 1938-1939 was, of course, the testing program.
Under Sister M. Immaculata and with the cooperation of subject-matter teachers and specialists, the work of constructing
the tests and evaluating the results of trial testing moved ahead
satisfactorily.[84] The thirteen objective tests, Form A, which
resulted, were considerably more impressive in format than
had been the old tests. Each booklet ran from five to eight
pages in length, carrying from 100 to 180 items of various
objective types: true-false, multiple-choice, matching, and
completion. The language tests included paragraph translation and the mathematics, physics, and chemistry tests required substantial computation work. The student answered
directly in the test booklets, and these were returned by the

schools for scoring in the office of Affiliation.[85]

For the testing program, 1939 was a transitional year. Tests which had been passed by students under the old plan were recognized, and the old course outlines were taken into consideration in making up the new tests. The gradual change-over to the new requirements would take four years, but the 1939 tests were strictly on an optional basis.[86] Under these conditions, 101 affiliated schools participated that year, administering a total of 5,072 tests to 2,480 students, and 489 of the new diplomas were issued as a result.[87] While this was a considerable drop from the thousands administered in former years, the Committee was gratified by the number and more so by the unanimous approval of the new tests.[88] The report made by the Committee was modest in its claims but reflected the optimistic feeling that the potential value of the tests was most promising.[89] The belief that the 1939 testing program had gotten this service to affiliated high schools off to a good start was well-founded. Although the increases in the number of tests distributed each year and the number of diplomas issued were not overwhelming, the continuing growth of both over the years attested to a general acceptance of the new tests.[90]

Throughout the literature of the reorganized Affiliation program, mention was made of special institutes and meetings to be conducted by Affiliation to permit the discussion of the common problem of various groups of academic officers. The first example of this service took the form of a conference for the registrars of the affiliated colleges, held on the University campus on Saturday and Sunday, August 12-13, in 1939. Having presented a tentative program and having sought advice from the colleges themselves,[91] Harriman and Deferrari formulated a final program that included speakers from the University of Pennsylvania and Villanova University as well as Drs. Campbell, Deferrari, and Harriman of the Catholic University. Topics discussed were the then new Evaluative Criteria of the Cooperative Study of Secondary School Standards, college transcripts, and academic record keeping. A special discussion period on Affiliation was also held and two of the University's special series of Jubilee Lectures completed the program.[92] Attendance must have been sufficiently good and the response in general enthusiastic to warrant the continuing of this service. In June of 1940 similar conferences were held for diocesan superintendents of schools, principals of secondary schools, and administrative officers of nursing schools. These also were reported as successful.[93]

The perfecting of the most important of the Affiliation services, the personal visitation of affiliates, was also keeping the Committee busy in 1938-1939. Deferrari was making frequent trips for this purpose, and the minutes of Committee meetings recorded other inspections by Dr. Campbell, Sister M. Immaculata, and Sister M. Olivia. This work was indeed a burden, one which was to worry the Committee for years to come, since the number of qualified evaluators was never large.[94] At the same time, the work of inspecting and reporting was shaping up well, and the results were gratifying. Both affiliates and the Committee were finding the procedure effective in providing a sound basis for individualized advisement.[95] Checking old affiliates as well as studying new applications was a part of the agenda of each meeting. Questionnaires were sent to many of the institutions of higher education on the list,[96] and the action taken on those showing serious weaknesses was specific and demanding: of one, a definite program of improvement for the next two years was required if Affiliation was to be continued;[97] on another, unless specified improvements were evident within one year, Affiliation would be discontinued;[98] two were advised to change their status from that of a four-year college to a junior college[99] and one, to discontinue its junior college altogether.[100] Satisfactory written reports and approval by regional accrediting associations were sufficient reasons for the postponement of an Affiliation inspection until a later date.[101]

The inspection work at the high school level was less heavy during this time, probably because the high school plan itself was still undergoing reorganization and no final announcement of the new high school scheme was made until in January of 1939. Several visitations were made and several applicants were granted Affiliation; some, however, "with an inspection to be made at the convenience of the Committee."[102] The latter became a regular policy of the Committee as the number of high school inspections increased and considerable distances were often involved. Such a procedure permitted the more systematic visiting of several affiliates in a general area of the country and was economical both in terms of the evaluator's time and the affiliate's money.

Thus by the end of the academic year 1938-1939, Dr. Deferrari was able to report not only that the reorganizational work on the Program of Affiliation had been completed, but that the beginning services also were functioning well.[103] While his report on the number of affiliates showed a decrease from the previous year, this in no way reflected on the work of his new Committee. A total of 304 affiliates had been reported for 1937-1938,[104] but several experiences had caused Deferrari to question the accuracy of the list. A more thorough check with each affiliate on the list revealed that the actual number of affiliates in each category, except the college, was below the number listed. The high schools especially were far below, sixty-eight of the regular and thirteen of the novitiate high schools having withdrawn from Affiliation without having been deleted from the official list.[105] The 1938-1939 report, therefore, showed a total of only 243 affiliates, but in spite of the losses, this figure represented an increase of fourteen colleges, two junior colleges, one teacher training institution, and three nursing schools.[106] It was evident that within the new Affiliation plans for higher education, all was going well.

By the end of the next year, the total number of affiliates had increased to 278. Colleges were up by twelve, teacher training institutions by three, schools of nursing by seven, and the regular high schools by eighteen.[107] A year later, at the end of 1940-1941, the successful renewal of Affiliation under the reorganized plan became even more apparent: the total number of affiliates was 301.[108]

Thus it was just twenty-five years after Dr. Shields had initiated so ably his 1912 program of Affiliation that the University under Dr. Deferrari began the work of reorganizing and revitalizing this plan in keeping with the new needs of Catholic education. It was in the fiftieth anniversary year of the University that this work was brought to a successful close. Like in 1912, there was still pioneering work to be done in the expanding and strengthening of the program, but Affiliation was once again dedicated to meeting the current problems of Catholic high schools and colleges and was solidly founded on principles and procedures that would permit growth and development in an even more complex educational era. In Dr. Deferrari the University had found another Catholic educator with the vision and energy of Dr. Shields.

FOOTNOTES

[1]Deferrari, Memoirs . . . , pp. 260-262.

[2]By interview with Roy J. Deferrari, August 24, 1963.

[3]Hogan, op. cit., pp. 83-86; Barry, op. cit., pp. 218-219.

[4]See pp. 38-41 of this study.

[5]ACUA, BTEM, November 5, 1929.

[6]Deferrari, Memoirs. . . , p. 200.

[7]ACUA, MMCAE, February 25, 1938, p. 3.

[8]Ibid., p. 2. Additional members were to be appointed as required.

[9]Ibid., pp. 3-4. The revised statutes cited by the Rector refer to the 1937 revision, Constitutions of the Catholic University of America, translated from the Latin (Washington: 1937). For Affiliation the major change consisted in a transfer of control from the Trustees to the Rector and the Academic Senate. With the new Committee on Affiliation and Extension, matters of policy and the final approval of new affiliates were to be submitted routinely to the Academic Senate (ibid., January 20, 1939, p. 24).

[10]Ibid., pp 4-8. The Affiliation Office had been moved to the Library from the third floor of McMahon Hall in 1932, in order to give the Department of Psychology more room (ACUA, RF, Ryan to McVay, September 17, 1932).

[11]ACUA, MMCAE, March 4, 1938, pp. 4-5.

[12]Ibid., pp. 5-7.

[13]By interview with Roy J. Deferrari, July 30, 1963.

[14]ACUA, RF, Deferrari to Corrigan, April 12, 1939.

[15]The implementing of the new Affiliation purpose in the late 1930's anticipated the regional accrediting agencies' acceptance of service as a secondary aim of the accrediting process. Thus while Deferrari drew heavily on his firsthand knowledge of Middle States procedures, his own contribution was substantial. The adapting of the principles to Affiliation and the modification of principles and policies in terms of Catholic education represented pioneering efforts in the Catholic system. Cf. Deferrari, Memoirs. . . , p. 262.

[16]OAF, "Principles and Standards for Affiliating Institutions of Higher Education" (original typescript). Cf. Appendix B.

[17]Ibid.

[18]Ibid.

[19]ACUA, MMCAE, March 10, 1938, p. 7.

[20]Ibid., March 17, 1938, p. 8. The question was raised at the meeting as to whether the religion of faculty members should be requested; it was agreed that this should be ascertained by the evaluator at the time of the visit rather than by the questionnaire.

[21]OAF, "Questionnaire for Colleges" (original typescript).

[22]By interview with Roy J. Deferrari, July 30, 1963.

[23]OAF, "Guide for Inspectors of Colleges" (original typescript).

[24]ACUA, MMCAE, March 24, 1938, p. 9.

[25]Ibid., March 17, 1938, p. 8.

[26]ARR, 1937-1938 (October 31, 1938), p. 83.

[27]ACUA, MMCAE, March 31, 1938, p. 10.

[28]At a little later date, additional space was provided in the quarters of the Greek and Latin Department on the second floor of McMahon, and the test and bulletin work was carried on there; by interview with Roy J. Deferrari, July 30, 1963.

[29]ACUA, AF, "Proposals for reorganization of system of affiliation of high schools," written in Deferrari's hand.

[30]ACUA, MMCAE, March 24, 1938, p. 9.

[31]OAF, "Principles and Standards for Affiliating Secondary Schools" (original typescript). Cf. Appendix B.

[32]ACUA, MMCAE, June 2, 1938, p. 17.

[33]OAF, "Application for Affiliation of Secondary Schools" (mimeographed).

[34]ACUA, MMCAE, May 12, 1938, p. 14.

[35]Ibid., March 17 to May 25, 1938, pp. 8-17.

[36]Ibid., April 28 to June 2, 1938, pp. 12-17.

[37]ACUA, MMBT, April 26, 1933, p. 469.

[38]ARR, 1937-1938 (October 31, 1938), p. 83.

[39]Ibid., p. 85; OAF, "Report of the Chairman of the Committee on Affiliation and Extension" (1938-1939), p. 4 (typescript).

[40]ACUA, MMCAE, March 31, 1938, p. 10.

[41]ACUA, AF, August 5, 1938.

[42]Ibid. The sixth point referred to extension centers and branch summer sessions primarily. For a similar list of benefits for all affiliates, see "Foreword," Program of Affiliation (1939), pp. 5-6.

[43]Ibid., Keefe to Deferrari, October 14, 1938.

[44]Ibid., Deferrari to Keefe, October 21, 1938.

[45]Ibid., Keefe to Deferrari, November 18, 1938.

[46]Ibid., Deferrari to Keefe, November 23, 1938.

[47]The first Affiliation bulletins ran an editorial, "Affiliation vs. Accreditation," Bulletin for Institutions of Higher Learning, I (January, 1939), 1-2; Bulletin for Secondary Schools, I (January, 1939), 1-2; Bulletin for Schools of Nursing, I (March, 1939), 1.

[48]ACUA, MMCAE, March 10, 1938, p. 7.

[49]Ibid., December 9, 1939, p. 35.

[50]ARR, 1937-1938 (October 31, 1938), p. 84.

[51]ACUA, MMCAE, October 14, 1938, p. 19.

[52]Program of Affiliation (1939), p. 68.

[53]Ibid., p. 69. The diploma fee was set at fifty cents (ibid., p. 24).

[54]OAF, "A Report of the 1939 Objective Examination Testing Program" (mimeographed).

[55]Ibid., pp. 1-2.

[56]Deferrari, Memoirs. . . , p. 197.

[57]Program of Affiliation (1939), p. 27.

[58]ACUA, MMCAE, December 2, 1938, pp. 21-22. The only major change made by the Committee was in civics: this

outline was to be tentative, pending a special study by the
University's School of Social Sciences.

[59]Ibid., December 9, 1939, p. 23.

[60]Program of Affiliation (1939), pp. 25-67.

[61]OAF, "Inspection Blank -- Secondary Schools" (mimeographed).

[62]ACUA, MMCAE, October 18, 1938, p. 18.

[63]Ibid., October 18, 1939, p. 18.

[64]Ibid., December 9, 1938, p. 23. The policy adopted a
little later by the Committee maintained that a nursing program within a college was not covered by the Affiliation of the
college, but that the nursing program must be considered
separately. If such a program was not separately affiliated
and found inadequate, it would be recommended that it be eliminated from the college curriculum unless brought up to the
nursing standards (ibid., February 10, 1939, p. 26).

[65]Program of Affiliation (1939), pp. 14-22. The applica-
tion-questionnaires for both kinds of nursing schools were
probably also constructed at this time although no mention of
them is made in the minutes. Copies of these forms show that
considerable information of a professional nature as well as
the regular academic data was required: e.g., clinical services and facilities and nursing agencies which provided supplementary educational experiences. Cf. OAF, "Questionnaire
for Colleges Conducting Curricula in Nursing" and "Questionnaire for Hospital Schools of Nursing" (mimeographed).

[66]Program of Affiliation (1939), p. 10.

[67]Ibid., pp. 10-14. While the nature of the final examinations of these institutions continued to be checked by the
Committee, individual student papers were no longer examined,
as was last reported in the ARR, 1937-1938, p. 84. In 1939-
1940 a special service was added for these affiliates: an Affiliation certificate or diploma to those students who had
successfully fulfilled the approved course requirements of the
affiliate; cf. "Report of the Chairman of the Committee on
Affiliation and Extension" (1939-1940), p. 2, and ibid., (1940-
1941), p. 2 (typescripts).

[68]By interview with Roy J. Deferrari, July 30, 1963.

[69]ACUA, MMCAE, January 20, 1939, pp. 23-24.

[70]Ibid., February 10, 1939, p. 26.

[71]ACUA, AF, Deferrari to Rev. Carroll F. Deady, Detroit, Mich., March 21, 1939.

[72]ACUA, RF, Joseph Corrigan to the "secondary schools," January 23, 1939.

[73]Ibid., Joseph Corrigan to "schools of nursing," January 23, 1939.

[74]ACUA, MMCAE, February 10, 1939, p. 31.

[75]ACUA, AF, Deferrari to "Dear Superintendent," February 27, 1939.

[76]Cf. ACUA, AF, Superintendents' folder for 1939.

[77]Ibid., Rev. Paul E. Campbell to Deferrari, March 31, 1939.

[78]Ibid., Msgr. John R. Hagan to Deferrari, March 24, 1939.

[79]Ibid., Rev. Edward J. Gorman to Deferrari, April 1, 1939.

[80]Ibid., Rev. David C. Gildea to Deferrari, June 30, 1939.

[81]ACUA, MMCAE, October 14, 1938, p. 19.

[82]Bulletin for Institutions of Higher Learning, I (January, 1939), 1.

[83]Cf. Bulletin for Institutions of Higher Learning, I-III (January, 1939-April, 1941); Bulletin for Secondary Schools, I-III (January, 1939-April, 1941); Bulletin for Schools of Nursing (March, 1939-April, 1941). The bulletin format was a simple one: six pages of typescript, two folds, reproduced by the off-set method. The journals used were among the best for each level of education: e.g., Bulletin of the Association of American Colleges, Educational Record, Junior College Journal, Journal of Higher Education, Secondary Education, North Central Association Quarterly, School Review, Journal of Religious Education, Clearing House, Catholic Educational Review, Bulletin of the Department of Secondary-School Principals, Public Health Nursing, Hospitals, American Journal of Nursing, and American Journal of Public Health. Abstracts of articles by such well-known authors as Robert M. Hutchins, Harold L. Ickes, Guy Snavely, Norman Foerster, and others appeared regularly. Topics discussed were of a wide range, philosophical and practical, covering varying

aspects of educational work for the several kinds of affiliated institutions. Editorial comment was frequent and personalized in terms of Catholic education needs, and Affiliation announcements and original articles appeared with some regularity.

[84]OAF, "A Report of the 1939 Objective Examination Testing Program" (mimeographed), p. 1.

[85]Cf. OAF, Form A Battery (1939).

[86]ACUA, AF, Deferrari to McCormick, March 1, 1939.

[87]OAF, "A Report of the 1939. . . Testing Program," pp. 2, 14.

[88]Ibid. Gratification was justified by the fact that of the 107 then affiliated schools 101 voluntarily used the new tests. The actual drop in the number of tests taken in 1939 as compared to 1938 (17, 304) is also less significant in view of the following: the 1939 program covered 13 test fields of which a diploma candidate (optional) had to pass tests in only six prescribed fields over the four years of high school; under the old plan, some 50 different tests were issued annually, with all students required to take tests in all their prescribed courses -- which could run as high as 15-16 tests over the four-year period. Cf. Appendix D.

[89]Ibid., p. 7. This report is a sixteen page, mimeographed document consisting of a series of tables and a descriptive analysis of the nature and purposes of the tests. The tables presented "the mean scores in each of the thirteen subjects for each school and for all schools combined." Each school was listed by a code number only, making possible an impersonal comparison of its achievement with that of the other schools. The descriptive material was not entirely favorable to all aspects of the tests. For example, the religion test was admittedly too easy and lacking in sufficient comprehensiveness. In other cases, weaknesses in student achievement were pointed out and recommendations for improved teaching were made accordingly (pp. 7-15). A special table giving the percentile curve for the distribution of scores earned on the chemistry test was also included (p. 16).

[90]In 1940, there were 5,936 tests and 510 diplomas distributed; in 1941, 6,425 tests and 566 diplomas; OAF, "Report of the Chairman. . ." (1939-1940), p. 2; ibid. (1940-

1941), p. 2 (typescripts).

[91]ACUA, AF, Harriman to "Dear Registrar," March 1, 1939.

[92]Ibid., "Conference of Registrars of Affiliated Colleges" (mimeographed program). To encourage attendance, costs were kept at a minimum: accommodations were provided for the night of August 12th for one dollar and all delegates were the guests of the University at lunch on Sunday.

[93]OAF, "Report of the Chairman. . ." (1939-1940), p. 3.

[94]Ibid., p. 1.

[95]Ibid., (1938-1939), p. 1.

[96]ACUA, MMCAE, October 18, 1938, p. 18.

[97]Ibid., January 20, 1939, p. 25.

[98]Ibid., p. 24.

[99]Ibid., March 17, 1939, p. 29.

[100]Ibid., March 29, 1939, p. 30.

[101]Ibid., October 28, 1938, p. 20; December 2, 1938, p. 22; March 17, 1939, p. 29.

[102]Ibid., May 19, 1939, p. 32; June 2, 1939, p. 33.

[103]OAF, "Report of the Chairman. . ." (1938-1939), p. 1.

[104]ARR, 1937-1938, p. 84.

[105]OAF, "Report of the Chairman. . ." (1938-1939), p. 1.

[106]Ibid.

[107]Ibid. (1939-1940), p. 1. The number of junior colleges remained the same, probably because the junior college movement was not as yet actively supported by Catholic educators and there were comparatively few within the Catholic system. Among the novitiate high schools there was a drop of five, but this also was in keeping with the general Catholic educational scene. The growing practice of the sisterhoods to require a high school education of their applicants was gradually causing these schools to go out of existence. This trend continued until the few remaining affiliates of this group were absorbed in 1950-1951 by the regular high school list; ibid. (1950-1951), p. 1.

[108]Ibid. (1940-1941), p. 1. Steady growth has continued without interruption to the present time, with a total of 717 affiliates reported at the end of 1962-1963; ibid. (1962-1963), p. 2.

CONCLUSION

The concept of affiliation as a function of The Catholic University of America had its roots in the very foundation of the University itself. In an effort to complete and strengthen the emerging Catholic educational system of the United States, the Fathers of the Third Plenary Council of Baltimore, under Pope Leo XIII, not only established in 1884 a national Catholic pontifical university as the capstone of American Catholic education, but also gave to it the obligation and the authority to provide direct assistance to the other Catholic educational institutions of the country. Through a scheme of affiliation, which was to be unprejudicial to the autonomy of the affiliating seminary, college or school, the University was to promote and guide the unification and advancement of all branches of the system. To this end and to the general cause of Catholic education, the first three Rectors of the University were firmly dedicated. Despite early and often grave internal University developmental problems, each made a substantial contribution to educational unification under the central leadership of the University. Major initial efforts included the affiliation of theological curricula, the establishing of neighboring houses of study, and the organization of a national Catholic Educational Association.

By the beginning of the fourth rectorship in 1909, the urgency of the problems of unity, articulation, and standardization was generally recognized in Catholic educational circles as were the dangers in seeking solutions outside the Catholic system. It was in answer to this state of affairs that Dr. Thomas E. Shields, collaborating with Dr. Edward A. Pace and supported by the Rector, Thomas J. Shahan, led a direct and comprehensive attack on those factors which tended to undermine the Catholic character of the system: the training of Catholic school teachers under non-Catholic auspices, the use of secular textbooks and pedagogical literature, and the growing tendency toward the affiliating of Catholic schools

with state and other secular colleges and universities. Thus,
to stem the latter the Shields' plan of Affiliation of High
Schools and Colleges was approved by the University's Board
of Trustees on April 17, 1912.

The Shields' plan of Affiliation was basically a program
of standardization, the first under Catholic auspices in the
United States. Its emphasis, however, remained on institutional independence and initiative rather than on rigid uniformity, and on the translating of fundamental Catholic principles
into sound and up-to-date pedagogical practices, thus giving
it an objective beyond that of mere recognition. While its
standards and procedures were set realistically within reach
of those seeking academic approval, yet in application the
plan provided for the progressive qualitative development of
programs, courses, faculty, instruction, and resources. To
this far-seeing and far-reaching approach and to Dr. Shields
own greatness of spirit and abounding energy was due the
early success of Affiliation. By centering his standardization
techniques on the middle school and defining clearly the high
school's program and objectives, he sought to provide goals
at the same time for the Catholic elementary school and a
point of departure for the Catholic college. Testing became
an important sanction as a means both to raise and to maintain
institutional and classroom standards within the Catholic high
school.

With Dr. Shields' untimely death in 1921, the original
Affiliation program was carried on by his faithful disciples.
The pioneering work of standardization in the Catholic field,
however, had been accomplished, and the scope and purpose
of each level of Catholic education had been clarified. These
old problems were being steadily replaced by newer ones
dealing with state and regional accreditation and the maintaining of maximum academic efficiency. Failure to adjust the
Affiliation process to cope with these new needs and to
modernize its structural procedures in keeping with new
evaluative trends and techniques brought its effectiveness,
especially in relation to high school testing, into question by
the end of the 1920's.

The University, although slow and cautious to act on the

complex academic and financial problems involved, gave considerable attention to the matter in the 1930's. Through
Rectors James Hugh Ryan and Joseph M. Corrigan, the matter
was finally brought to a head in the academic year 1937-1938.
At that time a new Committee on Affiliation and Extension was
appointed under the chairmanship of Dr. Roy J. Deferrari.
Like Dr. Shields, Dr. Deferrari's background and knowledge
of current educational and accreditation conditions and his
driving energy gave the new Committee the direction and
leadership needed to bring about a complete reorganization of
Affiliation. The old concept of standardization was discarded
and replaced by one strictly of service. The prime criterion
was capability and willingness on the part of the affiliate's
administrators to use University Affiliation to promote the
development of their institution as a Catholic educational endeavor and thus, at the same time, to seek systematically
for whatever accreditation by the secular agencies as was
deemed advisable. Tied directly to this idea of assistance
in securing accreditation was the inspection and evaluation
technique through which Affiliation was to function. Not only
was the original and basic principle of institutional autonomy
to be fully respected under the new process, but maximum
flexibility was to be attained through adapting the process to
the needs of each affiliate and by offering a variety of services
to meet a variety of educational needs. High school testing
became merely one of these services; bulletins and conferences on educational problems were initiated early under the
new plan, and other services were promised as their desirability became evident. The 1938 and 1939 years were also
productive in widening the scope of Affiliation to include junior
colleges, teacher training schools, and schools of nursing as
well as the four-year general college and the regular and novitiate high schools. Minor seminaries and the philosophy divisions of major seminaries were absorbed within these appropriate academic classifications.

The first efforts of the Committee in promoting and
implementing the new plan met with immediate, though modest
success in the form of a favorable response by Catholic educators. By the time that the total reorganization of Affiliation

had been completed in 1939, the first swing upward in the
number of new affiliates was evident, and the following year's
statistics confirmed that the optimism of the University to
bring about a renewal of the values of Affiliation was not ill-
founded. As the intervening years have shown, once again the
Catholic University through its Program of Affiliation was
prepared to fulfill the early hopes of its founding Fathers:
dedicated to the Christian educational ideal, a flexible and cooperative program to assist realistically and practically other
Catholic schools and colleges to meet the contemporary problems of American education.

APPENDIX A

THE 1912 PLAN OF AFFILIATION

For the Affiliation of Colleges and High Schools to the University*

Pope Leo XIII, the founder of the Catholic University, says in his Apostolic Letter, "Magna Nobis Gaudia, " of March 7, 1887 [sic]: "We exhort you all that you shall take care to affiliate with your university, your seminaries, colleges, and other Catholic institutions according to the plan suggested in the Constitutions, in such a manner as not to destroy their autonomy. "

The Pope in these words seems to have realized what has since become an urgent need in our educational system and to have anticipated a movement that is now quite general among our teaching communities. The establishment of the Schools of Philosophy, Letters and Science, offering courses of special interest and utility to lay students, naturally suggested some sort of articulation between the University and the colleges. On the other hand, the Sisters who attended the first session of the University Summer School in 1911, have frequently expressed their desire for affiliation with the University in preference to any arrangement that might be offered by other universities, and some of our institutions have already applied for affiliation.

In view of these facts, and in order to establish a standard for our colleges and schools, as well as to secure due recognition for the institutions that are doing good work, the Trustees of the University, at their meeting on April 17, prescribed the following conditions for affiliation:

*AHSC (1912), pp. [i-iv] .

Affiliation of Colleges

Any Catholic college may be affiliated to the University on these conditions:

1. The college must include at least seven chairs or departments and each chair or department must be under the separate direction of at least one professor or instructor.
2. Every instructor in the faculty must have at least the A.B. degree from a college of recognized standing, and every head of a department must have at least an M.A. degree from a college in good standing.
3. The equipment of the college in libraries and laboratories must be sufficient to secure effective work in the branches offered.
4. The college must require for entrance the completion of a four years' successful course in an accredited secondary school (high school), or the passing of entrance examinations on the subjects required in the curriculum of accredited secondary schools.
5. The college course must include 2,160 hours of class work distributed over four years. Two hours of laboratory work are to be regarded as equivalent to one hour of class work.

Affiliation of High Schools

Any Catholic high school may be affiliated on the following conditions:

1. The high school must give a course extending over four years and including a total of 15 units, of which at least three must be devoted to English and three to some other one subject.
Meaning of unit. A subject, e.g., English, pursued four or five hours a week for a school year of from 36 to 40 weeks, constitutes a unit.
2. The subjects required with their respective values are: Religion, 2 units; English, 3 units; some other language,

2 units; mathematics, 2 units; social science (including history), 1 unit; natural science, 1 unit. Four units to be elective. They must be selected in such a way, however, as to give another course of 3 units; i.e., one or more units must be advanced work in one of the subjects, other than English, enumerated above. Where Latin is to be pusued [sic] in college, at least 2 units of Latin must be taken in the high school.

3. Reasons for this curriculum:

(a) The high school has two functions: one is to give an education to students who will not go beyond the high school, the other is to give a proper preparation to students who will go to college. Hence some subjects are necessary for both classes of students, while other subjects are necessary for only the one or the other class. All students need: Religion, English, mathematics, and a second language in addition to English. The student going on to college with a view to theology or law will need Latin, Greek and modern language, together with social science; if he contemplates the study of medicine he will need more in the line of natural science, e.g., biology and chemistry. The student who goes no farther than the high school will need more in the way of mathematics, modern languages, economics and the vocational subjects.

(b) The proposed curriculum, by requiring advanced work in at least two subjects, prevents the smattering which gives the student a little of many things and not much of any thing.

(c) At the same time sufficient latitude is allowed to enable the student to determine his vocation and to begin his preparation for it before he leaves the high school.

(d) The curriculum does not prescribe Latin for four years; hence a student, who after one or two years in the high school, may discover a vocation for a career in which Latin is specially required, e.g., the priesthood, can, without loss of time, take up

Latin, say in the third and fourth years, and complete his study of that language during his four
years at college.

Execution of the Plan of Affiliation

With these standards of high school and college in view,
the University will proceed as follows in affiliating any institution:

1. The school or college applying for affiliation shall
submit to the University, on blanks supplied by the University,
a detailed statement of its curriculum and equipment and of the
qualifications of its professors or instructors.

2. If this statement is satisfactory it shall be verified by
personal inspection through some person delegated by the University for that purpose.

3. Should this report be favorable, the institution in
question shall be placed on the list of affiliated institutions.

4. The University shall then send to the institution an
assignment of the matter for each subject offered in the curriculum of the institution and, at the end of the year, a set of
examination questions sealed and to be opened in the class
when assembled for examination. The papers are then to be
sealed in the presence of the class and forwarded to the University, where they will be examined and marked according to
a certain scale.

5. All students who successfully pass the examinations
held during the four years in the high school shall be admitted
without further examination to any college affiliated by the
University. All students who successfully pass the examinations held during the four years in college shall be admitted,
without further examination, into the courses in the University
leading to the higher degrees. They must, however, reside
in colleges approved by the University.

6. If it should appear, either from the statement submitted or from inspection, that some modification is needed in
order to comply with the requirements, the institution shall be
placed on the list of tentative affiliation and, when the require-

ment is fulfilled, the institution shall be placed on the list of permanent affiliation.

7. In all cases, either of permanent or of tentative affiliation, a record, as shown by examination papers, shall be kept by the University of the work done each year by each student in each affiliated institution, and a copy of this record shall be sent to the institution in which the student resides and to the high school or college from which the students graduated. Should it appear from such records that the work of an institution is unsatisfactory, the University shall endeavor to discover the cause of the defect and to indicate the remedy.

APPENDIX B

THE 1939 PLAN OF AFFILIATION

Principles and Standards for Affiliating Institutions of
Higher Education*

I. INTRODUCTION

In establishing and maintaining the plan of affiliation,
the University authorities have especially in mind the first
part of Article 71, Section 2, of the Statutes of the University
as approved by the Sacred Congregation of Seminaries and
Universities. This article reads: "Colleges, Seminaries,
and other Catholic Institutions may, without prejudice to their
autonomy, be affiliated to the University by the authority of
the Rector and the Academic Senate, upon the fulfillment of
conditions to be prescribed by said Rector and Senate."

It should be understood, from the outset, that the University authorities do not regard "affiliation" as the equivalent of "accreditation." Certain minmum requirements are
of course necessary for the proper maintenance of an institution of higher education, but the main emphasis will be placed
on the administrators' understanding of the purpose of their
foundation as a Catholic institution and on their zeal and on the
resources at their command to enable their institution to attain
the aims proposed. Neither is it the wish of the University
authorities to "Standardize" in the usual sense of the term.
It is understood that every Catholic institution of higher education will have many general aims and principles in common
with other similar Catholic institutions. It is expected that in
addition to these general aims and principles, each Catholic
institution of higher education will have special objectives
peculiar to itself and these the University authorities would
preserve and assist the institution in question to achieve.

*OAF, 1938 typescript.

In the affiliation of an institution, attention will be centered on the manner in which the institution as a Catholic institution performs its task of instruction as a whole. Consideration of course must be given to matters which have an important bearing on instructional efficiency such as the financial resources; buildings and grounds; the organization of the curriculum; the administration; the library; laboratories; admission policy; graduation requirements; student activities, and faculty competence.

II. PRINCIPLES AND STANDARDS

1. <u>Purpose</u>. It is essential that an institution seeking affiliation make a public statement of its general and special aims. This must give evidence of having been carefully thought out and must be thoroughly understood by all those responsible in any way for the direction of the institution. The institution must show, by its whole organization and activities, that it is directed toward these objectives.

2. <u>Admissions</u>. The general practice of an institution in the admission of students is a reliable index of its academic character. Notice will be taken of the extent to which a system of selective admission is used and how carefully announced entrance requirements are observed. The admission of patently unqualified students or of any large number of special or non-matriculated or probationary students will be considered as evidence of unsound admission practice.

3. <u>Faculty</u>. In judging the competence of a faculty, no specific and rigid standards will be followed. The actual training of the members of the staff, i.e., the courses which they have pursued, and the institutions in which these courses were successfully completed, is of more importance than the degrees themselves. Successful experience and sound classroom teaching are of great importance. Intellectual alertness as shown by scholarly productions and by participation in the activities of learned societies will also be considered. In general, however, it is highly desirable that members of a college faculty possess nothing less than a doctor's degree from a recognized graduate school or have the real equivalent in training.

4. Instruction. The quality of instruction will be evaluated only in part by observation. The institution will be expected to furnish objective evidence through the achievement of its students in standardized tests and the quality of the work of its graduates in leading graduate, professional and research institutions. Special attention will be paid to the success which the institution is attaining in achieving its objectives as shown by the results of instruction.

5. Curriculum. It is understood that the curriculum will form a unit so organized as to achieve best the avowed aims of the institution and to meet the needs of the student today. The curriculum should be flexible enough for adaptation to the talents and interests of the student without failing of the objectives of the institution as a whole. Furthermore, care should be taken in a college of liberal arts not to permit an over-emphasis in the curriculum on professional or preprofessional studies. Specialized vocational curricula should be undertaken with caution.

Ordinarily it is expected that at least two full time faculty members will devote all their time to work in a single department in which major work is offered. At least one of the two should be of professorial rank and should have the doctor's degree or its equivalent.

The size of the classes and the teaching load of the individual members of the faculty should be such as to promote effective teaching and at the same time not to interfere with productive scholarship.

6. Library. The library is of course the centre of any institution of higher education. The main consideration is to what extent the collection of books supports the program of the college, and to what extent the teaching staff and the students make use of it. It is understood that a professionally trained librarian will be in charge who will be asked to furnish accurate information on these and other matters pertaining to the library. The librarian should have faculty rank and should have wide discretion in the expenditure of funds for the library.

Important factors in the administration of the library which will be taken into account are: Its general organization, the policies relative to the accessioning and discarding of books, the accessibility and usefulness of the book collection, the amount and the apportionment of money appropriated for library purposes.

7. Laboratories. Adequate laboratory space and scientific equipment for the teaching of the sciences as well as for independent studies on the part of the teachers are essential. The Laboratories must be under the control of teachers genuinely interested in the advancement of science, and trained in the methods and spirit of scientific research.

8. Graduation. No less than 120 or more than 135 semester hours of work should be required for the bachelor's degree. It is understood that all this work will be of college grade, implying at least two hours of private study for every hour of class. Qualitative as well as quantitative standards for graduation are strongly recommended. All institutions applying for affiliation will be expected to state their residence requirements and the limit set on the amount of credit applicable toward a degree for extra-mural courses and for work by correspondence. Strict conformity is expected in the carrying out of the announced requirements for graduation.

9. The Catalogue. The catalogue is an official statement of the purpose of the institution. It should not contain material designed primarily to secure publicity. Such material may be published separately. It should be written in clear, concise English, and should be carefully edited.

The catalogue should contain at least the following: (1) The names of all the faculty members showing degrees earned in course, the institutions granting them and the dates when granted. (2) Entrance requirements. (3) Graduation requirements. (4) Brief descriptions of all courses to be offered during the year for which the catalogue is issued. Courses given in rotation should be definitely indicated as such. The listing of any large number of courses to be given on demand is not approved. Whenever possible each department should announce the names of all its members, and indicate the instructors of each course offered.

An annual roster of students should be published either as a part of the catalogue or separately.

10. Professional Courses. Professional courses offered

by a college seeking affiliation should be so conducted as to merit the approval of the particular professional group. In a college of liberal arts, professional courses should not be emphasized to such an extent that they enroll the majority of the student body or require for their maintenance a disproportionate share of available funds.

11. Graduate Work. Graduate instruction should be offered only by institutions properly qualified to do so. When offered they should be separately organized, separately administered, and separately taught. Hours of credit accumulated in an undergraduate curriculum, beyond the requirements of the bachelor's degree are not regarded as of graduate character.

12. Student Activities. Religious, cultural and social activities play an important role in the education of college students. It is expected, however, that these activities will be carefully planned with reference to the objectives of the college, and will be assigned proper and effective part in the general program. Over emphasis on any of these activities is not approved.

13. Administration. A sound academic program can be effectively carried out only if it is supported by an efficient administration. Hence, in affiliation, officers' understanding of the aims and purposes of their institution, and the efforts they are making to realize them will be given careful consideration.

The functions of trustees, faculty members and administrative officers should be clearly defined, and the Committee will require evidence of the careful performance of their respective duties.

14. Finances. The Committee does not specify detailed requirements in the matter of resources and endowment. It does, however, look for an income sufficient to carry out the professed program of the institution without embarrassment. Furthermore it believes that no satisfactory college program can long be sustained without a substantial income over and above that realized from student fees. The Committee will look at least for the definite planning of such a source of income. Attention will be given also to the manner in which the

income is expended, specifically, what proportion is assigned
to instruction, administration, maintenance, equipment and
supplies, library and student activities. It is understood that
the business management of the institution will be in the hands
of a properly qualified officer.

15. Buildings and Grounds. The physical plant of an institution must be adequate for the attainment of the institution's
objectives. Specifically, by its beauty it should contribute a
good share to the general programs. The campus and buildings should also be designed to promote the health, the recre-
ation, and the general welfare of faculty and students.

16. The Junior College. The general principles outlined above are applicable also to the Junior College, allowance
being made for the shorter curriculum and the more elementary nature of the program.

N.B. After all available information has been
assembled by means of the Questionnaire and the
visitation and inspection, the institution's fitness
to be affiliated will be determined by the total
effect upon the Committee.

Principles and Standards for Affiliating Secondary Schools*

I. INTRODUCTION

In establishing and maintaining the plan of affiliation,
the University authorities have especially in mind that part of
Article 71, Section 2, of the Statutes of the University as approved by the Sacred Congregation of Seminaries and Universities, which reads: "Colleges, Seminaries, and other
Catholic institutions may, without prejudice to their autonomy,
be affiliated to the University by the authority of the Rector
and the Academic Senate, upon the fulfillment of conditions to
be prescribed by said Rector and Senate."

It must be understood from the outset that the University
authorities do not regard "affiliation" as the equivalent of
"accreditation." Some requirements must, of course, be
laid down to insure a certain minimum of excellence for a

*OAF, 1938 typescript.

secondary school, but the main emphasis will be placed on the administrators' understanding of the purpose of their institution as a Catholic secondary school and their eagerness and resources for developing and improving their institution as a Catholic secondary school. Neither is it the wish of the University authorities to "standardize" in the usual sense of the term. It is understood that every Catholic secondary school will have many general aims and principles in common with other Catholic secondary schools. It is expected that in addition to these general aims and principles, every Catholic secondary school will have certain worthy purposes peculiar to itself. It will be the aim of affiliation to preserve and assist the secondary school in achieving them.

In the process of affiliation, emphasis will be placed on the manner in which the institution as a Catholic secondary school performs its task of instruction as a whole. Attention, however, must be given to matters which have an important bearing on instructional efficiency such as the grounds and buildings, the curriculum, the administration, the library, the laboratories, the graduation requirements, and faculty competence.

II. PRINCIPLES AND STANDARDS

1. Organization and Administration. A school to be affiliated must require for graduation the completion of a four-year secondary school course. A unit is a year's work in one subject requiring about one-fourth of the student's time, and includes not less than 120 sixty-minute hours of prepared classroom work. The minimum length of a recitation period should be forty minutes exclusive of time used in the changing of classes or teachers. A school year of at least thirty-six weeks is recommended. Exception to these requirements will be permitted only when the school can definitely show that its work is efficient and satisfactory under other conditions.

The general intellectual and moral level of a school, the efficiency of instruction, the success with which habits of thought and study are acquired are fundamental factors in determining the worthiness of a school to be affiliated. A school will be evaluated in these matters by a competent and

sympathetic inspection and by the quality of the work of graduates in institutions of higher education.

A sufficiently large number of qualified teachers will be
required to meet adequately the task of giving the instruction
offered. A staff equivalent to at least four full-time teachers
must be maintained.

2. Preparation of Teachers. The preparation of a
teacher of academic subjects should be the completion of a
four year course in a college affiliated with the Catholic University of America or of equal standing. Teachers without
this training will be given consideration by reason of successful teaching experience, provided that at least three-fourths
of the teachers of academic subjects meet this requirement.
Teachers must have had either professional training or
successful teaching experience.

In the case of lay teachers, it is expected that salaries
will be paid sufficient to secure teachers with required qualifications.

3. Teaching Load. A teacher should not teach more
than five periods daily. Any school requiring that a teacher
conduct more than six teaching periods daily, or carry a daily
teaching load of more than 150 pupil-periods, must present
convincing evidence of the wisdom and success of such action.
A double period of laboratory work or of study room supervision is considered as the equivalent of one period of teaching.

The Committee recommends thirty as the maximum
number of pupils per class. No school with an excessive number of pupils per class will be affiliated.

4. Curriculum. The Committee recommends that
every affiliated school offer units in Religion, English, Mathematics, Foreign Languages (Latin is strongly recommended),
Social and Natural Sciences, Practical and Fine Arts, and
Physical Education.

5. Physical Equipment. The location, building, and
equipment shall be such as to insure proper conditions of
health for teachers and pupils. The laboratories and library
shall be adequate to meet the needs of the curriculum offered.

6. Final Evaluation of School. The Committee is pri-

marily concerned with the so-called college-preparatory
secondary school, although it does not question the value of
such training for students who are not preparing for college.
Consequently it will consider of prime importance the records
of graduates of a secondary school in institutions of higher
education. The other requirements of Standard 1 will also be
given special consideration. The final evaluation of a school,
however, will be determined by the combined effect on the
Committee of the report of the inspector and the information
obtained from the questionnaire submitted by the school.

7. Revision of List of Affiliated Schools. A revised
list of affiliated schools will be published annually. The
Committee reserves the right to require a report from a
school annually or as often as it sees fit, and to drop a school
from the list at any time for the violation of any standard.

8. Certificates. A Certificate of Affiliation will be issued to any affiliated school upon application to the Chairman
of the Committee and the payment of a fee of two dollars.

A Secondary School Diploma will also be issued by the
University to those students in the senior class who pass
successfully comprehensive written examinations in six subjects, namely Religion, English, Mathematics, a foreign language, History, and a natural science. More detailed information regarding these examinations may be obtained on application to the Chairman of the Committee.

9. Fees. When a school applies for affiliation it must
deposit with the Chairman of the Committee a fee of ten dollars
($10.00). This fee includes the annual fee for the first year.
All schools retaining their affiliation with the University must
pay an annual fee of five dollars ($5.00), payable on January
1st. of each year. Before an inspection is made, the school
must agree to pay the inspector's fee of fifteen dollars
($15.00) and his traveling expenses. On fees for certificates,
see Section 8 above.

TABLE SHOWING NUMBER OF AFFILIATES BY ACADEMIC CLASSIFICATIONS, 1913-1939*

End of Academic Year	High Schools	Novitiate H.S.	Colleges	Junior Colleges	T.Tr. Instit.	Nursing Schools
1912-1913	33	--	3	--	--	--
1913-1914	70	--	4	--	--	--
1914-1915	89	--	8	--	--	--
1915-1916	112	--	10	--	--	--
1916-1917	127	--	10	--	--	--
1917-1918	145	--	10	--	--	--
1918-1919	155	--	13	--	--	--
1919-1920	176	--	13	--	--	--
1920-1921	177	46	15	--	--	--
1921-1922	198	58	18	--	--	--
1922-1923	203	60	18	--	--	--
1923-1924	212	55	20	--	--	--
1924-1925	227	53	22	--	--	--
1925-1926	229	52	23	--	--	--
1926-1927	228	55	25	--	--	--
1927-1928	229	54	25	--	--	--
1928-1929	225	55	26	--	--	--
1929-1930	217	53	27	--	--	--
1930-1931**						
1931-1932	200	51	29	--	--	--
1932-1933**						
1933-1934	201	52	32	--	--	--
1934-1935	202	54	33	--	--	--
1935-1936	182	53	35	--	--	--
1936-1937**						
1937-1938	131	44	40	--	--	--
1938-1939	107	44	54	6	6	3

*These figures were collected from the annual lists of affiliated high schools and colleges as given in the Year Book of the Catholic University of America, 1913-1914 through 1922-1923 and in General Information, 1923-1924 through 1939-1940.

**The annual list for these years was not available.

APPENDIX D

TABLE SHOWING NUMBER OF HIGH SCHOOL TESTS AND CERTIFICATES DISTRIBUTED FROM 1913-1939*

Academic Year	Tests	Certificates
1912-1913	1,318	--
1913-1914	4,699	--
1914-1915	9,093	--
1915-1916	13,662	--
1916-1917	17,116	--
1917-1918	22,114	442
1918-1919	26,479	385
1919-1920	31,907	469
1920-1921	37,359	719
1921-1922	43,770	1039
1922-1923	48,265	1222
1923-1924	61,214	1829
1924-1925	61,746	1959
1925-1926	61,406	2065
1926-1927	60,404	1897
1927-1928	53,880	1644
1928-1929	50,177	1497
1929-1930	47,813	1437
1930-1931	41,531	1392
1931-1932	34,982	1233
1932-1933	28,332	1101
1933-1934	23,539	932
1934-1935	19,771	752
1935-1936	19,641	582
1936-1937**		
1937-1938	17,304	629
1938-1939	5,072	489

*These figures were collected from the Report on Affiliated High Schools (1920), the Annual Report of the Rector, 1923-1924 through 1937-1938, and "A Report of the 1939 Objective Testing Program" (OAF, mimeographed).

**Data were not given for 1936-1937.

BIBLIOGRAPHY

Manuscript Sources

Archives of The Catholic University of America. Academic
Senate Files to 1907; Affiliation Files, General 1933-
1949; Board of Trustees Exhibits of Meetings, 1887-
1929; Catholic Sisters College, Correspondence 1909-
1920; Keane, John J., "Chronicles of Catholic University
of America from 1885"; Minutes of the Meetings of the
Board of Trustees, 1885-1933; Minutes of the Meetings
of the Committee on Affiliation and Extension, 1938-
1945; Pace's Papers; Rector's Files, Correspondence
1903-1947; Vice Rector's Files, 1916-1934.

Office of Affiliation Files. Reports of the Committee on
Affiliation and Extension, 1938-1940; Test Files, 1939-
1940; Bulletin Files, 1939-1940; miscellaneous correspondence and material.

Printed Sources

Affiliation of High Schools and Colleges, 1913-1914.

Affiliation of High Schools and Colleges, 1914.

Affiliation of High Schools and Colleges, 1916.

Affiliation of High Schools and Colleges, 1917.

Affiliation of High Schools and Colleges, 1919.

Affiliation of High Schools and Colleges, 1920.

Affiliation of High Schools and Colleges, 1922. Washington.

Affiliation of High Schools and Colleges, 1923. Washington.

Affiliation of High Schools and Colleges, 1924. Washington.

Affiliation of High Schools and Colleges, 1926.

Affiliation of High Schools and Colleges, 1928.

Affiliation of High Schools and Colleges, 1930.

Affiliation of High Schools and Colleges, 1933.

Affiliation of High Schools and Colleges, 1934.

Affiliation of High Schools and Colleges, 1936.

Affiliation of High Schools and Colleges, 1939. Washington:
    Catholic University of America Press, 1939.

An Appeal to the Catholics of the United States in Behalf of the
    University which the Late Council of Baltimore Resolved
    to Create. New York: Catholic Publications Society
    Co., 1885.

Annual Report of the Rector of The Catholic University of
    America Including Report of the Treasurer, June 30,
    1923. Washington, October, 1923.

(Thirty-fifth) Annual Report of the Rector, covering the Aca-
    demic Year June 30, 1923, to June 30, 1924. Washington,
    October, 1924.

(Thirty-sixth) Annual Report of the Rector, covering the Aca-
    demic Year June 30, 1924, to June 30, 1925. Washington,
    October, 1925.

(Thirty-seventh) Annual Report of the Rector, covering the
    Academic Year June 30, 1925, to June 30, 1926.
    Washington, September, 1926.

(Thirty-eighth) Annual Report of the Rector, covering the
    Academic Year June 30, 1926, to June 30, 1927.
    Washington, September, 1927.

(Thirty-ninth) Annual Report of the Rector, covering the Aca-
    demic Year June 30, 1927, to June 30, 1928. Washington,
    September, 1928.

Annual Reports of the Rector and Treasurer to the Trustees
    with Reports of Deans and Other University Officials
    for the Year Ending June 30, 1929. Washington,
    October, 1929.

Annual Reports of the Rector and Treasurer to the Trustees
    with Reports of Deans and Other University Officials
    for the Year Ending June 30, 1930. Washington,
    October, 1930.

Annual Reports of the Rector and Treasurer to the Trustees
    with Reports of Deans and Other University Officials
    for the Year Ending June 30, 1931. Washington,
    October, 1931.

Annual Reports of the Rector and Treasurer to the Trustees
    with Reports of Deans and Other University Officials
    for the Year Ending June 30, 1932. Washington,
    October, 1932.

Annual Reports of the Rector and Treasurer to the Trustees
    with Reports of Deans and Other University Officials
    for the Year Ending June 30, 1933. Washington,
    October, 1933.

Annual Reports of the Rector and Treasurer to the Trustees
    with Reports of Deans and Other University Officials
    for the Year Ending June 30, 1934. Washington,
    October 31, 1934.

Annual Reports of the Rector and Treasurer to the Trustees

with Reports of Deans and Other University Officials
for the Year Ending June 30, 1935. Washington,
October 31, 1935.

Annual Reports of the Rector and Treasurer to the Trustees
with Reports of Deans and Other University Officials
for the Year Ending June 30, 1936. Washington,
October 15, 1936.

Annual Reports of the Rector and Treasurer to the Trustees
with Reports of Deans and Other University Officials
for the Year Ending June 30, 1937. Washington,
October 30, 1937.

Annual Reports of the Rector and Treasurer to the Trustees
with Reports of Deans and Other University Officials
for the Year Ending June 30, 1938. Washington,
October 31, 1938.

The Catholic Sisters College at The Catholic University of
America: Year Book, 1914-1915. Washington, 1914.

The Catholic Sisters College at The Catholic University of
America: Year Book, 1917-1918. Washington, 1917.

The Catholic Sisters College at The Catholic University of
America: Year Book, 1918-1919. Washington, 1918.

The Catholic University of America: General Information,
1923-1924. Washington, 1923.

The Catholic University of America: General Information,
1924-1925. Washington, 1924.

The Catholic University of America: General Information,
1925-1926. Washington, 1925.

The Catholic University of America: General Information,
1926-1927. Washington, 1926.

The Catholic University of America: General Information, 1927-1928. Washington, 1927.

The Catholic University of America: General Information, 1928-1929. Washington, 1928.

The Catholic University of America: General Information, 1929-1930. Washington, 1929.

The Catholic University of America: General Information, 1930-1931. Washington, 1930.

The Catholic University of America: General Information, 1932-1933. Washington, 1932.

The Catholic University of America: General Information, 1933-1934. Washington, 1933.

The Catholic University of America: General Information, 1934-1935. Washington, 1934.

The Catholic University of America: General Information, 1935-1936. Washington, 1935.

The Catholic University of America: General Information, 1936-1937. Washington, 1936.

The Catholic University of America: General Information, 1938-1939. Washington, 1938.

The Catholic University of America: General Information, 1939-1940. Washington, 1939.

Constitutions of The Catholic University of America, translated from the Latin. Washington, n. d.

Courses of Study for Affiliated High Schools, 1912-1913.

Programs of Affiliation of The Catholic University of America.

Washington, 1960.

Report on Affiliation of High Schools. 1920.

The Sisters College Messenger, I (April, 1915).

The Sisters College Messenger, II (April, 1916).

The Statutes of The Catholic University of America. Washington: The Catholic University, 1937.

Year Book of The Catholic University of America, 1913-1914. Washington, 1913.

Year Book of The Catholic University of America, 1914-1915. Washington, 1914.

Year Book of The Catholic University of America, 1915-1916. Washington, 1915.

Year Book of The Catholic University of America, 1916-1917. Washington, 1916.

Year Book of The Catholic University of America, 1917-1918. Washington, 1917.

Year Book of The Catholic University of America, 1918-1919. Washington, 1918.

Year Book of The Catholic University of America, 1919-1920. Washington, 1919.

Year Book of The Catholic University of America, 1920-1921. Washington, 1920.

Year Book of The Catholic University of America, 1921-1922. Washington, 1921.

Year Book of The Catholic University of America, 1922-1923.

Washington, 1922.

Books

Ahern, Patrick Henry. The Catholic University of America, 1887-1896: The Rectorship of John J. Keane. Washington: The Catholic University of America Press, 1948.

Barry, Colman J., O.S.B. The Catholic University of America, 1903-1909: The Rectorship of Denis J. O'Connell. Washington: The Catholic University of America Press, 1950.

Burns, Rev. J. A., C.S.C. Catholic Education: A Study of Conditions. New York: Longmans, Green and Co., 1912.

_____. The Growth and Development of the Catholic School System in the United States. New York: Benziger Brothers, 1912.

Burns, V. Rev. J. A.; Kohlbrenner, Bernard J.; and Peterson, Most Rev. John B. A History of Catholic Education in the United States. New York: Benziger Brothers, 1937.

Deferrari, Roy J. Memoirs of The Catholic University of America, 1918-1960. Boston: Daughters of St. Paul, 1962.

Ellis, John Tracy. The Formative Years of The Catholic University of America. Washington: American Catholic Historical Association, 1946.

Hogan, Peter E., S.S.J. The Catholic University of America, 1896-1903: The Rectorship of Thomas J. Conaty. Washington: The Catholic University of America Press, 1949.

Maynard, Theodore. The Story of American Catholicism.

New York, Macmillan Co., 1951.

O'Dowd, Rev. James T. Standardization and Its Influence on Catholic Secondary Education in the United States. ("Catholic University of America, Educational Research Monographs," Vol. IX, No. 1.) Washington: Catholic Education Press, 1935.

Shields, Thomas Edward. The Education of Our Girls. New York: Benziger Brothers, 1907.

_____. The Making and the Unmaking of a Dullard. Washington: Catholic Education Press, 1909.

_____. Philosophy of Education. Washington: Catholic Education Press, 1921.

Ward, Justine. Thomas Edward Shields. New York: Charles Scribner's Sons, 1947.

Articles and Periodicals

"The Association of Catholic Colleges, Report of the First Annual Conference of the Association of Catholic Colleges of the United States, Chicago, April 12-13, 1899," Catholic University Bulletin, V (July, 1899), 357-362.

Bede, Brother. "The Aims and Purposes of Catholic Secondary Education, Cultural and Vocational: What Part Must the High School Take in Their Attainment," Catholic Educational Association Bulletin, VIII (November, 1911), 87-97.

Brown, Robert W. "The Organization of Catholic High Schools," Catholic Educational Review, I (May, 1911), 387-392.

Burns, James A., C.S.C. "A History of Catholic Parochial Schools in the United States," Catholic University

Bulletin, XIII (October, 1906), 434-452.

_____. "Report of the Committee on High Schools," Catholic
Educational Association Bulletin, VIII (November, 1911),
45-66.

"Cardinal Gibbons Sermon on the Occasion of the 'Silver
Jubilee of the Catholic University of America',"
Catholic Educational Review, IX (May, 1915), 385-395.

Cassidy, Francis P. "Catholic Education in the Third Plenary
Council of Baltimore," Catholic Historical Review,
XXXIV (January, 1949), 257-327.

"The Catholic Sisters College," Catholic Educational Review,
VII (May, 1914), 437-444.

"The Catholic University and Its Constitutions," The Catholic
World, XLIV (July, 1889), 427-432.

"Colleges and High Schools Affiliated with the University,"
Catholic Educational Review, V (May, 1913), 417-418;
VI (September, 1913), 181-182.

"Commencement Exercises, 1914," Catholic University
Bulletin, XX (October, 1914), 564-565.

Commission on American Citizenship. "Dr. Shields, a
Pioneer Catholic Educator," Catholic Action, XXII
(October, 1940), 9-10.

Conaty, Thomas J. "The Catholic College of the Twentieth
Century," Catholic University Bulletin, VII (July, 1901),
304-319.

_____. "The College Teacher," Catholic University Bulletin,
VI (July, 1900), 275-293.

" 'The Condition of Catholic Secondary Education in the United

States,' Report of the Advisory Board of the Executive Board of the Catholic Educational Association," Catholic Educational Review, X (October, 1915), 204-223.

Culemans, J. B. "A Plea for Diocesan School Superintendents," Catholic Educational Review, XI (January, 1916), 33-44.

Cummings, James E. "Pertinent Facts on Catholic Secondary Education," Catholic Educational Review, XXVIII October, 1930), 447-454.

"Current Events," Catholic Educational Review, III (May, 1912), 459.

Dean, James J., O.S.A. "The High School -- Its Relation to the Elementary School and to the College," Catholic Educational Association Bulletin, VIII (November, 1911), 74-81.

Deferrari, Roy J. "The Affiliation of Catholic Educational Institutions with The Catholic University of America," Catholic University of America Bulletin, XXVIII (October, 1960), 1ff.

_____. "Education and Accrediting Today," National Catholic Educational Association Bulletin, XXXVIII (August, 1941), 272-287.

_____. "Institutional Affiliation with the Catholic University of America," National Catholic Educational Association of America, XXXIX (August, 1942), 303-307.

"Educational Conference of Seminary Presidents," Catholic University Bulletin, IV, 397-405.

"For the Affiliation of Colleges and High Schools to the University," Catholic Educational Review, III (May, 1912), 445-449.

Garrigan, Rev. P. J. "The First Lustrum of the Catholic University," American Ecclesiastical Review, I (September, 1889), 338-347.

Gibbons, James Cardinal. "The Anthony Nicholas Brady Memorial: Address at Dedication on May 4, 1916," Catholic Educational Review, XII (June, 1916), 3-9.

Green, James F., O.S.A. "Catholic Education above the Grammar Grades," Catholic Educational Association Bulletin, VIII (November, 1911), 169-175.

Gorham, Joseph A. "Looking Back Fifty Years," Catholic Educational Review, LIX (March, 1961), 145-154.

[Hueser, Herman.] "Present Aspects of the Catholic University," American Ecclesiastical Review, I (August, 1889), 280-298.

Jeannette, Sister Mary, O.S.B. "Vocational Preparation of Youth in Catholic Schools," Catholic Educational Review, XVII (April, 1919), 211-221.

Johnson, George. "Ad Multos Annos," Catholic Educational Review, XXXI (November, 1933), 532-539.

_____. "Present Developments and Tendencies in the American High School," Catholic Educational Review, XX (February, 1922), 73-83.

_____. "Dedication," Catholic Educational Review, XXXVII (January, 1939), 3-9.

_____. "Fundamentals of Catholic Teacher Training," Catholic Educational Review, XXI (October, 1923), 449-460.

_____. "A Plan of Teacher Certification," Catholic Educational Review, XIX (September, 1921), 446-452.

_____. "Thomas E. Shields," Catholic Historical Review, VIII (January, 1929), 582-585.

Jordan, Edward B. "Some Problems of the Catholic College," Catholic Educational Review, XXII (March, 1924), 129-140; (November, 1924), 513-522; XXIV (February, 1926), 65-75.

Klinkhamer, Sister Marie Carolyn, O.P. "The Catholic University of America, 1889-1905: Ideological Foundations," Catholic Educational Review, LII (March, 1954), 162-182.

_____. "Historical Reasons for Inception of the Parochial School System," Catholic Educational Review, LII (February, 1954), 73-94.

"Letters of Cardinal Martinelli and Cardinal Gibbons," Catholic University Bulletin, VII (July, 1901), 386-387.

Marique, Pierre J. "T. E. Shields, Apostle of Progress in Education," Thought, II (December, 1927), 360-374.

McCormick, Patrick J. "Bishop Shahan: American Catholic Educator," Catholic Educational Review, XXX (May, 1932), 257-265.

_____. "Roman Catholic Parochial Schools," Catholic Educational Review, VIII (September, 1914), 138-152.

_____. "Standards in Education," Catholic Educational Review, XIV (September, 1917), 97-108.

McKenna, Bernard A. "The Alumni Association," Catholic Educational Review, V (May, 1913), 413-416.

McVay, Leo L. "Affiliated High School and College Section," Catholic Educational Review, XXI (November, 1923), 565-567; (December, 1923), 619-622; XXII (January,

1924), 49-52; (February, 1924), 118-121; (March, 1924), 177-179; (April, 1924), 242-244; (May, 1924), 304-306; (June, 1924), 373-375; (November, 1924), 562-564; (December, 1924), 618-621; XXIII (January, 1925), 49-53; (February, 1925), 113-116; (March, 1925), 180-183; (April, 1925), 231-234; (May, 1925), 304-307; (June, 1925), 370-373; (November, 1925), 559-562; (December, 1925), 632-635; XXIV (January, 1926), 47-51; (February, 1926), 111-114; (March, 1926), 179-182;(April, 1926), 237-241; (May, 1926), 301-305; (June, 1926), 371-373; (September, 1926), 423-425; (October, 1926), 492-494; (November, 1926), 554-558; XXV (January, 1927), 43-46; (February, 1927), 112-114; (March, 1927), 178-182; (April, 1927), 239-242; (May, 1927), 299-304; (June, 1927), 368-370; (November, 1927), 558-561; XXVI (January, 1928), 45-48; (February, 1928), 108-112.

_____. "Catholic High Schools and Affiliation," Catholic Educational Review, XX (February, 1922), 84-92.

_____. "Dr. Shields and Affiliation," Catholic Educational Review, XIX (April, 1921), 269-273.

_____. "Educational Notes," Catholic Educational Review, XX (February, 1922), 112-115.

_____. "The Problems of Affiliation," Catholic School Interests, III (June, 1924), 90-91.

"Monsignor Pace, Eminent Educator and Philosopher," Catholic Educational Review, XXXVI (June, 1938), 326-336.

Murphy, John T., C.S.Sp. "The New Catholic University and the Existing Colleges," The Catholic World, L (December, 1889), 302-306.

O'Gorman, Thomas. "Leo XIII and the Catholic University,"

Catholic University Bulletin, I (January, 1895), 8-24.

O'Mahoney, J. P., C.S.V. "Number of Units Required and Elective for College Entrance," Catholic Educational Association Bulletin, VIII (November, 1910), 157-174.

Pace, Edward A. "The Holy Father's Letter," Catholic Educational Review, III (February, 1912), 104-113.

_____. "The Present State of Education," Catholic Educational Association Bulletin, V (November, 1908), 32-45.

_____. "Religion and Education," Catholic Educational Association Bulletin, VIII (November, 1911), 98-104.

_____. "The University: Its Growth and Its Needs," Catholic Educational Review, IV (October, 1912), 353-358.

"Pastoral Letter of the Archbishops and Bishops of the United States," Catholic Educational Review, XVIII (May, 1920), 255-266.

"Pius X, Pope, Letter to James Gibbons, Cardinal, Chancellor of Catholic University of America," Catholic Educational Review, III (February, 1912), 100-103.

"Professor." "Standardization of Catholic Colleges," American Ecclesiastical Review, LV (September, 1916), 302-303.

_____. "Standardization of Catholic Colleges," Catholic Educational Review, XIII (March, 1917), 193-199.

Purcell, Richard J. "Thomas Edward Shields," Dictionary of American Biography, XVIII (New York, 1935), 107-108.

_____. "Thomas Joseph Shahan," Dictionary of American Biography, XVIII (New York, 1935), 16-17.

[_____.] The Catholic University of America -- A Half Century of Progress. Washington, 1939.

Roche, Rayson E. "The Sisters College: The Summer School -- Affiliation of Schools and Colleges," The University Symposium, V (April, 1915), 356-362.

Schumacher, Matthew, C.S.C. "The Affiliating and Accrediting of Catholic High Schools and Academies to Colleges," Catholic Educational Association Bulletin, VI (November, 1909), 132-142.

_____. "College Entrance Requirements," Catholic Educational Association Bulletin, IX (November, 1912), 162-166.

_____. "What Next?" Catholic Educational Review, XII (October, 1916), 204-210.

Schwitalla, Alphonse M., S.J. "The Affiliation of Schools of Nursing with Our Catholic Colleges," National Catholic Educational Association Bulletin, XXXIII (August, 1937), 186-202.

Shahan, Thomas J. "Archbishop Spalding and the Catholic University," Catholic Educational Review, VII (February, 1914), 138-144.

_____. "The Catholic University of America (1889-1916)," The Catholic World, CIII (June, 1916), 364-383.

_____. "The Pastor and Education," Catholic Educational Association Bulletin, VII (November, 1910), 45-59.

Shields, Thomas E. "The Catholic Sisters College," Catholic Educational Review, XII (June, 1916), 10-17.

_____. "Catholic Teachers and Educational Progress," The Catholic World, LXXXIII (April, 1906), 93-101.

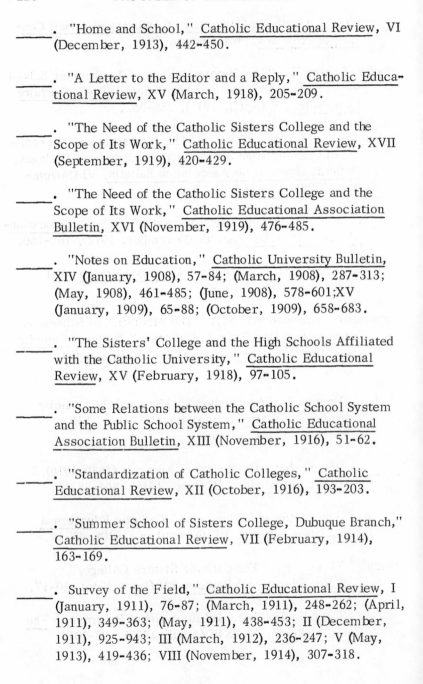

_____ . "Home and School," Catholic Educational Review, VI (December, 1913), 442-450.

_____ . "A Letter to the Editor and a Reply," Catholic Educational Review, XV (March, 1918), 205-209.

_____ . "The Need of the Catholic Sisters College and the Scope of Its Work," Catholic Educational Review, XVII (September, 1919), 420-429.

_____ . "The Need of the Catholic Sisters College and the Scope of Its Work," Catholic Educational Association Bulletin, XVI (November, 1919), 476-485.

_____ . "Notes on Education," Catholic University Bulletin, XIV (January, 1908), 57-84; (March, 1908), 287-313; (May, 1908), 461-485; (June, 1908), 578-601;XV (January, 1909), 65-88; (October, 1909), 658-683.

_____ . "The Sisters' College and the High Schools Affiliated with the Catholic University," Catholic Educational Review, XV (February, 1918), 97-105.

_____ . "Some Relations between the Catholic School System and the Public School System," Catholic Educational Association Bulletin, XIII (November, 1916), 51-62.

_____ . "Standardization of Catholic Colleges," Catholic Educational Review, XII (October, 1916), 193-203.

_____ . "Summer School of Sisters College, Dubuque Branch," Catholic Educational Review, VII (February, 1914), 163-169.

_____ . Survey of the Field," Catholic Educational Review, I (January, 1911), 76-87; (March, 1911), 248-262; (April, 1911), 349-363; (May, 1911), 438-453; II (December, 1911), 925-943; III (March, 1912), 236-247; V (May, 1913), 419-436; VIII (November, 1914), 307-318.

_____. "Syllabus for Music in Affiliated Schools, " Catholic Educational Review, XV (February, 1918), 106-108.

_____. "Teachers College of the Catholic University of America, " Catholic Educational Review, VI (November, 1913), 314-337.

Sister of the Congregation de Notre Dame. "The Second Summer Session of the Sisters College, " Catholic Educational Review, IV (September, 1912), 152-157.

"Sisters College Erects Shrine to the Memory of Doctor Shields, " Sisters College Messenger, XVII (January, 1929), 1-5.

Smith, V. Rev. Ignatius, O.P. "Monsignor Edward Aloysius Pace -- Apostle of Truth, " Catholic Educational Review, XXXVI (June, 1938), 321-325.

"Third Annual Conference of Catholic Colleges, " Catholic University Bulletin, VII (July, 1901), 383-385.

"Thomas Edward Shields: Illness -- Death -- Funeral, " Catholic Educational Review, XIX (April, 1921), 193-222.

"Tribute to the Memory of Monsignor Pace, " Catholic Educational Review, XXXIX (November, 1941), 562-564.

"University Chronicle, " Catholic University Bulletin, XVIII (May, 1912), 477; (June, 1912), 550-553; XIX (June, 1913), 430-432; (October, 1913), 573-574; XXI (January, 1915), 26-27.

"University Degrees for Sisters, " Catholic Educational Review, IV (June, 1912), 53-60.

Unpublished Material

McInerney, Sister St. Thomas, S.S.J. "A Study of the Educational Outcomes of Affiliation with the Catholic University of America upon a Typical Academy." Unpublished Master's dissertation, Department of Education, Catholic University of America, 1934.

Murphy, Daniel J., O.S.F.S. "The National Catholic Educational Association and Standardization." Unpublished Master's dissertation, Department of Education, Catholic University of America, 1930.

O'Connor, Sister M. Augustine. "The Influence of Very Reverend Doctor Thomas E. Shields on Catholic Education in the United States." Unpublished Master's dissertation, Department of Education, Catholic University of America, 1941.

Spencer, Rev. James P. "Standardization in American Education with Special Reference to the Elementary Schools." Unpublished Master's dissertation, Department of Education, Catholic University of America, 1925.

Strelecky, Richard John. "A History of the Catholic Educational Review." Unpublished Master's dissertation, Department of Education, Catholic University of America, 1961.

accreditation, 1-2, 23, 26, 38-41, 43, 75, 90-91, 102-103, 138-139, 157, 170, 173, 188n, 194, 195.

affiliates, statistics on, 89-90, 95, 106-107, 114n, 115n, 122, 140-141, 185, 192n, 211, 212.

Affiliation plan, of 1907, 31-33n, 57n; of 1912, 46-54, 60-88, 197-201; of 1939, 178-186, 202-210.

American Council on Education, 35, 136.

American Ecclesiastical Review, 8-9, 90.

application forms, college, 77-78, 163-164; high school, 78-79, 166-167; nursing schools, 189n.

articulation, 12-13, 22, 64, 67, 105; see also Catholic school system.

Association of American Universities, 62, 103, 117n, 154.

Association of Catholic Colleges, 15-16, 17, 19, 23.

Benedictine Sisters, 89, 166.

benefits of Affiliation, 102-107, 109, 145-147, 170-171, 173, 179-180.

Bisleti, Cardinal, 129-130.

Board of Studies and Discipline, 98, 100.

Bowles, Frank, 161.

bulletins of Affiliation, 157, 181-182, 190n.

Burns, James A., C.S.C., 25-26, 44, 45, 105-106.

business courses, 100-102, 123-124.

Campbell, James M., 142, 156, 168, 182.

Carnegie Foundation, 54n.

Catholic Education Press, 35, 42.

Catholic Educational Association, 14-17, 23-27, 43-46, 47, 62-63, 66, 90-91, 105, 119n, 136, 193; see also National Catholic Education Association.

Catholic Educational News Service, 42.

Catholic Educational Review, 35, 36, 43, 47, 48, 51, 83, 105, 106, 126, 127, 128.

Catholic University Bulletin, 35, 51, 90, 105.

Catholic University of America, founding of, 3-9; Constitutions of, 4-7, 8, 13, 14, 118, 130-131, 157; growth of, 9-10, 12, 20-21, 23, 34, 38-43, 129-131.

Catholic World, 7, 10.

Catholic school system, 2, 7-9, 14-17, 24-27, 36-37, 43-46, 48-49, 60-61, 113-114, 193; see also articulation.

Catholic Sisters College, 23, 35, 36, 38-42, 47, 49, 53, 64, 89, 90, 94, 100, 103, 104, 105, 107, 110-113, 120n, 121, 128, 155, 156.

certificate of Affiliation, 166, 177.

chemistry, 70-71, 177.

college Affiliation, 13-14, 18-19, 21, 49, 61-64, 77-78, 91, 103-104, 122, 129, 136-137, 158-159, 161-165, 169-173, 184, 194, 198, 202-207.

College Entrance Examination Board, 138.

college entrance examinations,
129.
Committee of Nine (N.E.A.), 67,
74.
Committee on Affiliation, 51-53,
58n, 73, 79, 81-83, 89, 94,
106, 110-111, 121-123, 131-
135, 143-144; and Extension,
156-161, 163-169, 173-179,
181-185, 195.
Conaty, Thomas J., 12-20.
conferences for affiliates, 128-
129, 183-184.
Cooper, John M., 177.
correspondence courses, 155.
Corrigan, Joseph M., 144, 154-
155, 156, 163, 169, 179,
180, 195.
Council of Baltimore, Second
Plenary, 3, 12; Third
Plenary, 3, 36, 193.
course outlines, high school, 68-
74, 81, 98-102, 123, 128,
134, 137-138, 175-177; see
also syllabus.
Curley, Michael J., 129, 130.

Deferrari, Roy J., 121, 131,
137, 142, 154-186, 195.
diploma, high school, 95-96, 122,
166, 212.
Dunwoodie Seminary, 21.

Education, Department of, 19-20,
22, 23, 35, 41, 47, 48, 94,
112, 121, 155-156.
elementary education, 2, 94-95,
112, 194.
English, 69, 177.
Euphrasia, Sr., S.N.D., 72-73.
Evaluative Criteria, 160, 183.
extension, 20, 22, 155-156, 157-
158, 169.

Farley, John Cardinal, 22-50.

finances, 110-111, 112-113, 133,
134, 141-142, 152n, 165, 166.

Garrigan, P. J., 10.
Gibbons, James Cardinal, 4, 11,
16, 17, 18, 48, 105.

Harriman, Arthur J., 156, 160,
165, 183.
Hewitt, Augustine F., 11.
high school Affiliation, 19, 50,
65-75, 78-84, 95-102, 104-
107, 122-129, 137-138, 139-
142, 159-160, 165-167, 180-
181, 184-185, 194, 195, 198-
200, 207-210.
high school movement, 1-2;
Catholic, 19-20, 24-25, 44-
45, 66, 119n, 141, 144.
history, 70, 72-74.
houses of study, 10-12, 29n, 142,
193.

Immaculata, Sister M., O.S.B.,
167, 173, 176, 182, 184.
inspections, 75, 78, 124-126,
132, 133, 137, 162, 164, 168,
177, 184-185.
Ireland, John, 4, 11, 18, 21, 35.

Johnson, George, 36-37, 156, 159,
160.
Jordan, Edward B., 142, 156, 159.
junior colleges, 132, 134, 135-
136, 178.

Keane, John J., 4-6, 9-12, 18,
28n.
Keefe, Anselm M., 171-173.

Landry, Aubrey E., 121, 131,
147n.
Latin, 70, 137-138.
Leo XIII, Pope, 6, 17, 48, 91,
193.

Lucy, Mother, O.S.B., 166.

McCormick, Patrick J., 35, 51, 52, 81, 89, 90, 121, 126, 131.
McVay, Leo L., 90, 95, 107, 108, 113, 115n, 116n, 121, 122, 123, 124-126, 128, 131, 132, 138, 142, 154, 156, 159, 165.
Magni Nobis Gaudii, 6-7, 125.
Martinelli, Sebastian Cardinal, 15-16.
Middle States Association of Colleges and Secondary Schools, 154, 161-162, 173.
Moore, Thomas V., O.S.B., 150n.
Murphy, John T., C.S.Sp., 9.
music, 98-100, 117n.

National Catholic Educational Association, 154; see also Catholic Educational Association.
National League of Nursing Education, 178.
New York State Council of Catholic School Superintendents, 181.
Notre Dame of Maryland, College of, 18.
novitiates, high schools, 95, 116n; normal schools, 94-95, 132, 134-136, 168; see also teacher training institutions.
nursing schools, 169, 177-178, 179-180, 182, 189n.

O'Connell, Denis J., 20-27, 130.
O'Connor, James, 5-6.
O'Dowd, James T., 102.
Olivia, Sister M., O.S.B., 169, 173, 177, 182, 184.

Pace, Edward A., 10, 12, 13-14, 18, 19, 20, 21, 22-23, 25, 27, 34-36, 37, 38-41, 42-43, 45, 46, 47-48, 50, 51-52, 60, 62, 90, 91-94, 97-98, 102, 103-104, 108-112, 113-114, 121, 123, 124, 126, 130, 131, 132, 134, 141, 154, 155, 193.
Paulist Fathers, 10-11.
Pedagogy, New York Institute of, 20, 22.
Pius X, Pope, 48.
Pius XI, Pope, 129.
procedures of Affiliation, 75-84, 124-126, 168, 184.
Program of Affiliation, 176, 179.
Purcell, Richard J., 121, 131.
purpose of Affiliation, 60-61, 102-104, 133, 138-139, 157, 162, 169-170, 187n.

religion, 68, 84n, 138, 177.
reorganization, need of, 110-112, 132-134, 143-144, 169-170, 194-195; work of, 154-186.
Ryan, James Hugh, 131, 133, 135, 141-144, 154, 195.
Ryan, John A., 142.

St. Cecilia Normal School, 150n.
St. Joseph Seminary, 92.
St. Paul Seminary, 11-12, 13, 14.
Schaaf, Valentine, 142.
Schrembs, Joseph, 44, 56n, 130.
Schumacker, Matthew, 26, 43, 45-46.
Scientific Study, Institute of, 22-23.
seminary Affiliation, 11, 12-13, 14, 17-18, 21-22, 28n, 56n, 103-104, 142, 193.
seminary conference, 14, 17.
seminaries, preparatory, 91-94, 132, 134-135, 136, 179.

Senate, Academic, 12, 13-14, 18, 19, 20, 49-50, 58-59n, 89, 98, 100, 114n, 132, 142, 186n.

Shahan, Thomas J., 10, 20, 21, 26, 27, 32n, 34, 35, 41, 42, 43, 44, 47, 64, 92, 98, 106, 113, 121, 123, 129-131, 141, 152n, 155, 193.

Shields, Thomas E., passim, especially 34-120.

Sisters College Messenger, 112.

Spalding, John Lancaster, 3, 4, 18, 20.

Spalding, Martin John, 3.

standardization, 60-61, 75, 109, 145-147, 194; see also accreditation and Catholic school system.

standards, 61-67, 74-75, 136-137, 138, 162-163, 166, 171-172, 198-200, 202-210.

State Board of Nurse Examiners, 178.

Summer School, 35, 36, 38-42, 47.

superintendents, 180-181.

syllabus, 53-54, 56n, 81, 138; see also courses of study.

teacher certification, 95, 116n.

teacher training, 19-20, 22-23, 37, 38-41, 74-75, 155; institutions of, 178-179; see also novitiate normal schools.

testing, college, 76, 78, 135-136, 189n; high school, 76, 80-84, 87n, 95-98, 116n, 122-123, 129, 130, 132, 133, 134, 137, 140-142, 143-144, 145, 159-160, 165, 167, 173-175, 182-183, 191n, 194, 195.

textbooks, 40-42, 74-75, 102, 126, 138.

Trinity College, 18, 38, 108, 109.

Trustees, Board of, 13, 14, 18-20, 21-22, 31-33n, 41, 46, 48, 50-51, 52-53, 57-58n, 129-131, 132, 141, 143, 156, 169, 194.

Turner, William, 130, 143.

University of the State of New York, 181.

Volkert, Anthony, 82-94.

Ward, Justine, 52-53, 99, 108.

Weber, Nicholas A., 142.

Zook, George F., 161.